Captain John Smith's America

AMERICAN PERSPECTIVES

EDITED BY BERNARD WISHY AND
WILLIAM E. LEUCHTENBURG

* in preparation

Captain John Smith's America

Selections From His Writings

Edited by

JOHN LANKFORD

HARPER TORCHBOOKS ❦ The University Library
Harper & Row, Publishers
New York, Evanston, & London

CAPTAIN JOHN SMITH'S AMERICA

Designed by Darlene Starr Carbone

This book is for my parents,
who live on Tabbs Creek, Lancaster County, Virginia,
in the heart of Captain John Smith's America.

Contents

Introduction to the Torchbook Edition

by

JOHN LANKFORD

The motto which Captain John Smith (1579/80–1631) bore on his coat of arms read *Vincere est vivere,* to overcome is to live. The epitaph over his grave in St. Sepulchre's Church in London begins

> Here lies one conquer'd that hath conquer'd Kings,
> Subdu'd large Territories, and done things
> Which to the World impossible would seeme,
> But that the truth is held in more esteeme.[1]

Yet the world at large, and American historians in particular, have not often held John Smith in the esteem he deserves. His truthfulness has been at issue. Beginning in the middle of the nineteenth century American historians like Henry Adams, influenced by the new German textual criticism, raised serious doubts concerning the authenticity of the events Smith recounted in *The Generall Historie of Virginia, New England, and the Summer Isles* (1624) and *The True Travels, Adventures, and Observations of Captain John Smith* (1630). The Captain's rescue by Pocahontas was said to be but an invention of his later years. The travels in the Mediterranean, Hungary, Turkey, and Russia were characterized as pure fantasy; his hairbreadth escapes both by land and sea

---

[1] Edward Arber, ed., with a new introduction by A. G. Bradley, *Travels and Works of Captain John Smith* (2 vols., Edinburgh, 1910), II, p. 971.

and his victories in single combat against Turkish champions but fiction based on Elizabethan melodramas.[2]

If such a critical view is adopted, both the man and his contributions are lost. This is a sad mistake, for Smith was one of the first Englishmen to see America as more than a get-rich-quick scheme. He was one of the first to fall in love with the land and to see its potential. Beyond the forests and Indian fields, Smith envisioned growing towns and cities and thriving trade and commerce. To him, America was the setting for a new civilization.

Recent scholarship has cleared away much of the confusion surrounding the Captain. As a result of the work of Laura P. Striker, Bradford Smith, and Philip Barbour, the nineteenth century view has been revised.[3] It is now certain that Smith's story of his exploits during the years 1600 to 1604 is more than plausible. In spite of his phonetic spelling of Hungarian, Russian, and Turkish names and places, and the changing political geography of the region over the centuries, John Smith's story holds up when checked against the available sources. The battles he chronicled were fought and the commanders under whom he served did lead the armies. It may all sound strange to the ears of Western scholars, but this does not diminish its validity. As Bradford Smith and Laura P. Striker conclude, the Captain "would have been hopelessly entangled had he tried to fake an account" of the Turkish wars during these years. "Not only does Hungarian history corroborate Smith wherever he can be checked, but his own account clarifies an area of Hungarian history that is full of obscurity in the Hungarian sources. His writings make him an authority on Hungarian history!"[4]

[2] A summary of these criticisms is found in Jarvis M. Morse, "John Smith and His Critics: A Chapter in Colonial Historiography," *Journal of Southern History*, I (1935), pp. 123–137.

[3] The best guide to the revisionist literature on John Smith is Laura P. Striker and Bradford Smith, "The Rehabilitation of Captain John Smith," *Journal of Southern History*, XXVIII (1962), pp. 474–481. Two recent biographies sum up the new findings: Bradford Smith, *Captain John Smith: His Life and Legend* (Philadelphia and New York, 1953), with an appendix by Laura P. Striker, "Captain John Smith's Hungary and Transylvania," pp. 311–342; and Philip L. Barbour, *The Three Worlds of Captain John Smith* (Boston, 1964). The bibliography in the Barbour volume, pp. 493–527, is the best starting place for those who wish to pursue John Smith in greater detail.

[4] Striker and Smith, "The Rehabilitation of Captain John Smith," p. 477.

The young Henry Adams began his career as a professional historian in 1867 with a critical analysis of John Smith's Virginia career, paying special attention to the Pocahontas episode. Following the advice of the dean of New England historians, John Gorham Palfrey, who suggested to Adams that an attack on Smith "would attract as much attention, and probably break as much glass, as any other stone that could be thrown by a beginner," the young scholar set out to achieve "nothing less than the entire erasure of one of the more attractive portions of American history."[5] Adams used a simple technique. He reprinted in parallel columns the accounts of Smith's capture by the Indians in the *True Relation* (1608) and *The Generall Historie* written sixteen years later. In this manner, Adams demonstrated that the Pocahontas story appeared only in the second version. Assuming with the German textual critics that the account written closest to the event is the accurate report, Adams concluded that in the later version Smith "embodied everything that could tend to the increase of his own reputation," and that "His own share in the affairs of the colony was magnified at the expense of his companions."[6] The difficulty with this documents-centered approach is that it ignores the larger historical context, especially the circumstances in which the documents were composed. John Smith would have incurred the wrath of the directors of the Virginia enterprise in London had he given a full account of Indian hostility just as the colony was getting under way. Such news would have damaged the image of the project in the eyes of potential investors and settlers. Smith himself was an investor and hoped to profit through both dividends and promotion for his services in Virginia. He could ill afford to lose the respect of the London backers by such adverse reports.

To get at the real John Smith and thereby see his importance for America, one must begin with his times and his social background. Only by establishing the nature of his historical milieu and his position in the social structure can the documents be made to yield their full meaning. Smith was born just as the Age of Elizabeth approached full flower. To say that he was an Elizabethan is to say something very special, for this

[5] Quoted in Edwin C. Rozwenc, "Captain John Smith's Image of America," *William and Mary Quarterly*, 3rd ser., XVI (1959), p. 27.
[6] Henry Adams, "Captain John Smith: Sometime Governour in Virginia, and Admirall of New England," reprinted in Elizabeth Stevenson, ed., *A Henry Adams Reader* (New York, 1959), p. 50. The essay was published originally in the *North American Review* for January 1867.

was a time of rapid social change in England. Society was opening up. Position and family counted for less, talent and ability for more. There was greater opportunity for social mobility in Elizabeth's England than there ever had been before.[7]

The son of a lower middle-class farmer in Lincolnshire, young John Smith wanted to rise in the world. After a grammar school education and a brief apprenticeship with a wealthy merchant of King's Lynn, which might have provided a route for improving his status in English society, Smith set out to win fame and fortune as a soldier in the Low Countries.[8]

[7] While it is no easy matter to grasp the very texture, fabric, and meaning of life in a bygone age, see for example the following: J. B. Black, *The Reign of Elizabeth, 1558–1603* (2nd ed., Oxford, 1959), especially chapter VII, "The Expansion of England and the Economic and Social Revolution," pp. 235–279 and *passim;* Joan Simon, *Education and Society in Tudor England* (Cambridge, 1966), especially part III, "The Place of Education in the Elizabethan Age," pp. 291–403 and *passim;* Louis B. Wright, *Middle-Class Culture in Elizabethan England* (Ithaca, 1958), especially part I, "The Background," pp. 1–118 and *passim;* and A. L. Rowse, *The Elizabethans and America* (New York and Evanston, 1965 [Harper Torchbook]), *passim.* The importance of these English backgrounds for America in the seventeenth century and after is stressed by Louis Hartz in his brilliant and controversial *The Founding of New Societies: Studies in the History of the United States, Latin America, South Africa, Canada, and Australia* (New York, 1964), see especially pp. 3–122.

[8] The biographies by Bradford Smith and Philip Barbour provide the best summary of John Smith's early life. The will of George Smith, John's father, is printed by Bradford Smith, *Captain John Smith,* pp. 343–345. It shows an inventory of goods and chattels which amounted to a little over £77. While it is almost impossible to translate this into a measure of contemporary purchasing power, it should be made clear that the elder Smith was not a poor man. Further, he was respected in his community. See Bradford Smith, *op. cit.,* pp. 16–17. Like most Englishmen of the day, he held his land in copyhold from the local Lord of the Manor. For further details of land tenure and status among the yeoman class see Mildred Campbell, *The English Yeoman Under Elizabeth and the Early Stuarts* (New Haven, 1942), especially chapter IV, "Copyhold and Freehold," pp. 105–155 and *passim.* That young John Smith had a grammar school education, though it probably ended when he was about fourteen since he was not destined for the University, also points out the relatively solid status of his family. See Simon, *Education and Society,* p. 369. In 1685 the scholar Henry

In selecting the military life rather than trade and commerce as a method for achieving upward mobility, Smith followed his heart's desire and, at the same time, demonstrated the influence of the local Lord of the Manor, Peregrine Bertie, Lord Willoughby de Eresby, a nationally renowned military leader. After two years abroad, in 1599 Smith was back from the wars and preparing to accompany the sons of Lord Willoughby on a French tour. While he soon returned to England because of the excessive expenses incurred by the young gentlemen, this evidence points to the early and close connection between Smith and the Bertie family. If Lord Willoughby never formally acted as John's patron, his friendship proved invaluable. It provided the aspiring young man with a model and a style of life to copy and with connections which often would be useful in later life.[9] Smith went back to Lincolnshire *via* Paris, the Netherlands, and Scotland, demonstrating at the age of twenty his keen desire to see the world and expand his horizons through travel.[10]

Early in 1600 John Smith "retired himself into a little woody pasture," on land probably owned by Lord Willoughby. "Here by a fair brook he built a pavilion of boughs, where only in his clothes he lay." In this pastoral retreat, "His study was Machiavelli's [The] Art of War and Marcus Aurelius; his exercise a good horse, with his lance and ring; his food was thought to be more of venison than anything else; what he wanted, his man brought him." There the would-be knight with his nameless serving man strengthened mind and body in

---

Wharton characterized Smith as "an Englishman of a reputable family [who], after having spent his youth in literary exercises, upon reaching manhood desired to learn the art of warfare by journeying to France and Belgium. . . ." Henry Wharton, *The Life of John Smith, English Soldier,* translated by Laura P. Striker (Chapel Hill, 1957), pp. 39–40. Samuel Eliot Morison accepts this evaluation of Smith's social origins in his *Builders of the Bay Colony* (Boston, 1964 [Sentry Edition]), p. 7.

[9] Barbour, *The Three Worlds of Captain John Smith,* p. 11. For biographical details on Peregrine Bertie see Leslie Stephen and Sidney Lee, eds., *The Dictionary of National Biography* (22 vols., London, 1908–9), II, pp. 404–407.

[10] Next to formal education in the schools or an apprenticeship with a merchant or craftsman, the Elizabethans viewed foreign travel as an important way of acquiring an education and improving one's social position. See Simon, *Education and Society,* p. 346.

the arts of war. Though the country folk scoffed and called Smith a
hermit, "His friends persuaded one Signor Theodore Paleologue, Rider
to Henry, Earl of Lincoln, an excellent horseman, and noble Italian
gentleman, to insinuate into his woodish acquaintances; whose languages
and good discourse, and exercise of riding, drew him [John Smith] to
stay with him at Tattershall [Lord Willoughby's castle]."[11]

While some might seek to use this passage as evidence that John
Smith was a romantic in the Don Quixote tradition of knight-errantry,
the evidence points in another direction. The young man retired into
his "little woody pasture" to escape distractions and study war. Smith's
connection with Paleologue can be regarded only as great good fortune.
Apparently the man was as competent as Smith describes him and
proved an able tutor to his apt pupil.

This episode illustrates Smith's intensely practical approach to life.
At later periods it is clear that he mastered the available literature on
such topics as colonization and exploration. Yet child of the age that he
was, Smith would doubtless have agreed with Lawrence Keymis, one of
Raleigh's associates in the disastrous Guiana expedition, "that the true
commendation of virtue consists in action."[12] Reading books or practic-
ing horsemanship in peaceful Lincolnshire was not enough. The rapid
alternation between thought and action with the accent most often on
action characterized the personality type so recurrent in the Elizabethan
period.

If the social matrix of Elizabethan life was complex, the personality
type which often appeared is even more difficult to understand.
Professor A. L. Rowse has suggested that many Elizabethans showed
a strong tendency toward megalomania.[13] To them life was a drama,
and it is not surprising that the theater was the art form *par excellence*
of the age. To these men the drama of life was written in bold, clear
characters. Elizabethans were quick to act and react. Their thought was
often secondary to their action or a rationalization for it. They lived
in a world with no middle ground. Men were either Catholics or
Protestants, friends of England or allies of Spain. One day a man was
in favor at Court and the next, a tenant in the Tower of London. This
instability and tendency toward megalomania came from the social

[11] Arber, ed., *True Travels and Works,* II, p. 823. See also Barbour, *The
Three Worlds of Captain John Smith,* pp. 14–16 and 401–402.
[12] Quoted in Black, *The Reign of Elizabeth,* p. 280.
[13] Rowse, *The Elizabethans and America,* pp. 39–40 and *passim.*

milieu in which they grew up. A period of rapid social and cultural change produced character and personality which were not well integrated.

During Elizabeth's reign (1558-1603), England emerged as a nation-state and in economic life laid the foundations for a modern capitalistic society. She entered the international arena and started on the long road to empire. Religious tensions ran deep and were intertwined with foreign affairs. English cities took on new importance and new routes for social mobility developed which offered individuals almost un-dreamed-of opportunities. These Elizabethans were reckless and willing to venture everything, including their lives, on grand designs. Whether they sought gold in the new world, searched for the northwest passage, became leading members of the London guilds or trading companies, or plotted intrigues at Court, they were restless and striving.[14] Something of this state of mind rubbed off in America. With modifications it appeared again and again as America developed along her own special path. Captain John Smith was a link between the world of Elizabeth and the men who followed "the western star" across a continent far removed in time and space from the old Queen's London.

After a few months in Lincolnshire, John Smith decided that the pleasures of study and exercise "could not content him . . . [and] he returned again to the Low Countries."[15] In the summer of 1600, however, the Netherlands was enjoying an uneasy peace so the young Englishman pushed on looking for adventure. Smith soon fell in with four young men who posed as French nobles and together they decided to make their way to Hungary and join the struggle against the Turks. These rogues fleeced Smith, made away with his baggage, and left him stranded in France. This was the first of many scrapes from which he had to extricate himself.

After a long series of adventures and near disasters, Smith arrived at Graz in Austria in the summer of 1601 and quickly demonstrated his mastery of *The Art of War* in the battle of Limbach. Promotion followed as he continued to prove his talent and valor. At the end of

[14] If these generalizations cannot be easily documented, the following works offer at least a starting point: Clarence L. Ver Steeg, *The Formative Years, 1607–1763* (New York, 1964), especially chapter 1, "England and the Age of Discovery," pp. 1–28; Black, *The Reign of Elizabeth, passim;* and Rowse, *The Elizabethans and America, passim.*

[15] Arber, ed., *True Travels and Works,* II, p. 823.

the campaigning season in 1602 the Imperial Army under the Count
of Modrusch, with which Smith was serving, was virtually annihilated
in a battle before the Red Tower Pass in Rumania. Smith, though
wounded, survived and was sold into slavery by the Turks. Eventually
he ended up somewhere east of the Black Sea serving a sadistic master.
Undaunted, Smith watched his chance and killed his owner with a
threshing bat. Hiding the body under a pile of straw, he took his
oppressor's clothes and horse and escaped into the barren steppe country.
By great luck he stumbled on a caravan route and made his way to a
Muscovite outpost. By the Christmas season of 1603 Smith reached
Leipzig and secured a kind of discharge paper from the Transylvanian
Prince, Zsigmond Báthory. This paper, which Smith always treasured,
proved his position as a Captain in the Imperial Army and referred
to its owner as a gentleman. In addition, Smith's coat of arms was
confirmed and the Prince granted him fifteen hundred gold ducats.
Filled with pride, Captain Smith used his new wealth to indulge in a
tour of Germany and Spain. Pushing on to North Africa, he enjoyed
a stint of privateering with a French sea captain. He returned to
England late in 1604.[16]

While it is difficult to account for John Smith's movements from the
time he arrived back from the continent until he left for Virginia in
December 1606, some things are clear. All that he learned about
fighting and horsemanship in Lincolnshire had been augmented by
several years of battlefield experience. Marching, the details of combat,
strategy, and, most important, the ability to command men—these
things Smith brought away from his experience in the Turkish wars.
Further, he had been seasoned by his adventures. They taught the
young Captain self-confidence and self-reliance and he admirably
demonstrated these virtues in his escape from slavery. Travel in Europe
during 1603 and 1604 added further dimension and depth to his abilities.
It is also reasonable to assume that building on the foundation of his
grammar school Latin and whatever brief training Theodore Paleologue
provided in languages, Smith developed a certain feeling for foreign

[16] It is impossible to give more than these few brief examples from Smith's
career during the years 1600 to 1604. The Captain tells it in his *True
Travels*, Arber, ed., *True Travels and Works*, II, pp. 821–880. Philip
Barbour has accomplished a masterful bit of detective work in putting
together the details of these years in *The Three Worlds of Captain John
Smith*, pp. 17–77.

tongues. In some part, this must account for his ability to master the rudiments of the Virginia Indian language. His experiences as a privateer introduced the landsman to ships and navigation. Smith would later use this knowledge to advantage. At every step during his four years away from England, Smith had the opportunity to sharpen his powers of observation and critical judgment. Finally, it must be stressed that he returned home with a new status. He had risen to the position of Captain in the Imperial Army, and the Prince of Transylvania had referred to him as a gentleman. Smith even had an authorized coat of arms to prove his new standing.

As Philip Barbour conjectures, John Smith must have made good use of his new status when he returned to his native Lincolnshire.[17] In the two years before he sailed for Virginia Smith extended his circle of friends. Working through his connection with the Bertie family, he met Samuel Purchas, who would carry on the work of the great geographer and propagandist for colonization, Richard Hakluyt; possibly Hakluyt himself; and Thomas Hariot, who had firsthand experience with the new world. Smith may even have received lessons in map-making from Henry Hudson. Perhaps the most important of all his new acquaintances was the shadowy historical figure, Bartholomew Gosnold, who explored the New England coast for Walter Raleigh in 1602. Gosnold occupied an important position in organizing the expedition which founded Jamestown. At all events, Smith invested in the Virginia venture and had enough reputation and backing to be selected as one of the members of the Council which would govern the new colony.

On 20 December 1606, the *Susan Constant, Godspeed,* and *Discovery* dropped down the Thames from London outward bound for Virginia. The voyage was abnormally long, for the fleet was held up in the Downs by adverse winds. By the time they reached the Canaries trouble was brewing and in some obscure way, John Smith was at the center of it. He was confined as a prisoner on suspicion of mutiny, and remained an outcast until after they reached Virginia. Probably the young veteran ran afoul of certain gentlemen on board. Edward Maria Wingfield, a well connected soldier who became the first President at Jamestown, and John Smith more than likely disagreed on some issue. Smith, never one to suffer fools gladly, may have insulted the older

[17] Barbour, *The Three Worlds of Captain John Smith,* pp. 78–108.

man. Reading between the lines of Smith's description of life at
Jamestown under Wingfield's presidency, it is clear that Smith respected
performance rather than rank and privilege. Wingfield may have
demanded deference because of his superior status where Smith would
only recognize merit based on ability and performance. Conjecture
aside, here was one of the first factions and it set the pattern of conflict
and divisive disagreements which would plague the Virginia enterprise
for years to come.[18]

After stops in the Caribbean, the little fleet entered the Chesapeake
Bay on 26 April 1607 and on the morning of 14 May the men went
ashore on a marshy peninsula in the James River to found the first
English city in North America. Even after the establishment of
Jamestown Smith was excluded from the Council and kept under
surveillance. Not until the tenth of June was he finally admitted to
the government of the colony. From this point on, the reader can
follow the details of John Smith's Virginia career in the Captain's
own words.[19]

These years can be divided into two periods. From June 1607 until
September 1608 Smith concerned himself with the practical problems
of feeding the adventurers, providing for their safety and defense
against the Indians, and exploring Chesapeake Bay and its environs.
Throughout this first period his power and influence grew. He
continually blocked developing factions among the colonists and did
his best to quell mutinies. Almost from the beginning some wished to
jettison the colony and return to England. When the difficult nature
of the enterprise became clear, the fainthearted thought only of creature
comforts and were willing to pay any price for food. Save for a few
brief periods of calm, social disorganization was the order of the day
at Jamestown until the arrival of Governor Dale in 1611. After that
date, a new set of laws and administrative procedures slowly pulled
the colonists into a cohesive unit. Also by 1611, the reorganized
Virginia Company started sending over men with skills which would
be useful in the wilderness. As the lists of colonists printed by Smith
show, many who came in the early years were unfit by temperament
or talent to carve out a plantation in the wilds of Virginia. They were,

[18] See below, pp. 37, 38–39. Barbour, *The Three Worlds of Captain
John Smith,* pp. 109–120, provides the general outlines of this interpretation. I have followed his reconstruction of the events.
[19] See below, pp. 3–124.

in large part, gentlemen and gallants, not farmers and mechanics.[20]

The key note of this first period of Smith's activities in Virginia is the stress he placed on solving practical problems. To a man with the Captain's temperament and background, the first step toward action was to collect the necessary hard facts on which sensible policy could be based. Thus it was that he met the Indians, learned their language, established procedures for trade, and made notes on Indian life. His policy toward the natives was realistic. It was neither tenderhearted nor was it brutal after the fashion of later Virginia leaders. He quickly realized the vast cultural distance which separated the red man from the white, and tried to bridge the gap by a mixture of firmness, patience, and good will. In all these activities Smith was forced to draw upon his reserve of martial courage and his skill as an observer. His observations of the Indians in the Chesapeake Bay region earned him a reputation for excellence as an anthropologist. The descriptions are clear, detailed, and cover most important aspects of Indian society, from religion through political structure and agriculture.

While on an expedition in December 1607 Smith was captured by the Indians and taken to the camp of the great Powhatan, overlord of the Indians in the Chesapeake area. Here, his life in peril, Smith set about reconciling Powhatan to the presence of the English in Virginia. The climax of this adventure came in his rescue by Pocahontas, the favorite daughter of the Indian despot. Whether Powhatan really intended to kill Smith, or was simply subjecting him to a form of the rites of passage, will never be known. The point is, there is enough collateral evidence from other Indian cultures in North America to make it clear that Pocahontas was exercising her prerogative in saving the bearded Captain from the Indian cudgels.[21]

From June to September of 1608 Smith and a small group of adventurers explored the Bay in an open boat as far north as the

[20] For a penetrating sociological analysis of the early years at Jamestown see Sigmund Diamond, "From Organization to Society: Virginia in the Seventeenth Century," *American Journal of Sociology*, LXIII (1958), pp. 457–475.

[21] Barbour, *The Three Worlds of Captain John Smith,* pp. 167–168 and Bradford Smith, *Captain John Smith,* pp. 115–118. See also the sketch of John Smith by James T. Adams in Allen Johnson and Dumas Malone, eds., *The Dictionary of American Biography* (22 vols., New York, 1928–44), XVII, p. 295.

mouth of the Susquehanna River. On two successive trips they made
their way up the major rivers flowing into the Bay from the west
and examined the Eastern Shore in some detail. Smith busied himself
collecting information on the several Indian tribes, their languages,
customs, and fighting strength. He noted the topography of the land
and the coastline, later publishing his observations as a map which
remained useful throughout the colonial period.[22]

In the autumn of 1608 Smith was elected President of the Council
at Jamestown and the second phase of his Virginia career opened. Four
months after his election the English population of Virginia numbered
about four hundred. Approximately thirty counted themselves among
the original group which arrived in 1607. Small in numbers, torn by
faction and mutiny, and at cross-purposes with the directors in London
and the Indians in Virginia, such was the colony which Smith governed
from September 1608 to September 1609. Three overlapping types of
issues confronted him during this second period of his Virginia career.
Stability had to be maintained at Jamestown and the colonists had to
learn to live with each other and their new environment. The natives
had to be brought into line and some degree of stability attained in
Indian-English relations. The investors and directors in London had
to be given satisfaction and proof that the colony was a profitable
economic venture. In his tenure as President, Smith could not hope to
effect lasting solutions to any of these problems. He did, however, point
the way and as later events like the starving time of 1609-1610 and
the massacre of 1622 demonstrate, Smith's administration was more
competent than those of many of his successors.

The first crisis President Smith faced was brought on by the arrival
of Captain Christopher Newport, who commanded the original fleet
in 1607 and served the London directors as Admiral in charge of
transporting men to Virginia and bringing back valuable cargo.
Newport's instructions included a number of items which Smith
thought impossible. The Admiral was not to return without achieving
at least one of the following: find a passage to the South Seas, bring
samples from gold mines which he was also to discover, or locate
any survivors of Raleigh's lost colony at Roanoke. In addition, he was
to crown Powhatan King by permission of the English government on

[22] The Virginia map is reproduced in Arber, ed., *True Travels and Works,*
II, p. 384.

the assumption that this act would make the despot dependent on English authority. Further, Newport was to see that the colonists took a soft line with the Indians. Finally, the Admiral let Smith know that the London investors wanted a return cargo worth at least £2000 to defray the expenses of the voyage.

The confusion which followed these orders is described by Smith in vivid detail.[23] The results included the pathetically humorous coronation of Powhatan, a renewed search for precious metals, and the abortive attempt to explore the James River above the falls at present-day Richmond. Relations between the English and the Indians were undermined as a result of unauthorized trading by colonists and sailors from the ships. Difficulties mounted because Newport stayed on in Virginia until December 1608 and his sailors consumed most of the food brought from England for the colonists. At length, he returned with samples of worthless ore and a cargo of logs and shingles. Smith and the settlers at Jamestown faced the new year with depleted food supplies, and Indian relations were hardly cordial.

Only hard work and swift action by President Smith saved the colony from starvation or annihilation during the winter of 1608-1609. Powhatan ordered all the Indians to refuse to trade with the English for corn. Smith boldly forced them to do so by threatening war as the immediate alternative. Then he visited Powhatan at his winter camp and narrowly escaped death at the hands of the wily chief. In the end, Smith got what he wanted, but Powhatan fled into the woods and the two leaders never met again. As difficulties increased, some colonists went over to the Indians. A few remained at Jamestown as a kind of fifth column while others simply decamped. They must have reasoned that Powhatan had both food and numerical superiority and felt they would be on the winning side if it came to open conflict. Smith moved up the Pamunkey River after his interview with the great chief and demanded corn of Opechancanough, Powhatan's brother. Only by luck and a continual show of force did Smith avoid battle and get the food he needed.

Turning his attention to the situation in Jamestown, President Smith adopted a strong line with the gentlemen and gallants who formed the largest single group of the population. He insisted that those who did not work would not eat. Within three months pitch, tar, and soap

[22] See below, pp. 76–86.

ashes were being produced in quantity, and samples had come from the glasshouse. A well was dug in the fort and the church roof mended, while the general defenses were strengthened and a continuous watch kept against surprise attack. Thirty to forty acres were readied for crops, fishing operations expanded, and the livestock, consisting of chickens and hogs, given better care.

Just as the situation seemed to be improving, the settlers discovered that their corn had rotted in the storehouse and what was not spoiled had been attacked by rats. Smith acted swiftly and divided his forces, sending small parties out to live off the land. Obviously it was his last hope, since no more food supplies could be gained from the Indian trade. Further plans for mutiny followed as a result of this catastrophe, but Smith managed to squelch them. The most serious problem, apparently, was a growing desire on the part of many to abandon the colony and fly to Newfoundland or to the south. Not until the first week in July did relief appear in the form of Captain Samuel Argall and a ship sent out to trade and fish. Argall brought news of the reorganization of the Virginia enterprise and the creation of the Virginia Company. In August part of the fleet arrived, but the new leaders, together with the official orders and instructions, had apparently been lost in a great storm at sea.[24] This precipitated a constitutional crisis at Jamestown. There was a new government, but it was not on hand. President Smith's term ran until September, but his enemies made the most of the situation and his effectiveness was weakened. Charges were brought against Smith by all those with complaints concerning his management of the colony. At this point, Smith suffered a serious wound when a bag of gunpowder exploded. Sick and disappointed at the course of events in Jamestown, he left for England in the early fall of 1609. John Smith never returned to Virginia and would visit America only once more, though he lived on for twenty-two years.

The last phase of Smith's career extends from his return to England until his death in 1631. On the surface it appears as a long period of frustration. He saw America again only for a few months in 1614 when he mapped the New England coast. His voyage of 1615 was

[24] Actually the ship with Sir Thomas Gates and other administrators together with the official documents had been wrecked in the Bermudas and would not reach Virginia until the spring of 1610.

interrupted by a storm which nearly wrecked his ship and then, after refitting, he was captured by French pirates. In 1617 the Captain was held in Plymouth harbor by adverse winds for three months and the trip cancelled. Yet this last phase was by no means barren of accomplishment. During these years Smith published his most important works.[25] It was he who gave New England its name. Through his writings and map of the region, the best made to that date, Smith served as press agent for New England and can claim credit for indirectly advising both the Pilgrims and Puritans. Much of his energy and time went into an attempt to find support for the exploration and colonization of New England, and he sought to interest the London guilds in investing in his schemes. Further, he attempted to work out a plan of cooperation by which the London merchant adventurers and those of the West Country could pool their resources in such enterprises. The sharp commercial rivalries between these two groups prevented any real success in this direction.

Smith's 1614 voyage was made under the auspices of the London adventurers. It was, however, an economic failure and after 1614 he served the Plymouth Company merchants in the west, working closely with Sir Ferdinando Gorges. The abortive 1615 attempt saw Smith intent on setting up a colony in New England. In spite of his efforts, all he ever received for his cooperation was the worthless title of Admiral of New England. Yet, out of these later years came John Smith's mature vision of America. He developed a social theory which would be much closer to the reality of the future American scene than that of any other Elizabethan.

Smith's discussion of New England in *The Generall Historie* differs strikingly from the sections on Virginia.[26] He lacked time and resources to make such detailed observations and explorations as he had in Virginia. Further, there are numerous digressions in these pages which to the casual reader may seem remote from the topic at hand. Yet in

[25] *A Map of Virginia, with a Description of its Commodities, People, Government, and Religion* (1612), *A Description of New England; or, Observations and Discoveries in North America* (1616), *New England Trials* (1620), *New England Trials* (1622), *The Generall Historie* (1624), *An Accidence; or, The Pathway to Experience for Young Seamen* (1626), *The True Travels, Adventures, and Observations of Captain John Smith* (1630), and *Advertisements for the unexperienced Planters* (1631).
[26] See below, pp. 125–148.

these apparent digressions Smith developed his vision of America's future. His ideas are worth examining in some detail.

The origins of Smith's view of society and social life can be traced back to his own experience. In less than thirty years he put a good deal of social distance between himself and the Lincolnshire copyhold farm of his father. It was not unnatural, then, that Smith believed in mobility and the importance of new men making their way into higher levels of English society. Indeed, he fashioned a view of history which stressed the renewal of the old establishment with talent from the lower classes.

John Smith's idea of society was not the medieval conception of fixed social orders. He recognized, to be sure, the existence of a class system. Yet in Smith's mind, young men from the lower classes could become gentlemen. Industry and discretion might do for a man of humble origins what his parents failed to do for him at birth.[27] Although England provided many avenues for mobility, her social and economic resources were limited. Smith realized that a new geographical stage was necessary for the social drama he envisioned. New England provided what he sought.

In reflecting on New England's future, Smith observed that it was a country without "hard landlords to rack us with high rents, or extorting fines," where there were neither "tedious pleas in law to consume us with their many years' disputation for justice" nor mob violence. "Here every man may be master of his own labor and land, . . . and if he have nothing but his hands, he may set up his trade; and by industry quickly grow rich."[28] Clearly he saw the importance of the fact that certain encumbering social institutions would not be transplanted to New England and that the new society which developed there would not be hindered by feudal remains. Moreover, New England seemed to have the best combination of natural endowments in the new world. The northern winter might be harsher than that to the south, but in diversity of economic opportunity New England more than made up for this defect. Fertile soil, minerals, timber and naval stores, deep harbors, and the rich harvest of the sea—all these spelled wealth and social advancement for those willing to work.

[27] See below, p. 169. The *Advertisements* also contain some of John Smith's ideas on the future of America. These observations can best be understood only in conjunction with the material in *The Generall Historie*.
[28] See below, pp. 128–129.

Thus Smith developed his scheme for a New England colony.[29] Fishing would provide commodities for a staple trade with Europe. He carefully detailed the success that European fishermen had in the waters off New England and argued that a permanent English base there would extend the profit margin and soon the Dutch and French would be outdistanced by the English. With timber, pitch, tar, and iron available, New England would soon be building her own ships. It took the economic crash at the end of the 1630's and many years of painful trial and error before the Puritans of Massachusetts Bay learned this lesson which John Smith pointed out so clearly for them.

In a later consideration of the problem of a New England colony, John Smith advised that land be distributed with a lavish hand. "In so doing," he reasoned, "a servant that will labor, within four or five years may live as well there [in New England] as his master did here [in England]." Smith desired to see all the settlers own their land as freeholders rather than be encumbered with any lesser status. "For it is the greatest comfort you can give them, where the very name of servitude will breed much ill blood and become odious to God and man."[30]

If the individual would profit from the opportunities held out by New England, so would the state. Smith felt that the abundance of resources and opportunities in the new world would eliminate individual poverty and thus relieve the state of one of its most aggravating burdens.[31] Moreover, English society itself would be invigorated as a result of overseas colonial development. A new moral vitality would be infused into the very heart of English life. Where idle wealth and moral corruption now held sway, Smith contended, new vision and strength would appear. This argument was backed up with an interpretation of history. The Captain claimed that the great empires of earlier epochs fell because they lost means for training their youth in productive activities. Colonies offered the right training ground. Without them, England would succumb to the kind of dry rot that destroyed Rome.[32] Young men could prove themselves in the colonies and return home, if they wished, to occupy improved social positions. Indeed, Smith viewed this as so important that he suggested the English

[29] See below, pp. 131–132.
[30] See below, p. 180.
[31] See below, p. 143.
[32] See below, pp. 138–141.

gentry might well consider financing colonization if for no other reason than to protect themselves from the dual threat of rebellion by the disaffected at home and foreign invasion. He also echoed the traditional argument that overseas activities would build up the army and navy to protect England in time of war.

John Smith tried to keep his attention on the idea that colonization would be beneficial to both individual Englishmen and the society as a whole. There is some evidence, however, that even at this early date in American colonial history he realized that life in the new world might change a man in subtle ways. "Here [New England] nature and liberty affords us that freely which in England we want, or it costeth us dearly. What pleasure can be more than being tired with any occasion ashore, in planting vines, fruits, or herbs, in contriving their own grounds to the pleasure of their own minds, their fields, gardens, orchards, buildings, ships, and other works, &c., to recreate themselves before their own doors in their own boats upon the sea." Such activities, he reasoned, would bring pleasure as well as economic gain to "both servant, master and merchant."[33] This intertwining of pride in ownership, material profit, and the control over nature, all presage the psychological independence of the colonist. In a long and almost passionate passage, Smith summed up his vision of a properous middle-class colony and touched on many elements of the yet unformed American character:

> Who can desire more content that hath small means, or but only his merit to advance his fortunes, than to tread and plant that ground he hath purchased by the hazard of his life; if he have but the taste of virtue and magnanimity, what to such a mind can be more pleasant than planting and building a foundation for his posterity, got from the rude earth by God's blessing and his own industry without prejudice to any . . . what so truly suits with honor and honesty, as the discovering things unknown, erecting towns, peopling countries, informing the ignorant, reforming things unjust, teaching virtue and gain to our native mother country . . . find employment for those that are idle, because they know not what to do: so far from wronging any, as to cause posterity to remember thee; and remembering thee, ever honor that remembrance with praise.[34]

[33] See below, p. 142.
[34] See below, p. 138.

Even the gentleman found a new role in John Smith's scheme for New England. Hunting and fishing to supply food for individuals and the community was to take the place of idle hunting and hawking for mere sport. The dramatic challenge of the unknown wilderness was to replace the pale challenge of ritualized sport which was the gentleman's lot in old England. If this were not enough, the wonders of nature would offer compensations which the average English sportsman had not imagined possible.[35]

In John Smith's vision of America, prosperity and personal advancement were the key themes. Among the freeholders and members of a new and growing community, true virtue and honor were to be found. Finally, nature was so remarkable in her generosity, her contrasts, and the opportunities she afforded that like John Smith, settlers in New England might fall in love with the land.

Historians know very little about John Smith's relations with the Puritan leaders who founded Massachusetts Bay. There is no evidence that John Winthrop and John Smith ever met. Probably Winthrop read *The Generall Historie,* or at least heard it summarized at the meetings where the Massachusetts enterprise was planned. It is clear, however, that Smith was well informed on the activities of the Puritan leaders. His deep interest in their scheme is illustrated by the last work he wrote, *Advertisements for the unexperienced Planters of New England* (1631). Essentially a long memorandum intended for John Winthrop and the other Puritan leaders, the *Advertisements* is filled with practical advice and information for those who would settle in New England.[36] In it John Smith sums up his life and thought in a compact and often compelling form. Clearly he was aware that the Puritans were left of center in religion, but he tried to escape the consequences of his knowledge. Nothing could dissuade him from the desire to render whatever service he could. After all, Smith's last and deepest interest was in Virginia and New England, "his children that never had a mother."[37]

> And John Smith went exploring.
> He is one of the first Americans we know,
> And we can claim him, though not by the bond of birth,
> For we've always bred chimeras.

[35] See below, pp. 142–143.
[36] See below, pp. 164–195.
[37] Quoted in Barbour, *The Three Worlds of Captain John Smith,* p. 84.

And he was one,
This bushy-bearded, high-foreheaded, trusting man
Who could turn his hand to anything at a pinch,
Bragging, canny, impatient, durable
And fallen in love with the country at first sight.
For that is something which happens or does not.
It did to him.[38]

A Note on This Edition

The selections included in this volume are from *The Generall Historie* of 1624 and the *Advertisements for the unexperienced Planters of New England* of 1631, edited by Edward Arber and contained in his *Travels and Works of Captain John Smith,* published in Edinburgh in 1910. As suggested earlier in this introductory essay, *The Generall Historie* was selected because it stands as the mature summing-up of Smith's experience and observations. To be sure, he acted as a kind of general editor, incorporating the writings of other men as well as his own earlier writings into this final production. The incorporations of others are indicated as Smith originally did in the 1624 text.

It has been my aim to edit and annotate these early seventeenth century writings in a form that will make them intelligible to contemporary readers. I have by no means, however, attempted a translation into twentieth century English. The text will present certain difficulties to the reader attuned to the prose style of his own day. The Elizabethans wrote and talked to be listened to with care and attention. The changes in the form of written communication, so evident when Smith is compared to today's news media or most of the fiction writers now in vogue, indicate the wide gap which separates us from the seventeenth century. His sentences run on in long, unhurried periods which double back upon themselves, so that the reader is sometimes reminded of a translation from the Latin. Indeed, the Latin classics which John Smith studied in grammar school formed his own style and that of his contemporaries. If the reader brings his undivided attention to Smith's writings, he will soon develop the necessary facility to follow the pattern of thought.

If the prose style has changed since the founding of Jamestown, so has the very meaning of words. English has always been a voracious

[38] Stephen Vincent Benét, *Western Star* (New York, 1943), p. 72.

language; it has always relished adding new words to its massive storehouse. As a result, some words seem to fall into disfavor and are gradually abandoned. Others are emptied of their former meaning and given new content. I have identified words of this type so that the reader will not have to turn continually to the multi-volume *Oxford English Dictionary.* Where necessary, idioms are also identified. Generally, strange or archaic words have been identified at their first appearance.

In addition to the problem of meaning there are also difficulties with spelling, punctuation, and capitalization. I have modified the text as printed by Edward Arber in the following ways. Spelling has been brought into conformity with twentieth century usage, as have capitalization and the use of the italics of which the Elizabethan was so fond. In most instances, the punctuation remains the same as in the Arber text. The exception has been the insertion of commas in series. Where verb forms, prepositions, and adverbs have been altered they appear in brackets. On a few occasions verbs have been added in brackets to help clarify a particularly long sentence. Occasional footnotes have been provided to help identify persons, places, or events mentioned in the text. A few of these footnotes refer the reader to other passages in this edition. Some identifications have also been placed in the text in brackets.

Aside from these changes, passages which are repetitious have been deleted and all the poetry which Smith inserted for didactic purposes has been excised. In the Virginia chapters I have substituted the contemporary names for major rivers, putting the Indian name in brackets the first time the river is mentioned. Where possible, I have identified places and things by their twentieth century names.[39] This has been especially difficult for the geography of the New England coast, since Smith's observations were not as well organized and reported as were those he made in Virginia.

---

[39] Of special value here is Barbour, *The Three Worlds of Captain John Smith, passim;* Philip Alexander Bruce, *Economic History of Virginia in the Seventeenth Century* (2 vols., New York, 1907), especially vol. I, chapters I–IV; William B. Weeden, *Economic and Social History of New England, 1620–1789* (2 vols., New York, 1963), especially vol. I, chapters I–II; and Lewis C. Gray, *History of Agriculture in the Southern United States to 1860* (2 vols., Gloucester, Mass., 1958), especially vol. I, chapters I–II.

I am indebted to the following libraries whose collections proved of special value in the course of this project: the Brady Memorial Library, Manhattanville College of the Sacred Heart, Purchase, New York; the Columbia University Library; and the New York Public Library. During the academic year 1965-1966 my research assistant at Manhattanville College, Miss Maria Tymoski, cheerfully performed innumerable tasks from xeroxing to locating citations with skill and patience. Nancy Lankford not only demonstrated the usual wifely devotion by acting as typist, but also provided invaluable assistance in the process of editing the seventeenth century texts. Any sins of commission or omission rest, of course, on my head alone.

University of Missouri
Columbia, Missouri
November 10, 1966

PART ONE

Captain John Smith Reports on the American Scene

1. Virginia: The Land and its Native Inhabitants

Selections from Book II of
The Generall Historie of Virginia, New England, and the Summer Isles

. . . Virginia is a country in America between the degrees of 34 and 45 of the north latitude. The bounds thereof on the east side are the great ocean: on the south lieth Florida: on the north *nova Francia:* as for the west thereof, the limits are unknown. Of all this country we purpose [propose] not to speak, but only of that part which was planted by the Englishmen in the year of our Lord, 1606[-1607]. And this is under the degrees 37, 38, and 39. The temperature of this country doth agree well with English constitutions, being once seasoned to the country. Which appeared by this, that though by many occasions our people fell sick; yet did they recover by very small means, and continued in health, though there were other great causes, not only to have made them sick, but even to end their days, &c.

The summer is hot as in Spain; the winter cold as in France or England. The heat of summer is in June, July, and August, but commonly the cool breezes assuage the vehemency of the heat. The chief of winter is half [of] December, January, February, and half [of] March. The cold is extreme[ly] sharp, but here the proverb is true, that no extreme long continueth.

In the year 1607[-1608] was an extraordinary frost in most of Europe, and this frost was found as extreme in Virginia. But the next year for 8 or 10 days of ill weather, [an]other 14 days would be as summer.

The winds here are variable, but the like thunder and lightning to purify the air, I have seldom either seen or heard in Europe. From the southwest came the greatest gusts with thunder and heat. The northwest wind is commonly cool and bringeth fair weather with it. From the north is the greatest cold, and from the east and southeast as from the Bermudas, fogs and rains.

Sometimes there are great droughts, other times much rain, yet great necessity of neither, by reason we see not but that all the rarity of needful fruits in Europe, may be there in great plenty, by the industry of men, as appeareth by those we there planted.

There is but one entrance by sea into this country, and that is at the mouth of a very goodly bay, 18 or 20 miles broad. The cape on the south is called Cape Henry, in honor of our most noble Prince. The land, white hilly sands like unto the Downs, and all along the shores great plenty of pines and firs.

The north cape is called Cape Charles, in honor of the worthy Duke of York. The isles before it, Smith's Isles, by the name of the discover[er].

Within is a country that may have the prerogative [natural advantage] over the most pleasant places known, for large and pleasant navigable rivers, heaven and earth never agreed better to frame a place for man's habitation; were it fully manured [cultivated] and inhabited by industrious people. Here are mountains, hills, plains, valleys, rivers, brooks, all running most pleasantly into a fair bay, compassed but for the mouth, with fruitful and delightsome land. In the bay and rivers are many isles both great and small, some woody, some plain, most of them low and not inhabited. This bay lieth north and south, in which the water floweth near 200 miles, and hath a channel for 140 miles, of depth betwixt 6 and 15 fathoms, holding in breadth for the most part 10 or 14 miles. From the head of the bay to the northwest, the land is mountainous, and so in a manner from thence by a southwest line; so that the more southward, the farther off from the bay are those mountains. From which fall certain brooks which after come to five principal navigable rivers. These run from the northwest into the southeast, and so into the west side of the bay, where the fall [mouth] of every river is within 20 or 15 miles one of another.

The mountains are of divers natures: for at the head of the bay the rocks are of a composition like millstones. Some of marble, &c. And many pieces like crystal we found, as thrown down by water from those mountains. For in winter they are covered with much snow, and when it dissolveth the waters fall with such violence, that it causeth great inundations in some narrow valleys, which is scarce[ly] perceived being once in the rivers. These waters wash from the rocks such glistering tinctures, that the ground in some places seemeth as gilded, where both the rocks and the earth are so splendent to behold, that better judgments than ours might have been persuaded, they contained more than probabilities.

The vesture [vegetation] of the earth in most places doth manifestly prove the nature of the soil to be lusty and very rich. . . . Generally for the most part it is a black, sandy mold, in some places a fat, slimy clay, in other places a very barren gravel. But the best ground is known by the vesture it beareth, as by the greatness of trees, or abundance of weeds, &c.

The country is not mountainous, nor yet low, but such pleasant plain hills, and fertile valleys, one prettily crossing another, and watered so conveniently with fresh brooks and springs, no less commodious than delightsome. By the rivers are many plain marshes, containing some 20, some 100, some 200 acres, some more, some less. Other plains there are few, but only where the savages inhabit: but all [is] overgrown with trees and weeds, being a plain wilderness as God first made it.

On the west side of the bay, we said were 5 fair and delightful navigable rivers.

The first of those, and the next to the mouth of the bay hath his course from the west northwest. It is called [the] James [*Powhatan*], according to the name of a principal country that lieth upon it. The mouth of this river is near[ly] three miles in breadth, yet do the shoals force the channel near the land. . . . It is navigable 150 miles. . . . It falleth from rocks far west in a country inhabited by a nation they call *Monacans*. But where it cometh into our discovery it is [the] James. In the farthest place that was diligently observed, are falls, rocks, shoals, &c. which make it past navigation any higher. Thence in the running downward, the river is enriched with many goodly brooks, which are maintained by an infinite number of small rundles and pleasant springs, that disperse themselves for best service, as do the veins of a man's body.

From the south there falls into it: first, the pleasant river [the] Appomattox [*Apamatuck*]. . . .

From the north side is the river of Chickahominy [*Chickahamania*], the back river of Jamestown; another by the Cedar Isle, where we lived ten weeks upon oysters, then a convenient harbor for fisher boats at Old Point Comfort [*Kecoughtan*], that so turneth itself into bays and creeks, it makes that place very pleasant to inhabit; their cornfields being girded therein in a manner [as] peninsulas.

The most of these rivers are inhabited by several nations, or rather families, of the name of the rivers. They have also over those some governor, as their king, which they call *Werowances*.

In a peninsula on the north side of this river are the English planted in a place by them called Jamestown, in honor of the King's most excellent Majesty.

The first and next [to] the river's mouth are the *Kecoughtans,* who besides their women and children, have not past 20 fighting men. The *Paspaheghs* (on whose land is seated Jamestown, some 40 miles from the bay) have not past 40. The river called Chickahominy [has] near[ly] 250. The *Weanocs* 100. The *Arrohattocs* 30. The place called *Powhatan,* some 40. On the south side [of] this river the *Appomattocs* have sixty fighting men. The *Quiyoughcohannocks* 25. The *Nansemonds* 200. The *Chesapeakes* 100. Of this last place the bay beareth the name. In all these places is a several [separate] commander, which they call [a] *Werowance,* except the *Chickahominies,* who are governed by the priests and their assistants, or their elders called *Caw-cawwassoughes.* In summer no place affordeth more plenty of sturgeon, nor in winter more abundance of fowl, especially in the time of frost. I took once 52 sturgeons at a draught [using a net], at another 68. From the latter end of May till the end of June are taken few, but young sturgeons of two feet or a yard long. From thence till the midst of September, them of two or three yards long and few others. And in 4 or 5 hours with one net were ordinarily taken 7 or 8: often more, seldom less. In the small rivers all the year there is good plenty of small fish, so that with hooks those that would take pains had sufficient.

Fourteen miles northward from the river James is the river Pamunkey [*Panaunkee*], which is navigable [for] 60 or 70 miles, but with catches and small barks 30 or 40 miles farther. At the ordinary flowing of the salt water, it divideth itself into two gallant branches [Pamunkey and Mattaponi].

On the south side inhabit the people of *Youghtanund,* who have about 60 men for wars. On the north branch *Mattapament,* who have 30 men. Where this river is divided the country is called Pamunkey, and nourisheth near[ly] 300 able men. About 25 miles lower on the north side of this river is *Werowocómoco,* where their great King inhabited when I was delivered him prisoner; yet there are not past 40 able men. Ten or twelve miles lower, on the south side of this river, is *Kiskiack,* which hath some 40 or 50 men. These, as also *Appomattoc, Irrohatock,* and *Powhatan,* are their great King's chief alliance, and inhabitants. The rest [are] his conquests.

Before we come to the third river that falleth from the mountains, there is another river (some 30 miles navigable) that cometh from the inland, called [the] Piankatank [*Payankatanke*], the inhabitants are about 50 or 60 serviceable men.

The third navigable river is called [the] Rappahannock [*Toppahanock*]. (This is navigable [for] some 130 miles.) At the top of it inhabit the people called *Manahoacs* amongst the mountains, but they are above the place we described.

Upon this river on the north side are the people *Cuttatawomen,* with 30 fighting men. Higher are the *Moraughtacunds,* with 80. Beyond them *Rappahannock* with 100. Far above is another *Cuttatawomen* with 20. On the south is the pleasant seat of *Nantaughtacund* having 150 men. This river also as the two former, is replenished with fish and fowl.

The fourth river is called [the] Potomac [*Patawomeke*], 6 or 7 miles in breadth. It is navigable [for] 140 miles, and fed as the rest with many sweet rivers and springs, which fall from the bordering hills. These hills many of them are planted, and yield no less plenty and variety of fruit, than the river exceedeth with abundance of fish.

It is inhabited on both sides. First on the south side at the very entrance is *Wighcocomoco* and hath some 130 men, beyond them *Sekacawone* with 30. The *Onawmanient* with 100. And the *Patawomekes* more than 200.

Here doth the river divide itself into 3 or 4 convenient branches. The greatest of the least is called Aquia Creek [*Quiyough*], trending northwest, but the river itself turneth northeast, and is still a navigable stream. On the western side of this bought [bend] is *Tauxenent* with 40 men. On the north of this river is *Secowocomoco* with 40. Somewhat further *Potapaco* with 20. In the east part is *Pamacaeack* with 60. After *Moyowance* with 100. And lastly, *Nacotchtanke* with 80. The river above this place maketh his passage down a low, pleasant valley over-shadowed in many places with high, rocky mountains; from whence distill innumerable sweet and pleasant springs.

The fifth river is called [the] Patuxent [*Pawtuxunt*], of a less proportion than the rest; but the channel is 16 fathoms deep in some places. Here are infinite skulls [schools] of divers kinds of fish more than elsewhere.

Upon this river dwell the people called *Acquintanacksuak, Pawtuxunt,* and *Mattapanient.* Two hundred men was the greatest strength that could be there perceived. But they inhabit together, and [are] not so dispersed as the rest. These of all other we found most civil to give entertainment.

Thirty leagues northward is a river not inhabited, yet navigable; for the red clay resembling *bole armeniac* we called it [the] Patapsco [*Bolus*].

At the end of the bay where it is 6 or 7 miles in breadth, it divides itself into 4 branches, the best [Susquehanna] cometh northwest from among the mountains, but though canoes may go a day's journey or two up it, we could not get two miles up it with our boats for rocks.

Upon it [are] seated the *Susquehannocks,* near it north and by west runneth a creek a mile and a half: at the head whereof the ebb left us on shore, where we found many trees cut with hatchets. The next tide keeping the shore to seek for some savages; (for within thirty leagues' sailing, we saw not any, being a barren country) we went up another small river like a creek 6 or 7 mile[s]. From thence returning we met 7 canoes of the *Massawomekes,* with whom we had conference by signs, for we understood one another scarce[ly] a word: the next day we discovered the small river [Sassafras] and people of *Tockwough* trending eastward.

Having lost our grapnel [anchor] among the rocks of [the] Susquehanna, we were then near[ly] 200 miles from home, and our barge about two tons, and had in it but 12 men to perform this discovery, wherein we lay above 12 weeks upon those great waters in those unknown countries, having nothing but a little meal, oatmeal, and water to feed us, and scarce[ly] half sufficient of that for half that time, but what provision we got among the savages, and such roots and fish as we caught by accident and God's direction; nor had we a mariner nor any [that] had skill to trim the sails but two sailors and myself, the rest being gentlemen, or them [that] were as ignorant in such toil and labor. Yet necessity in a short time by good words and examples made them do that that caused them ever after to fear no 'colors. What I did with this small means I leave to the reader to judge, and the map I made of the country, which is but a small matter in regard of the magnitude thereof.

But to proceed, 60 of those *Susquehannocks* came to us with skins, bows, arrows, targets [shields], beads, swords, and tobacco pipes for presents. Such great and well proportioned men are seldom seen, for they seemed like giants to the English, yea and to the neighbors, yet seemed of an honest and simple disposition, [and they were] with much ado restrained from adoring us as gods. Those are the strangest people of all those countries, both in language and attire; for their language it may well befit their proportions, sounding from them, as a voice in a vault. Their attire is the skins of bears, and wolves, some have cassocks made of bears' heads and skins, that a man's head goes through the skin's neck, and the ears of the bear fastened to his shoulders, the nose and teeth hanging down his breast, another bear's face split behind him, and at the end of the nose hung a paw, the half sleeves coming to the elbows were the necks of bears, and the arms through the mouth; with paws hanging at their noses. One had the head of a wolf hanging in a chain for a jewel, his tobacco pipe three quarters of a yard long, prettily carved with a bird, a deer, or some such devise at the great end, sufficient to beat out one's brains: with bows, arrows, and clubs, suitable to their greatness.

These are scarce[ly] known to Powhatan. They can make [muster] near[ly] 600 able men, and are palisaded in their towns to defend them[selves] from the *Massawomekes,* their mortal enemies. Five of their chief *Werowances* came aboard us, and crossed the bay in the barge. The picture of the greatest of them is signified in the map. The calf of whose leg was three quarters of a yard about, and all the rest of his limbs so answerable to that proportion, that he seemed the goodliest man we ever beheld. His hair, the one side was long, the other shorn close with a ridge over his crown like a cockscomb. His arrows were five quarters [one quarter was equal to nine inches] long, headed with the splinters of a white crystal-like stone, in [the] form of a heart, an inch broad, and an inch and a half or more long. These he wore in a wolf's skin at his back for his quiver, his bow, in the one hand and his club in the other, as is described.

On the east side [of] the bay, is the river Sassafras [*Tockwough*], and upon it a people that can make 100 men, seated some seven miles within the river: where they have a fort very well palisaded and mantelled with barks of trees. Next [to] them is *Ozinies* with sixty men. More to the south of that east side of the bay, the river Choptank [*Rapahanock*], near unto which is the river Nanticoke [*Kuskarawaock*]. Upon which is seated a people with 200 men. After that, is the river Pocomoke [*Tants Wighcocomoco*], and on it a people with 100 men.

The people of those rivers are of little stature, of another language from the rest, and very rude. But they on the river *Acohanock* with 40 men, and they of *Accomac* [located on Cherrystone Inlet] [with] 80 men doth equalize any of the territories of Powhatan, and speak his language; who over all those doth rule as King.

Southward we went to some parts of *Chawanoac* and the *Mangoaks* to search for them left by Master White [at Roanoke Island].

Amongst those people are thus many several nations of sundry languages, that environ Powhatan's territories. The *Chawanoacs*, the *Mangoaks*, the *Monacans*, the *Manahoacs*, the *Massawomekes*, the *Powhatans*, the *Susquehannocks*, the *Atquanachukes*, the *Tockwoughs*, and the *Kuskarawaocks*. [Of] all those not any one understandeth another but by interpreters. . . .

Of such things which are naturally in Virginia,
and how the[y] use them.

Virginia doth afford many excellent vegetables, and living creatures, yet [of] grass there is little or none, but what groweth in low marshes: for all the country is overgrown with trees, whose droppings continually turneth their grass to weeds, by reason of the rankness of the ground, which would soon be amended by good husbandry. The wood[s] that [are] most common [are] oak and walnut, many of their oaks are so tall and straight, that they will bear two feet and a half square of good timber for 20 yards long; of this wood there [are] two or three several kinds. The acorns of one kind, whose bark is more white than the other, and somewhat sweetish, which being boiled, at last afford a sweet oil, that they keep in gourds to anoint their heads and joints. The fruit they eat made in bread or otherwise.

There are also some elm, some black walnut tree[s], and some ash: [from] ash and elm they make soap ashes. If the trees be very great, the ashes will be good, and melt to hard lumps, but if they be small, it will be but powder, and not so good as the other.

Of walnuts there [are] 2 or 3 kinds; there is a kind of wood we called cypress, because both the wood, the fruit, and leaf did most resemble it, and of those trees there are some near[ly] three fathoms about at the foot, very straight, and 50, 60, or 80 [feet] without a branch.

By the dwelling of the savages are some great mulberry trees, and in some parts of the country, they are found growing naturally in pretty groves. There was an assay [attempt] made to make silk, and surely the worms prospered excellent[ly] well, till the master workman fell sick. During which time they were eaten [by] rats.

In some parts were found some chestnuts, whose wild fruit equalize the best in France, Spain, Germany, or Italy.

Plums there are of three sorts. The red and white are like our hedge plums, but the other which they call *putchamins* [persimmons], grow as high as a palmetto: the fruit is like a medlar; it is first green, then yellow, and red when it is ripe: if it be not ripe, it will draw a man's mouth awry, with much torment, but when it is ripe, it is as delicious as an apricot.

They have cherries, and those are much like a damson, but [because of] their tastes and color we called them cherries. We saw some few crabs [wild apples], but [they were] very small and bitter.

Of vines [there is] great abundance in many parts that climb the tops of the highest trees in some places, but these bear but few grapes. Except by the rivers and savage habitations, where they are not over-shadowed from the sun, they are covered with fruit, though never pruned nor manured. Of those hedge grapes we made near[ly] twenty gallons of wine, which was like our French British wine, but certainly they would prove good were they well manured.

There is another sort of grape near[ly] as great as a cherry, this they call *messamins;* they be fat, and the juice thick. Neither doth the taste so well please when they are made in[to] wine.

They have a small fruit growing on little trees, husked like a chestnut, but the fruit most like a very small acorn. This they call *chechin-quamins* [chinquapins], which they esteem a great dainty. They have a berry much like our gooseberry, in greatness, color, and taste; those they call *rawcomens,* and do eat them raw or boiled.

[On] these natural fruits they live a great part of the year, which they use in this manner; the walnuts, chestnuts, acorns, and *che-chinquamins* are dried to keep. When they need walnuts they break them between two stones, yet some part of the shells will cleave to the fruit. Then do they dry them again upon a mat over a hurdle [grating]. After [that] they put it into a mortar of wood, and beat it very small: that done they mix it with water, that the shells may sink to the bottom. This water will be colored as milk, which they call *pawcohiccora,* and keep it for their use.

The fruit like medlars [which] they call *putchamins* [persimmons], they cast upon hurdles on a mat, and preserve them as prunes. [From] their chestnuts and *chechinquamins* boiled, they make both broth and bread for their chief men, or at their greatest feasts.

Besides those fruit trees, there is a white poplar, and another tree like unto it, that yieldeth a very clear and an odoriferous gum like turpentine, which some call balsam. There are also cedars and sassafras trees. They also yield gums in a small proportion of themselves. We tried conclusions to extract it out of the wood, but nature afforded more than our arts.

In the watery valleys groweth a berry which they call *ocoughta-namnis* [pokeberry?] very much like unto capers. These they dry in summer. When they eat them they boil them near[ly] half a day; for otherwise they differ not much from poison. *Mattoum* [wild rye] groweth as our bents. The seed is not much unlike to rye, though much smaller. This they use for a dainty bread buttered with deer suet.

During summer there are either strawberries, which ripen in April, or mulberries which ripen in May and June. Raspises [raspberries], hurts [hurtleberries]; or a fruit that the inhabitants call *maracocks* [squash], which is a pleasant, wholesome fruit much like a lemon.

Many herbs in the spring are commonly dispersed throughout the woods, good for broths and salads, as violets, purslane, sorrel, &c. Besides many we used whose names we know not.

The chief root they have for food is called *tockawhoughe* [tucka-hoe]. It groweth like a flag in marshes. In one day a savage will gather sufficient for a week. These roots are much of the greatness and taste of potatoes. They use to cover a great many of them with oak leaves and fern, and then cover all with earth in the manner of a coal pit; over it, on each side, they continue a great fire 24 hours before they dare eat it. Raw it is no better than poison, and being roasted, except it be tender and the heat abated, or sliced and dried in the sun, mixed with sorrel and meal or such like, it will prickle and torment the throat extremely, and yet in summer they use this ordinarily for bread.

They have another root which they call *wighsacan:* as th' other feedeth the body, so this cureth their hurts and diseases. It is a small root which they bruise and apply to the wound. *Puccoon* [bloodroot] is a small root that groweth in the mountains, which being dried and beat in[to] powder turneth red. And this they use for swellings, aches, anointing their joints, painting their heads and garments. They account it very precious, and of much worth. *Musquaspen* is a root of the bigness of a finger, and as red as blood. In drying, it will wither almost to nothing. This they use to paint their mats, targets, and such like.

There is also pellitory of Spain, sassafras, and divers other simples, which the apothecaries gathered, and commended to be good, and medicinable.

In the low marshes grow plots of onions, containing an acre of ground or more in many places; but they are small, not past the bigness of the top of one's thumb.

Of beasts the chief are deer, nothing differing from ours. In the deserts towards the heads of the rivers, there are many, but amongst the rivers few.

There is a beast they call *aroughcun* [raccoon], much like a badger, but useth to live [in] trees as squirrels do. Their squirrels some are near[ly] as great as our smallest sort of wild rabbits, some blackish or black and white, but the most are gray.

A small beast they have they call *assapanick,* but we call them flying squirrels, because spreading their legs, and so stretching the largeness of their skins, that they have been seen to fly 30 or 40 yards. An opossum hath a head like a swine, and a tail like a rat, and is of the bigness of a cat. Under her belly she hath a bag, wherein she lodgeth, carrieth, and suckleth her young. A *mussascus* [muskrat] is a beast of the form and nature of our water rats, but many of them smell exceeding[ly] strongly of musk. Their hares [are] no bigger than our conies, and few of them [are] to be found.

Their bears are very little in comparison [to] those of Muscovy and Tartary. The beaver is as big as an ordinary water dog, but his legs [are] exceeding[ly] short. His forefeet [are] like a dog's, his hinder feet like a swan's. His tail [is] somewhat like the form of a racquet, bare without hair, which to eat the savages esteem a great [delicacy]. They have many otters, which as the beavers they take with snares, and esteem the skins great ornaments; and of all those beasts they use to feed when they catch them.

An *utchunquoyes* is like a wild cat. Their foxes are like our silver haired conies, of a small proportion, and not smelling like those in England. Their dogs of that country are like their wolves, and cannot bark but howl; and the wolves not much bigger than our English foxes. Martens, polecats, weasels, and minks we know they have, because we have seen many of their skins, though very seldom any of them alive.

But one thing is strange, that we could never perceive their vermin destroy our hens, eggs, nor chickens, nor do any hurt, nor their flies nor serpents [to be] any way pernicious, where[as] in the south[ern] parts of America they are always dangerous, and often deadly.

Of birds the eagle is the greatest devourer. Hawks there be of divers sorts, as our falconers called them: sparrow hawks, lannerets, goshawks, falcons and ospreys, but they all prey most[ly] upon fish. Their partridges are little bigger than our quail. Wild turkeys are as big as our tame. There are woosels or blackbirds with red shoulders, thrushes and divers sorts of small birds, some red, some blue, scarce[ly] so big as a wren, but few in summer. In winter there are great plenty of swans, cranes gray and white with black wings, herons, geese, brants, ducks, widgeon, dotterel, oxeyes, parrots, and pigeons. [There was] of all those sorts great abundance, and some other strange kinds, to us unknown by name. But in summer [there were] not any, or a very few to be seen.

Of fish we were best acquainted with sturgeon, grampus, porpoise, seals, [and] stingrays whose tails are very dangerous. Brit, mullets, white salmon, trout, sole, plaice, herring, conyfish, rockfish, eels, lampreys, catfish, shad, perch of three sorts, crabs, shrimps, crayfish, oysters, cockles, and mussels. But the most strange fish is a small one, so like the picture of St. George his dragon, as possibl[y] can be, except his legs and wings; and the toadfish, which will swell till it be like to burst, when it cometh into the air.

Concerning the entrails of the earth, little can be said for certainty.

There wanted good refiners; for those that took [it] upon them[selves] to have skill this way, took up the washings from the mountains, and some moskered [crumbled] shining stones and spangles which the waters brought down, flattering themselves in their own vain conceits [fancies] to have been supposed what they were not, by the means of that ore, if it proved as their arts and judgments expected. Only this is certain, that many regions lying in the same latitude, afford mines very rich of divers natures. The crust also of these rocks would easily persuade a man to believe there are other mines than iron and steel, if there were but means and men of experience that knew the mine from spar.

Of their planted fruits in Virginia, and how they use them.

They divide the year into five seasons. Their winter some call *Popanow*, the spring, *Cattapeuk*, the summer, *Cohattayough*, the earing of their corn, *Nepinough*, the harvest and fall of leaf, *Taquitock*. From September until the midst of November are the chief feasts and sacrifice. Then have they plenty of fruits as well planted as natural, as corn green and ripe, fish, fowl, and wild beasts exceeding[ly] fat.

The greatest labor they take, is in planting their corn, for the country naturally is overgrown with wood. To prepare the ground they bruise the bark of the trees near the root, then do they scorch the roots with fire [so] that they grow no more.

The next year with a crooked piece of wood they beat up the weeds by the roots, and in that mold they plant their corn. Their manner is this. They make a hole in the earth with a stick, and into it they put four grains of wheat [corn] and two of beans. These holes they make four feet one from another; their women and children do continually keep it with weeding, and when it is grown middle high, they hill it about like a hop yard.

In April they begin to plant, but their chief plantation is in May, and so they continue till the midst of June. What they plant in April they reap in August, for May in September, for June in October; every stalk of their corn commonly beareth two ears, some three, seldom any four, many but one, and some none. Every ear ordinarily hath betwixt

200 and 500 grains. The stalk being green hath a sweet juice in it, somewhat like a sugar cane, which is the cause that when they gather their
corn green, they suck the stalks: for as we gather green peas, so do they
[gather] their corn being green, which excelleth their old.

They plant also peas they call *assentamens*. . . . Their beans are
. . . much esteeme[d] for dainties.

Their corn they roast in the ear green, and bruising it in a mortar
of wood with a polt [pestle], lap it in rolls in the leaves of their corn,
and so boil it for a dainty. They also reserve that corn late planted that
will not ripe[n], by roasting it in hot ashes, the heat thereof drying it.
In winter they esteem it being boiled with beans for a rare dish, they
call *pausarowmena*. Their old wheat [grains of corn] they first steep
a night in hot water, in the morning pounding it in a mortar. They use
a small basket for their temse [sieve], then pound again the great, and
so separating by dashing their hand in the basket, receive the flour in a
platter made of wood, scraped to that form with burning [coals] and
shells. Tempering [mixing] this flour with water, they make it either
in[to] cakes, covering them with ashes till they be baked, and then
washing them in fair water, they dry presently with their own heat:
or else boil them in water, eating the broth with the bread which they
call *ponap*.

The grouts [peeled grain] and pieces of the corn remaining, by
fanning, in a platter or in the wind, away the bran, they boil 3 or 4
hours with water, which is an ordinary food they call *ustatahamen*. But
some more thrifty than cleanly, do burn the core of the ear to powder,
which they call *pungnough,* mingling that in their meal; but it never
tasted well in bread, nor broth.

Their fish and flesh they boil either very tenderly, or boil it so long
on hurdles over the fire, or else after the Spanish fashion, putting it on
a spit, they turn first the one side, then the other, till it be as dry as their
jerkin [jerked] beef in the West Indies, that they may keep it a month
or more without putrifying. The broth of fish or flesh they eat as commonly as the meat.

In May also amongst their corn they plant pumpkins, and a fruit like
unto a muskmelon, but less and worse, which they call *maycocks*. These
increase exceedingly, and ripen in the beginning of July, and continue
until September. They plant also *maracocks* [squash], a wild fruit like
a lemon, which also increase infinitely. They begin to ripe[n] in September, and continue till the end of October.

When all their fruits be gathered, little else they plant, and this is done by their women and children; neither doth this long suffice them, for near[ly] three parts of the year, they only observe times and seasons, and live of[f] what the country naturally affordeth from hand to mouth, &c.

The commodities in Virginia, or that may be had by industry.

The mildness of the air, the fertility of the soil, and [the] situation of the rivers are so propitious to the nature and use of man, as no place is more convenient for pleasure, profit, and man's sustenance, under that latitude or climate. Here will live any beasts, as horses, goats, sheep, asses, hens, &c. as appeared by them that were carried thither. The waters, isles, and shoals, are full of safe harbors for ships of war or merchandise, for boats of all sorts, for transportation or fishing, &c.

The bay and rivers have much merchantable fish, and places fit for salt coats, building of ships, making of iron, &c. Muscovy and Poland do yearly receive many thousands, for pitch, tar, soap ashes, rosin, flax, cordage, sturgeon, masts, yards, wainscot, firs, glass, and such like; also Sweden for iron and copper. France in like manner, for wine, canvas, and salt. Spain as much for iron, steel, figs, raisins, and sacks [wines]. Italy with silks and velvets consumes our chief commodities. Holland maintains itself by fishing and trading at our own doors. All these temporize [trade] with other[s] for necessities, but all [are] as uncertain as peace or wars. Besides the charge, travel, and danger in transporting them, by seas, lands, storms, and pirates. Then how much hath Virginia the prerogative of all those flourishing kingdoms, for the benefit of our land, when as within one hundred miles all those are to be had, either ready provided by nature, or else to be prepared, were there but industrious men to labor. Only of copper we may doubt is wanting, but there is good probability that both copper and better minerals are there to be had for their labor. Other countries have it. So then here is a place, a nurse for soldiers, a practice for mariners, a trade for merchants, a reward for the good, and that which is most of all, a business (most acceptable to God) to bring such poor infidels to the knowledge of God and His holy gospel.

Of the natural inhabitants of Virginia.

The land is not populous, for the men be few; their far greater number is of women and children. Within 60 miles of Jamestown, there are
about some 5000 people, but of able men fit for their wars scarce[ly]
1500. To nourish so many together they have yet no means, because
they make so small a benefit of their land, be it never so fertile.

Six or seven hundred have been the most [that] hath been seen
together, when they gathered themselves to have surprised me at
Pamunkey, having but fifteen to withstand the worst of their fury. As
small as the proportion of ground that hath yet been discovered, is in
comparison of that yet unknown: the people differ very much in stature,
especially in language, as before is expressed.

Some being very great as the *Susquehannocks;* others very little, as
the *Wighcocomocos:* but generally tall and straight, of a comely proportion, and of a color brown when they are of any age, but they are
born white. Their hair is generally black, but few have any beards. The
men wear half their beards [heads] shaven, the other half long; for
barbers they use their women, who with two shells will grate away the
hair, of any fashion they please. The women['s hair is] cut in many
fashions, agreeable to their years, but ever some part remaineth long.

They are very strong, of an able body and full of agility, able to endure to lie in the woods under a tree by the fire, in the worst of winter,
or in the weeds and grass, in ambush in the summer.

They are inconstant in everything, but what fear constraineth them
to keep. [They are] crafty, timorous, quick of apprehension, and very
ingenuous. Some are of disposition fearful, some bold, most cautelous
[cautious], all savage. Generally [they are] covetous of copper, beads,
and such like trash. They are soon moved to anger, and so malicious,
that they seldom forget an injury: they seldom steal one from another,
lest their conjurers should reveal it, and so they be pursued and punished. That they are thus feared is certain, but that any can reveal their
offenses by conjuration I am doubtful. Their women are careful not to
be suspected of dishonesty without the leave of their husbands.

Each household knoweth their own lands, and gardens, and most live
of their own labors.

For their apparel, they are sometime[s] covered with the skins of
wild beasts, which in winter are dressed with the hair, but in summer

without. The better sort use large mantles of deer skins, not much
differing in fashion from the Irish mantles. Some [are] embroidered
with white beads, some with copper, other[s] painted after their manner. But the common sort have scarce to cover their nakedness, but with
grass, the leaves of trees, or such like. We have seen some use mantles
made of turkey feathers, so prettily wrought and woven with threads
that nothing could be discerned but the feathers. That was exceeding[ly] warm and very handsome. But the women are always covered
about their middles with a skin, and very shamefaced to be seen
bare.

They adorn themselves [most]ly with copper beads and paintings.
Their women, some have their legs, hands, breasts, and face cunningly
embroidered [tattooed] with divers works, as beasts, serpents, artificially
wrought into their flesh with black spots. In each ear commonly they
have 3 great holes, whereat they hang chains, bracelets, or copper. Some
of their men wear in those holes, a small green and yellow colored
snake, near[ly] half a yard in length, which crawling and lapping
[it]self about his neck oftentimes familiarly would kiss his lips. Others
wear a dead rat tied by the tail. Some on their heads wear the wing of
a bird, or some large feather with a rattle. Those rattles are somewhat
like the shape of a rapier but less, which they take from the tail of a
snake. Many have the whole skin of a hawk or some strange fowl,
stuffed with the wings abroad. Others a broad piece of copper, and
some the hand of their enemy dried. Their heads and shoulders are
painted red with the root *puccoon* [bloodroot] brayed [beaten] to
powder, mixed with oil, this they hold in summer to preserve them
from the heat, and in winter from the cold. Many other forms of paintings they use, but he is the most gallant that is the most monstrous to
behold.

Their buildings and habitations are for the most part by the rivers,
or not far distant from some fresh spring. Their houses are built like
our arbors, of small young springs [trees] bowed and tied, and so
close[ly] covered with mats, or the barks of trees very handsomely, that
notwithstanding either wind, rain, or weather, they are as warm as
stoves, but very smoky, yet at the top of the house there is a hole made
for the smoke to go into right over the fire.

Against the fire they lie on little hurdles of reeds covered with a mat,
born from the ground a foot and more by a hurdle of wood. On these
around about the house they lie heads and points one by th'other against

the fire, some covered with mats, some with skins, and some stark naked
lie on the ground, from 6 to 20 in a house.

Their houses are in the midst of their fields or gardens, which are
small plots of ground. Some [are] 20 acres, some 40, some 100, some
200, some more, some less. In some places from 2 to 50 of those houses
[are] together, or but a little separated by groves of trees. Near their
habitations is little small wood or old trees on the ground by reason of
their burning of them for fire. So that a man may gallop a horse
amongst these woods any way, but where the creeks or rivers shall
hinder.

Men, women, and children have their several names according to
the several humor of their parents. Their women (they say) are easily
delivered of child, yet do they love children very dearly. To make them
hardy, in the coldest mornings they wash them in the rivers, and by
painting and ointments so tan their skins, that after a year or two, no
weather will hurt them.

The men bestow their times in fishing, hunting, wars, and such man-
like exercises, scorning to be seen in any womanlike exercise, which is
the cause that the women be very painful [diligent], and the men often
idle. The women and children do the rest of the work. They make mats,
baskets, pots, mortars, pound their corn, make their bread, prepare
their victuals, plant their corn, gather their corn, bear all kind[s] of
burdens, and such like.

Their fire they kindle presently by chafing a dry, pointed stick in a
hole of a little square piece of wood, that firing itself, will so fire moss,
leaves, or any such like dry thing, that will quickly burn.

In March and April they live much upon their fishing weirs; and feed
on fish, turkeys, and squirrels. In May and June they plant their fields,
and live most[ly] on acorns, walnuts, and fish. But to amend their diet,
some disperse themselves in small companies, and live upon fish,
beasts, crabs, oysters, land tortoises, strawberries, mulberries, and such
like. In June, July, and August, they feed upon the roots of *tocknough,*
berries, fish, and green wheat [corn].

It is strange to see how their bodies alter with their diet, even as the
deer and wild beasts they seem fat and lean, strong and weak. Powhatan
their great King, and some others that are provident, roast their fish
and flesh upon hurdles as before is expressed, and keep it till scarce
times.

For fishing, hunting, and wars they use much their bow and arrows.

They bring their bows to the form of ours by the scraping of a shell. Their arrows are made, some of straight young sprigs, which they head with bone, some 2 or 3 inches long. These they use to shoot at squirrels on trees. Another sort of arrows they use made of reeds. These are pieced with wood, headed with splinters of crystal, or some sharp stone, the spurs of a turkey, or the bill of some bird. For his knife he hath the splinter of a reed to cut his feathers in form. With this knife also, he will joint a deer, or any beast, shape his shoes, buskins, mantles, &c. To make the nock of his arrow he hath the tooth of a beaver, set in a stick, wherewith he grateth it by degrees. His arrowhead he quickly maketh with a little bone, which he ever weareth at his bracer, of any splint of a stone, or glass in the form of a heart, and these they glue to the end of their arrows. With the sinews of deer, and the tops of deer horns boiled to a jelly, they make a glue that will not dissolve in cold water.

For their wars also they use targets that are round and made of the barks of trees, and a sword of wood at their backs, but oftentimes they use for swords the horn of a deer put through a piece of wood in [the] form of a pickax. Some [have] a long stone sharpened at both ends, used in the same manner. This they were wont to use also for hatchets, but now by trucking they have plenty of the same form of iron. And those are their chief instruments and arms.

Their fishing is much in boats. These they make of one tree by burning and scratching away the coals with stones and shells, till they have made it in [the] form of a trough. Some of them are an ell [one ell was equal to 45 inches] deep, and forty or fifty feet in length, and some will bear 40 men, but the most ordinary are smaller, and will bear 10, 20, or 30, according to their bigness. Instead of oars, they use paddles and sticks, with which they will row faster than our barges.

Betwixt their hands and thighs, their women use to spin the barks of trees, deer sinews, or a kind of grass they call *pemmenaw*, of these they make a thread very even and readily. This thread serveth for many uses. As about their housing, apparel, as also they make nets for fishing, for the quantity as formally braided as ours. They make also with it lines for angle[r]s.

Their hooks are either a bone grated as they notch their arrows in the form of a crooked pin or fishhook, or of the splinter of a bone tied to the cleft of a little stick, and with the end of the line, they tie on the bait.

They use also long arrows tied [to] a line, wherewith they shoot at fish in the rivers. But those of *Accomac* use staves like unto javelins headed with bone. With these they dart fish swimming in the water. They have also many artificial weirs, in which they get abundance of fish.

In their hunting and fishing they take extreme pains; yet it being their ordinary exercise from their infancy, they esteem it a pleasure and are very proud to be expert therein. And by their continual ranging, and travel, they know all the advantages and places most frequented with deer, beasts, fish, fowl, roots, and berries. At their huntings they leave their habitations, and reduce themselves into companies, as the Tartars do, and go to the most desert places with their families, where they spend their time in hunting and fowling up towards the mountains, by the heads of their rivers, where there is plenty of game. For betwixt the rivers the grounds are so narrow, that little cometh here which they devour not. It is a marvel they can so directly pass these deserts, some 3 or 4 days' journey without habitation. Their hunting houses are like unto arbors covered with mats. These their women bear after them, with corn, acorns, mortars, and all [the] bag and baggage they use. When they come to the place of exercise, every man doth his best to show his dexterity, for by their excelling in those qualities, they get their wives. Forty yards will they shoot level, or very near the mark, and 120 is their best at random. At their huntings in the deserts they are commonly two or three hundred together. Having found the deer, they environ [surround] them with many fires, and betwixt the fires they place themselves. And some take their stands in the midsts. The deer being thus feared by the fires, and their voices, they chase them so long within that circle, that many times they kill 6, 8, 10, or 15 at a hunting. They use also to drive them into some narrow point of land, when they find that advantage; and so force them into the river, where with their boats they have ambushes to kill them. When they have shot a deer by land, they follow him like bloodhounds by the blood and strain, and oftentimes so take them. Hares, partridges, turkeys, or eggs, fat or lean, young or old, they devour all they can catch in their power.

In one of these huntings they found me in the discovery of the head of the river of Chickahominy, where they slew my men, and took me prisoner in a bogmire; where I saw those exercises, and gathered these observations.

One savage hunting alone, useth the skin of a deer slit on the one side, and so put on his arm, through the neck, so that his hand comes to the head which is stuffed, and the horns, head, eyes, ears, and every part as artificially counterfeited as they can devise. Thus shrouding his body in the skin by stalking, he approacheth the deer, creeping on the ground from one tree to another. If the deer chance to find fault, or stand at gaze, he turneth the head with his hand to his best advantage to seem like a deer, also gazing and licking himself. So watching his best advantage to approach, having shot him, he chaseth him by his blood and strain till he get him.

When they intend any wars, the *Werowances* usually have the advice of their priests and conjurers, and their allies, and ancient friends; but chiefly the priests determine their resolution. Every *Werowance,* or some lusty fellow, they appoint captain over every nation. They seldom make war for lands or goods, but for women and children, and principally for revenge. They have many enemies, namely, all their westernly countries beyond the mountains, and the heads of the rivers. Upon the head of the *Powhatans* are the *Monacans,* whose chief habitation is at *Rassawek;* unto whom the *Mowhemenchughes,* the *Massinacacks,* the *Monahassanughs,* the *Monasickapanoughs,* and other nations pay tributes.

Upon the head of the river of Rappahannock is a people called *Manahoacs.* To these are contributers the *Tauxanias,* the *Shackakonias,* the *Ontponeas,* the *Tegninateos,* the *Whonkenteaes,* the *Stegaras,* the *Hassinungas,* and divers others, all confederates with the *Monacans,* though many different in language, and be very barbarous, living for the most part [on] wild beasts and fruits.

Beyond the mountains from whence is the head of the river Potomac, the savages report inhabit their most mortal enemies, the *Massawomekes,* upon a great salt water, which by all likelihood is either some part of Canada, some great lake, or some inlet of some sea that falleth into the South sea. These *Massawomekes* are a great nation and very populous. For the heads of all those rivers, especially the *Patawomekes,* the *Patuxents,* the *Susquehannocks,* [and] the *Tockwoughs* are continually tormented by them: of whose cruelty, they generally complained, and very importunate they were with me and my company to free them from these tormentors. To this purpose they offered food, conduct, assistance, and continual subjection.

Which I concluded to effect. But the Council then present [at James-town] emulating [jealous of] my success, would not think it fit to spare me forty men to be hazarded in those unknown regions, having passed (as before was spoken of) but with 12, and so was lost that opportunity.

Seven boats full of these *Massawomekes* we encountered at the head of the bay; whose targets, baskets, swords, tobacco pipes, platters, bows, and arrows, and everything showed, they much exceeded them of our parts; and their dexterity in their small boats, made of the barks of trees sewn with bark and well luted [cemented] with gum, argueth that they are seated upon some great water.

Against all these enemies the *Powhatans* are constrained sometimes to fight. Their chief attempts are by stratagems, treacheries, or surprisals. Yet the *Werowances,* women and children they put not to death, but keep them captives. They have a method in war, and for our pleasures they showed it [to] us, and it was in this manner performed at *Matta-panient.*

Having painted and disguised themselves in the fiercest manner they could devise. They divided themselves into two companies, near[ly] a hundred in a company. The one company [they] called *Monacans,* the other *Powhatans.* Either army had [its] captain. These as enemies took their stands a musket shot one from another; [they] ranked themselves 15 abreast, and each rank from another 4 or 5 yards, not in file, but in the opening betwixt their files. So the rear could shoot as conveniently as the front.

Having thus pitched the fields: from either part went a messenger with these conditions, that whosoever were vanquished, such as escape upon their submission in two days after should live, but their wives and children should be prize for the conquerors.

The messengers were no sooner returned, but they approached in their orders; on each flank a sergeant, and in the rear an officer for lieutenant, all duly keeping their orders, yet leaping and singing after their accustomed tune, which they only use in wars. Upon the first flight of arrows they gave such horrible shouts and screeches, as so many infernal hellhounds could not have made them more terrible.

When they had spent their arrows, they joined together prettily, charging and retiring, every rank seconding [the] other. As they got advantage they caught their enemies by the hair of the head, and down he came that was taken. His enemy with his wooden sword seemed to beat out his brains, and still they crept to the rear, to maintain the skirmish.

The *Monacans* decreasing, the *Powhatans* charged them in the form of a half moon; they unwilling to be enclosed, fled all in a troop to their ambushes, [to which] they led them very cunningly. The *Monacans* disperse[d] themselves among the fresh men, whereupon the *Powhatans* retired, with all speed to their seconds; which the *Monacans* seeing, took that advantage to retire again to their own battle[field], and so each returned to their own quarter.

All their actions, voices, and gestures, both in charging and retiring were so strained to the height of their quality and nature, that the strangeness thereof made it seem very delightful.

For their music they use a thick cane, on which they pipe as on a recorder. For their wars they have a great deep platter of wood. They cover the mouth thereof with a skin, at each corner they tie a walnut, which meeting on the backside near the bottom, with a small rope they twitch them together till it be so taut and stiff, that they may beat upon it as upon a drum. But their chief instruments are rattles made of small gourds, or pumpkin shells. Of these they have bass, tenor, countertenor, mean, and treble. These mingled with their voices sometimes twenty or thirty together, make such a terrible noise as would rather affright, than delight any man.

If any great commander arrive at the habitation of a *Werowance,* they spread a mat as the Turks do a carpet for him to sit upon. Upon another right opposite they sit themselves. Then do all with a tunable [harmonious] voice of shouting bid him welcome. After this do two or more of their chiefest men make an oration, testifying their love. Which they do with such vehemency, and so great passions, that they sweat till they drop, and are so out of breath they can scarce[ly] speak. So that a man would take them to be exceeding[ly] angry, or stark mad. Such victual as they have, they spend freely; and at night where his lodging is appointed, they set a woman fresh[ly] painted red with *puccoon* and oil, to be his bed fellow.

Their manner of trading is for copper, beads, and such like, for which they give such commodities as they have, as skins, fowl, fish, flesh, and their country corn. But their victuals are their chiefest riches.

Every spring they make themselves sick with drinking the juice of a root they call *wighsacan,* and water; whereof they pour so great a quantity, that it purgeth them in a very violent manner; so that in three or four days after, they scarce[ly] recover their former health.

Sometimes they are troubled with dropsies, swellings, aches, and such like diseases; for cure whereof they build a stove in the form of a dove house with mats, so close that a few coals therein covered with a pot, will make the patient sweat extremely. For swellings also they use small pieces of touchwood, in the form of cloves, which pricking on the grief they burn close to the flesh, and from thence draw the corruption with their mouth. With this root *wighsacan* they ordinarily heal green wounds. But to scarify a swelling, or make incision, their best instruments are some splintered stone[s]. Old ulcers, or putrified hurts are seldom seen cured amongst them.

They have many professed physicians, who with their charms and rattles, with an infernal rout of words and actions, will seem to suck their inward grief from their navels, or their grieved places; but of our surgeons they were so conceited, that they believed any plaster would heal any hurt. . . .

Of their religion.

There is yet in Virginia no place discovered to be so savage, in which they have not a religion, deer, and bow and arrows. All things that are able to do them hurt beyond their prevention, they adore with their kind of divine worship; as the fire, water, lightning, thunder, our ordnance, pieces [firearms], horses, &c.

But their chief god they worship is the Devil. Him they call *Okee,* and serve him more of fear than love. They say they have conference with him, and fashion themselves as near to his shape as they can imagine. In their temples they have his image evil favoredly carved, and then painted and adorned with chains of copper, and beads, and covered with a skin, in such manner as the deformity [moral ugliness] may well suit with such a god.

By him is commonly the sepulcher of their kings. Their bodies are first bowelled, then dried upon hurdles till they be very dry, and so about the most of their joints and neck they hang bracelets, or chains of copper, pearl, and such like, as they use to wear; their inwards they stuff with copper, beads, hatchets, and such trash. Then lap they them very carefully in white skins, and so roll them in mats for their winding sheets. And in the tomb which is an arch made of mats, they lay them orderly. What remaineth of this kind of wealth their kings have, they set at their feet in baskets. These temples and bodies are kept by their priests.

For their ordinary burials, they dig a deep hole in the earth with sharp stakes, and the corpse being lapped in skins and mats with their jewels, they lay them upon sticks in the ground, and so cover them with earth. The burial ended, the women being painted all their faces with black coal and oil, do sit twenty-four hours in the houses mourning and lamenting by turns, with such yelling and howling, as may express their great passions.

In every territory of a *Werowance* is a temple and a priest, two or three or more. Their principal temple or place of superstition is at *Uttamussak* at Pamunkey, near unto which is a house, temple, or place of Powhatan's.

Upon the top of certain red, sandy hills in the woods, there are three great houses filled with images of their Kings, and Devils, and tombs of their predecessors. Those houses are near[ly] sixty feet in length and built arbor[like], after their building. This place they count so holy as that [none] but the priests and Kings dare come into them; nor the savages dare not go up the river in boats by it, but they solemnly cast some piece of copper, white beads, or *puccoon* into the river, for fear their *Okee* should be offended and revenged of them. . . .

In this place commonly are resident seven priests. The chief differed from the rest in his ornaments, but inferior priests could hardly be known from the common people, but that they had not so many holes in their ears to hang their jewels at.

The ornaments of the chief priest were certain attires for his head made thus. They took a dozen, or 16, or more snakeskins and stuffed them with moss, and of weasels and other vermin skins a good many. All these they tie by their tails, so as all their tails meet in the top of their head like a great tassel. Round about this tassel is as it were a crown of feathers, the skins hang round about his head, neck, and shoulders, and in a manner cover his face.

The faces of all their priests are painted as ugly as they can devise, in their hands they had every one his rattle, some bass [in tone], some smaller. Their devotion was most[ly] in songs, which the chief priest beginneth and the rest followed him: sometimes he maketh invocations with broken sentences by starts and strange passions; and at every pause, the rest give a short groan. . . .

It could not be perceived that they keep any day as more holy than other[s]; but only in some great distress of want, fear of enemies, times of triumph and gathering together their fruits, the whole country of men, women, and children come together [for] solemnities. The manner of their devotion is, sometimes to make a great fire, in the house or fields, and all to sing and dance about it with rattles and shouts together, four or five hours. Sometimes they set a man in the midst, and about him they dance and sing, he all the while clapping his hands, as if he would keep time: and after their songs and dancings ended they go to their feasts. . . .

They have also divers conjurations, one they made when I was their prisoner. . . .

They have also certain altar stones they call *pawcorances*, but these stand from their temples, some by their houses, others in the woods and wildernesses, where they have had any extraordinary accident, or encounter. And as you travel, at those stones they will tell you the cause why they were there erected, which from age to age they instruct their children, as their best records of antiquities. Upon these they offer blood, deer suet, and tobacco. This they do when they return from the wars, from hunting, and upon many other occasions.

They have also another superstition that they use in storms, when the waters are rough in the rivers and seacoasts. Their conjurers run to the water sides, or passing in their boats, after many hellish outcries and invocations, they cast tobacco, copper, *puccoon,* or such trash into the water, to pacify that god whom they think to be very angry in those storms.

Before their dinners and suppers the better sort will take the first bit, and cast it in the fire, which is all the grace they are known to use.

In some part of the country they have yearly a sacrifice of children. Such a one was at *Quiyoughcohannock* some ten miles from Jamestown, and thus performed.

Fifteen of the properest young boys, between ten and fifteen years of age they painted white. Having brought them forth, the people spent the forenoon in dancing and singing about them with rattles.

In the afternoon they put those children to the root of a tree. By them all the men stood in a guard, every one having a bastinado [truncheon] in his hand, made of reeds bound together. This made a lane between them all along, through which there were appointed five young men to fetch these children: so every one of the five went through the guard to fetch a child each after other by turns, the guard fiercely beating them with their bastinadoes, and they patiently enduring and receiving all defending the children with their naked bodies from the unmerciful blows, that pay them soundly, though the children escape. All this while the women weep and cry out very passionately, providing mats, skins, moss and dry wood, as things fitting their children's funerals.

After the children were thus past the guard, the guard tore down the trees, branches and boughs, with such violence that they rent the body, and made wreaths for their heads, or bedecked their hair with the leaves. What else was done with the children, was not seen, but they were all cast on a heap, in a valley as dead, where they made a great feast for all the company.

The *Werowance* being demanded the meaning of this sacrifice, answered that the children were not all dead, but that the *Okee* or Devil did suck the blood from their left breast, who chanced to be his by lot, till they were dead; but the rest were kept in the wilderness by the young men till nine months were expired, during which time they must not converse with any: and of these were made their priests and conjurers.

This sacrifice they held to be so necessary, that if they should omit it, their *Okee* or Devil, and all their other *Quiyoughcosughes,* which are their other gods, would let them have no deer, turkeys, corn, nor fish: and yet besides, he would make a great slaughter amongst them.

They think that their *Werowances* and priests which they also esteem *Quiyoughcosughes,* when they are dead, do go beyond the mountains toward the setting of the sun, and ever remain there in [the] form of their *Okee,* with their heads painted with oil and *puccoon,* finely trimmed with feathers, and shall have beads, hatchets, copper, and tobacco, doing nothing but dance and sing, with all their predecessors.

But the common people they suppose shall not live after death, but rot in their graves like dead dogs.

To divert them from this blind idolatry, we did our best endeavors, chiefly with the *Werowance* of *Quiyoughcohannock,* whose devotion, apprehension, and good disposition, much exceeded any in those countries, with whom although we could not as yet prevail, to forsake his false gods, yet this he did believe that our God as much exceeded theirs, as our guns did their bows and arrows: and many times did send to me [at] Jamestown, entreating me to pray to my God for rain, for their gods would not send them any. And in this lamentable ignorance do these poor souls sacrifice themselves to the Devil, not knowing their Creator; and we had not language sufficient, so plainly to express it as [to] make them understand it; which God grant they may. . . .

Of the manner of the Virginians' government.

Although the country people be very barbarous, yet have they amongst them such government, as that their magistrates for good commanding, and their people for due subjection and obeying, excel many places that would be counted very civil.

The form of their commonwealth is a monarchical government, one as emperor ruleth over many kings or governors. Their chief ruler is called Powhatan, and taketh his name [from] his principal place of dwelling called *Powhatan*. But his proper name is *Wahunsonacock*.

Some countries he hath which have been his ancestors', and came unto him by inheritance, as the country called *Powhatan, Arrohattoc, Appomattoc, Pamunkey, Youghtanund,* and *Mattapanient.* All the rest of his territories . . . they report have been his several conquests.

In all his ancient inheritances, he hath houses built after their manner like arbors, some 30, some 40 yards long, and at every house provision for his entertainment according to the time. At *Werowocómoco* on the north side of the river Pamunkey, was his residence, when I was delivered him prisoner, some 14 miles from Jamestown; where for the most part, he was resident, but at last he took so little pleasure in our near neighborhood, that he retired himself to *Orapaks,* in the desert betwixt *Chickahominy* and *Youghtanund.*

He is of personage a tall, well proportioned man, with a sour look, his head somewhat gray, his beard so thin, that it seemeth none at all, his age near sixty; of a very able and hardy body to endure any labor. About his person ordinarily attendeth a guard of 40 or 50 of the tallest men his country doth afford. Every night upon the four quarters of his house are four sentinels, each from other a flight shoot [bow shot], and at every half hour one from the *corps du guard* doth hollow [call], shaking his lips with his finger between them; unto whom every sentinel doth answer round from his stand: if any fail[s], they presently send forth an officer that beateth him extremely.

A mile from *Orapaks* in a thicket of wood, he hath a house in which he keepeth his kind of treasure, as skins, copper, pearl, and beads, which he storeth up against the time of his death and burial. Here also is his store of red paint for ointment, bows and arrows, targets, and clubs. This house is fifty or sixty yards in length, frequented only by priests. At the four corners of this house stand four images as sentinels, one of a dragon, another a bear, the third like a leopard, and the fourth like a giant-like man: all made evil favoredly, according to their best workmanship.

He hath as many women as he will, whereof when he lieth on his bed, one sitteth at his head, and another at his feet; but when he sitteth, one sitteth on his right hand and another on his left. As he is weary of his women, he bestoweth them on those that best deserve them at his hands.

When he dineth or suppeth, one of his women, before and after meat, bringeth him water in a wooden platter to wash his hands. Another waiteth with a bunch of feathers to wipe them instead of a towel, and the feathers when he hath wiped are dried again.

His kingdoms descend not to his sons nor children, but first to his brethren, whereof he hath 3, namely, *Opitchapam, Opechancanough,* and *Catataugh,* and after their decease to his sisters. First to the eldest sister, then to the rest, and after them to the heirs male or female of the eldest sister, but never to the heirs of the males.

He nor any of his people understand any letters, whereby to write or read, only the laws whereby he ruleth is custom. Yet when he listeth his will is a law and must be obeyed: not only as a King, but as half a god they esteem him.

His inferior Kings, whom they call *Werowances,* are tied to rule by customs, and have power of life and death at their command in that nature. But this word *Werowance,* which we call and construe for a King, is a common word, whereby they call all commanders: for they have but few words in their language, and but few occasions to use any officers more than one commander, which commonly they call *Werowance,* or *Caucorouse,* which is Captain.

They all know their several lands, and habitations, and limits, to fish, fowl, or hunt in: but they hold all of their great *Werowance* Powhatan, unto whom they pay tribute of skins, beads, copper, pearl, deer, turkeys, wild beasts, and corn. What he commandeth they dare not disobey in the least thing. It is strange to see with what great fear and adoration, all these people do obey this Powhatan. For at his feet they present whatsoever he commandeth, and at the least frown of his brow, their greatest spirits will tremble with fear: and no marvel, for he is very terrible and tyrannous in punishing such as offend him.

For example, he caused certain malefactors to be bound hand and foot, then having of many fires gathered great store of burning coals, they rake[d] these coals round in the form of a cockpit, and in the midst they cast the offenders to broil to death. Sometimes he causeth the heads of them that offend him, to be laid upon the altar or sacrificing stone, and one with clubs beats out their brains. When he would punish any notorious enemy or malefactor, he causeth him to be tied to a tree, and with mussel shells or reeds, the executioner cutteth off his joints one after another, ever casting what they cut of[f] into the fire; then doth he proceed with shells and reeds to case the skin from his head and face; then do they rip his belly and so burn him with the tree and all. Thus themselves reported they executed George Cassen [see below, p. 44].

Their ordinary correction is to beat them with cudgels. We have seen a man kneeling on his knees, and at Powhatan's command, two men have beate[n] him on the bare skin, till he hath fallen senseless in a sound [swoon], and yet never cry nor complained. And he made a woman for playing the whore, sit upon a great stone, on her bare breech twenty-four hours, only with corn and water, every three days, till nine days were past; yet he loved her exceedingly: notwithstanding there are common whores by profession.

In the year 1608, he surprised the people of *Piankatank* his near neighbors and subjects. The occasion was to us unknown, but the manner was thus. First he sent divers of his men as to lodge amongst them that night, then the ambushe[r]s environed all their houses, and at the hour appointed, they all fell to the spoil: twenty-four men they slew; the long hair of the one side of their heads, with the skin cased off with shells or reeds, they brought away. They surprised also the women, and the children, and the *Werowance*. All these they presented to Powhatan. The *Werowance*, women and children became his prisoners, and do him service.

The locks of hair with their skins he hanged on a line betwixt two trees. And thus he made ostentation of his triumph at *Werowocómoco*, where he intended to have done as much to me and my company.

And this is as much as my memory can call to mind worthy of note; which I have purposely collected, to satisfy my friends of the true worth and quality of Virginia. Yet some bad natures will not stick to slander the country, that will slovenly spit at all things, especially in company where they can find none to contradict them. Who though they were scarce[ly] ever ten miles from Jamestown, or at the most but at the falls; yet holding it a great disgrace that amongst so much action, their actions were nothing, exclaim of all things, though they never adventured to know anything; nor ever did anything but devour the fruits of other men's labors. Being for [the] most part of such tender educations, and small experience in martial accidents, because they found not English cities, nor such fair houses, nor at their own wishes any of their accustomed dainties, with feather beds and down pillows, taverns and alehouses in every breathing place [every few feet], neither such plenty of gold and silver and dissolute liberty, as they expected, had little or no care of anything, but to pamper their bellies, to fly away with our pinnaces, or procure their means to return [to] England. For the country was to them a misery, a ruin, a death, a hell; and their reports here, and their actions there according[ly].

Some other[s] there were that had yearly stipends to pass to and again for transportation: who to keep the mystery of the business [to] themselves, though they had neither time nor means to know much of themselves; yet all men's actions or relations they so formally tuned to the temporizing time's simplicity, as they could make their ignorances seem much more, than all the true actors could by their experience. And those with their great words deluded the world with such strange promises, as abused the business much worse than the rest. For the business being built upon the foundation of their feigned experience, the planters, the money and means have still miscarried: yet they ever returning, and the planters so far absent, who could contradict their excuses? Which, still to maintain their vainglory and estimation, from time to time have used such diligence as made them pass for truths, though nothing [could be] more false. And that the adventurers might be thus abused, let no man wonder; for the wisest living is soonest abused by him that hath a fair tongue and a dissembling heart.

There were many in Virginia merely projecting, verbal, and idle contemplators, and those so devoted to pure idleness, that though they had lived two or three years in Virginia, lordly, necessity itself could not compel them to pass the peninsula, or palisades of Jamestown; and those witty spirits, what would they not affirm in the behalf of our transporters, to get victual from their ships, or obtain their good words in England, to get their passes.

Thus from the clamors, and the ignorance of false informers, are sprung those disasters that sprung in Virginia: and our ingenious verbalists were no less plague to us in Virginia, than the locusts to the Egyptians. For the labor of twenty or thirty of the best only preserved in Christianity by their industry, the idle livers of near[ly] two hundred of the rest: who living near[ly] ten months [October 1608–July 1609] on such natural means, as the country naturally of itself afforded.

Notwithstanding all this, and the worst fury of the savages, the extremity of sickness, mutinies, faction, ignorances, and want of victual; in all that time I lost but seven or eight men, yet subjected the savages to our desired obedience, and received contribution[s] from thirty-five of their Kings, to protect and assist them against any that should assault them, in which order they continued true and faithful, and as subjects to His Majesty, so long after as I did govern there, until I left the country.

John Smith writ this with his own hand.

2. The Beginnings of English Colonization in America: Virginia, 1607-1609

Selections from Book III of
The Generall Historie of Virginia, New England, and the Summer Isles

CHAPTER I.*

It might well be thought, a country so fair (as Virginia is) and a people so tractable, would long ere this have been quietly possessed, to the satisfaction of the adventurers, and the eternizing of the memory of those that effected it. But because all the world doe[s] see a defailment [failure] [in 1612]; this following treatise shall give satisfaction to all indifferent readers, how the business hath been carried: where[by] no doubt they will easily understand and answer to their question, how it came to pass there was no better speed and success in those proceedings.

Captain Bartholomew Gosnold, one of the first movers of this plantation, having many years solicited many of his friends, but found small assistance; at last prevailed with some gentlemen, as Captain John Smith, Master Edward Maria Wingfield, Master Robert Hunt, and divers others, who depended a year upon his projects, but nothing could be effected, till by their great charge and industry, it came to be apprehended by certain of the nobility, gentry, and merchants, so that

* Extracted from the authors following by William Simons, D. D.

His Majesty by his letters patent [10 April 1606], gave commission for establishing Councils, to direct here; and to govern, and to execute there. To effect this, was spent another year, and by that, three ships were provided, one of 100 tons, another of 40, and a pinnace of 20. The transportation of the company was committed to Captain Christopher Newport, a mariner well practiced for the western parts of America. But their orders for government were put in a box, not to be opened, nor the governors know until they arrived in Virginia.

On the 19 of December, 1606, we set sail from Blackwall, but by unprosperous winds, were kept six weeks in the sight of England; all which time, Master Hunt our preacher, was so weak and sick, that few expected his recovery. Yet although he [was] but twenty miles from his habitation (the time we were in the Downs) and notwithstanding the stormy weather, nor the scandalous imputations (of some few, little better than atheists, of the greatest rank amongst us) suggested against him, all this could never force from him so much as a seeming desire to leave the business, but preferred the service of God, in so good a voyage, before any affection to contest with his godless foes, whose disastrous designs (could they have prevailed) had even then overthrown the business, so many discontents did then arise, had he not with the water of patience, and his godly exhortations (but chiefly by his true, devoted examples) quenched those flames of envy, and dissension.

We watered at the Canaries, we traded with the savages at Dominica; three weeks we spent in refreshing ourselves amongst these West Indian isles; in Guadeloupe we found a bath so hot, as in it we boiled pork as well as over the fire. And at a little isle called Monica, we took from the bushes with our hands, near[ly] two hogsheads full of birds in three or four hours. In Nevis, Mona, and the Virgin Isles, we spent some time; where, with a loathsome beast like a crocodile, called a gwayn [iguana], tortoises, pelicans, parrots, and fishes, we daily feasted.

Gone from thence in search of Virginia, the company was not a little discomforted, seeing the mariners had 3 days passed their reckoning and found no land; so that Captain Ratcliffe (Captain of the pinnace) rather desired to bear up the helm to return for England, than make further search. But God the guider of all good actions, forcing them by an extreme storm to hull all night, did drive them by his providence to their desired port, beyond all their expectations; for never any of them had seen that coast.

The first land they made they called Cape Henry; where thirty of them recreating themselves on shore, were assaulted by five savages, who hurt two of the English very dangerously.

That night was the box opened, and the orders read, in which Bartholomew Gosnold, John Smith, Edward Wingfield, Christopher Newport, John Ratcliffe, John Martin, and George Kendall, were named to be the Council, and to choose a President amongst them for a year, who with the Council should govern. Matters of moment were to be examined by a jury, but determined by the major part of the Council, in which the President had two voices.

Until the 13 of May [1607] they sought a place to plant in; then the Council was sworn, Master Wingfield was chosen President, and an oration made, why Captain Smith was not admitted [to] the Council as the rest.

Now falleth every man to work, the Council contrive the fort, the rest cut down trees to make place to pitch their tents; some provide clapboard to relade the ships, some make gardens, some nets, &c. The savages often visited us kindly. The President's overweening jealousy would admit no exercise at arms, or fortification but the boughs of trees cast together in the form of a half moon by the extraordinary pains and diligence of Captain Kendall.

Newport, Smith, and twenty others, were sent to discover the head of the river: by divers small habitations they passed, in six days they arrived at a town called *Powhatan,* consisting of some twelve houses, pleasantly seated on a hill; before it three fertile isles, about it many of their cornfields, the place is very pleasant, and strong by nature, of this place the Prince is called Powhatan, and his people *Powhatans.* To this place the river is navigable: but higher within a mile, by reason of the rocks and isles, there is not passage for a small boat, this they call the falls. The people in all parts kindly entreated them, till being returned within twenty miles of Jamestown, they gave just cause of jealousy: but had God not blessed the discoverers otherwise than those at the fort, there had then been an end of that plantation; for at the fort, where they arrived the next day, they found 17 men hurt, and a boy slain by the savages, and had it not chanced a cross-bar shot from the ships struck down a bough from a tree amongst them, that caused them to retire, our men had all been slain, being securely all at work [when the attack came]. . . .

Hereupon the President was contented the fort should be palisaded, the ordnance mounted, his men armed and exercised: for many were

the assaults, and ambushes of the savages, and our men by their disorderly straggling were often hurt, when the savages by the nimbleness
of their heels well escaped.

What toil we had, with so small a power to guard our workmen adays,
watch all night, resist our enemies, and effect our business, to relade
the ships, cut down trees, and prepare the ground to plant our corn,
&c., I refer to the reader's consideration.

Six weeks being spent in this manner, Captain Newport (who was
hired only for our transportation) was to return with the ships.

Now Captain Smith, who all this time from their departure from the
Canaries was restrained as a prisoner upon the scandalous suggestions of
some of the chief (envying his repute) who feigned he intended to
usurp the government, murder the Council, and make himself King,
that his confederates were dispersed in all the three ships, and that
divers of his confederates that revealed it, would affirm it; for this he
was committed as a prisoner.

Thirteen weeks [24 March–10 June 1607] he remained thus suspected, and by that time [when] the ships should return they pretended
out of their commisserations, to refer him to the Council in England to
receive a check [rebuke], rather than by particulating [enumerating]
his designs [to] make him so odious to the world, as to touch [stain]
his life, or utterly overthrow his reputation. But he so much scorned
their charity, and publicly defied the uttermost of their cruelty; he
wisely prevented their policies, though he could not suppress their
envies; yet so well he demeaned [conducted] himself in this business,
as all the company did see his innocence, and his adversaries' malice,
and those suborned [induced] to accuse him, accused his accusers of
subornation [unlawful and corrupt practices]; many untruths were
alleged against him; but being so apparently disproved, begat a general
hatred in the hearts of the company against such unjust commanders,
that the President [Wingfield] was adjudged to give him £200; so that
all he had was seized upon, in part of satisfaction, which Smith presently returned to the store [common fund] for the general use of the
colony.

Many were the mischiefs that daily sprang from their ignorant (yet
ambitious) spirits; but the good doctrine and exhortation of our
preacher Master Hunt reconciled them, and caused Captain Smith to be
admitted [to] the Council [10 June 1607].

The next day all received the communion, the day following the
savages voluntarily desired peace, and Captain Newport returned [to]

England with news; leaving in Virginia 100 [men] the 15 [22] of June 1607. . . .

The names of them that were the first planters, were these following.

Council
Master Edward Maria Wingfield
Captain Bartholomew Gosnold
Captain John Smith
Captain John Ratcliffe
Captain John Martin
Captain George Kendall

Gentlemen
Master Robert Hunt, Preacher
Master George Percy
Anthony Gosnoll
George Flower
Captain Gabriel Archer
Robert Fenton
Robert Ford
William Brewster
Edward Harrington
Dru Pickhouse
Thomas Jacob
John Brookes
Ellis Kingston
Thomas Sands
Benjamin Beast
Jehu Robinson
Thomas Mouton
Eustace Clovill
Stephen Halthrop
Kellam Throgmorton
Edward Morish
Nathaniel Powell
Edward Browne
Robert Beheathland
John Penington

Jeremy Alicock
George Walker
Thomas Studley
Richard Crofts
Nicholas Houlgrave
Thomas Webbe
John Waller
John Short
William Tankard
William Smethes
Francis Snarsbrough
Richard Simons
Edward Brookes
Richard Dixon
John Martin
Roger Cooke
Anthony Gosnold
Thomas Wotton, Surgeon
John Stevenson
Thomas Gore
Henry Adling
Francis Midwinter
Richard Frith

Carpenters
William Laxon
Edward Pising
Thomas Emry
Robert Small

Laborers
John Laydon

William Cassen   William Garret, Bricklayer
George Cassen   Edward Brinto, Mason
Thomas Cassen   William Love, Tailor
William Rodes   Nicholas Scot, Drum[mer]
William White   William Wilkinson, Surgeon
Old Edward   Samuel Collier, boy
Henry Tavin   Nathaniel Pecock, boy
George Goulding   James Brumfield, boy
John Dods   Richard Mutton, boy
William Johnson
William Unger
James Read, Blacksmith
Jonas Profit, Sailor   With divers others to the
Thomas Cowper, Barber   number of 100.

CHAPTER II.

What happened till the first supply.

Being thus left to our fortunes, it fortuned that within ten days
scarce[ly] ten amongst us could either go, or well stand, such extreme
weakness and sickness oppressed us. And thereat none need marvel, if
they consider the cause and reason, which was this.

Whilst the ships stayed, our allowance was somewhat bettered, by a
daily proportion of biscuit, which the sailors would pilfer to sell, give,
or exchange with us, for money, sassafras, furs, or love. But when they
departed, there remained neither tavern, beer house, nor place of relief,
but the common kettle. Had we been as free from all sins as gluttony,
and drunkenness, we might have been canonized for saints; but our
President [Wingfield] would never have been admitted, for engrossing
to his private [use], oatmeal, sack, oil, aqua vitae, beef, eggs, or what
not, but the kettle; that indeed he allowed equally to be distributed, and
that was half a pint of wheat, and as much barley boiled with water for
a man a day, and this having fried some 26 weeks [December 1606–
June 1607] in the ship's hold, contained as many worms as grains; so
that we might truly call it rather so much bran than corn, our drink
was water, our lodgings castles in the air.

With this lodging and diet, our extreme toil in bearing and planting palisades, so strained and bruised us, and our continual labor in the extremity of the heat had so weakened us, as were cause sufficient to have made us as miserable in our native country, or any other place in the world.

From May, to September [1607], those that escaped, lived upon sturgeon, and sea crabs, fifty in this time we buried, the rest seeing the President's projects to escape these miseries in our pinnace by flight (who all this time had neither felt want nor sickness) so moved our dead spirits, as we deposed him [10 September 1607]; and established Ratcliffe in his place, (Gosnold being dead [22 August 1607]) Kendall deposed [September 1607?]. Smith newly recovered, Martin and Ratcliffe [were] by his care preserved and relieved, and the most of the soldiers recovered with the skillful diligence of Master Thomas Wotton our surgeon general.

But now was all our provision spent, the sturgeon gone, all helps abandoned, each hour expecting the fury of the savages; when God the patron of all good endeavors, in that desperate extremity so changed the hearts of the savages, that they brought such plenty of their fruits, and provision, as no man wanted.

And now where some affirmed it was ill done of the Council to send forth men so badly provided, this incontradictable reason will show them plainly they are too ill advised to nourish such ill conceits; first, the fault of our going was our own, what could be thought fitting or necessary we had; but [of] what we should find, or want, or where we should be, we were all ignorant, and supposing to make our passage in two months, with victual to live, and the advantage of the spring to work; we were at sea five months, where we both spent our victual and lost the opportunity of the time and season to plant, by the unskillful presumption of our ignorant transporters, that understood not at all, what they undertook.

Such actions have ever since the world's beginning been subject to such accidents, and everything of worth is found full of difficulties: but nothing so difficult as to establish a commonwealth so far remote from men and means, and where men's minds are so untoward as neither do well themselves, nor suffer others. But to proceed.

The new President [Ratcliffe], and Martin, being little beloved, of weak judgment in dangers, and less industry in peace, committed the managing of all things abroad to Captain Smith: who by his own example, good words, and fair promises, set some to mow, others to bind thatch, some to build houses, others to thatch them, himself always bearing the greatest task for his own share, so that in [a] short time, he provided most of them [with] lodgings, neglecting any for himself.

This done, seeing the savages' superfluity begin to decrease [he] (with some of his workmen) shipped himself in the shallop to search the country for trade. The want of the language, knowledge to manage his boat without sails, the want of a sufficient power (knowing the multitude of the savages), apparel for his men, and other necessaries, were infinite impediments; yet no discouragement.

Being but six or seven in company he went down the river to *Kecoughtan:* where at first they scorned him, as a famished man; and would in derision offer him a handful of corn, a piece of bread, for their swords and muskets, and such like proportions also for their apparel. But seeing by trade and courtesy there was nothing to be had, he made bold to try such conclusions as necessity enforced, though contrary to his commission: [he] let fly his muskets, [and] ran his boat on shore; whereat they all fled into the woods.

So marching toward their houses, they might see great heaps of corn: much ado he had to restrain his hungry soldiers from [the] present taking of it, expecting as it happened that the savages would assault them, as not long after they did with a most hideous noise. Sixty or seventy of them, some black, some red, some white, some parti-colored, came in a square order, singing and dancing out of the woods, with their *Okee* (which was an idol made of skins, stuffed with moss, all painted and hung with chains and copper) borne before them: and in this manner, being well armed with clubs, targets, bows and arrows, they charged the English, that so kindly received them with their muskets loade[d] with pistol shot, that down fell their god, and divers lay sprawling on the ground; the rest fled again to the woods, and ere long sent one of their *Quiyoughkasoucks* to offer peace, and redeem their *Okee*.

Smith told them, if only six of them would come unarmed and load his boat, he would not only be their friend, but restore them their *Okee*, and give them beads, copper, and hatchets besides: which on both sides was to their contents performed: and then they brought him venison, turkeys, wild fowl, bread, and what they had; singing and dancing in sign of friendship till they departed.

In his return he discovered the town and country of *Warraskoyack*.

Smith perceiving (notwithstanding their late misery) not any regarded but from hand to mouth: (the company being well recovered) caused the pinnace to be provided with things fitting to get provision for the year following; but in the interim he made 3 or 4 journeys and discovered the people of *Chickahominy:* yet what he carefully provided the rest carelessly spent.

Wingfield and Kendall living in disgrace, seeing all things at random [neglected] in the absence of Smith, the company's dislike of their President's weakness, and their small love to Martin's never mending sickness, strengthened themselves with the sailors and other confederates, to regain their former credit and authority, or at least such means aboard the pinnace, (being fitted to sail as Smith had appointed for trade) to alter her course and to go [to] England.

Smith unexpectedly returning had the plot discovered to him, [and] much trouble he had to prevent it, till with store of saker [cannon] and musket shot he forced them [to] stay or sink in the river: which action cost the life of Captain Kendall [after trial].

These brawls are so disgustful, as some will say they were better forgotten, yet all men of good judgment will conclude, it were better their baseness should be manifest to the world, than the business bear the scorn and shame of their excused disorders.

The President [Ratcliffe] and Captain Archer not long after intended also to have abandoned the country, which project also was curbed, and suppressed by Smith.

The Spaniard never more greedily desired gold than he [Smith] victual; nor his soldiers more to abandon the country, than he to keep it. But [he found] plenty of corn in the river of Chickahominy, where hundreds of savages in divers places stood with baskets expecting his coming.

And now the winter approaching, the rivers became so covered with swans, geese, ducks, and cranes, that we daily feasted with good bread, Virginia peas, pumpkins, and *putchamins* [persimmons], fish, fowl, and divers sorts of wild beasts as fat as we could eat them: so that none of our tuftaffaty [foppish] humorists desired to go [to] England.

But our comedies never endured long without a tragedy; some idle exceptions being muttered against Captain Smith, for not discovering the head of [the] Chickahominy River, and [being] taxed by the Council, to be too slow in so worthy an attempt. The next voyage he proceeded so far that with much labor by cutting of trees [a]sunder he made his passage; but when his barge could pass no farther, he left her in a broad bay out of danger of shot, commanding none should go ashore till his return: himself with two English and two savages went up higher in a canoe; but he was not long absent, but his men went ashore, whose want of government gave both occasion and opportunity to the savages to surprise one George Cassen, whom they slew, and much failed not to have cut of[f] the boat and all the rest.

Smith little dreaming of that accident, being got to the marshes at the river's head, twenty miles in the desert, had his two men slain (as is supposed) sleeping by the canoe, whilst himself by fowling sought them victual: who finding he was beset with 200 savages, two of them he slew, still defending himself with the aid of a savage his guide, whom he bound to his arm with his garters, and used him as a buckler, yet he was shot in his thigh a little, and had many arrows that stuck in his clothes but no great hurt, till at last they took him prisoner.

When this news came to Jamestown, much was their sorrow for his loss, few expecting what ensued.

Six or seven weeks those barbarians kept him prisoner, many strange triumphs and conjurations they made of him, yet he so demeaned himself amongst them, as he not only diverted them from surprising the fort, but procured his own liberty, and got himself and his company such estimation amongst them, that those savages admired him more than their own *Quiyoughkasoucks*.

The manner how they used and delivered him, is as followeth.

The savages having drawn from George Cassen whither Captain Smith was gone, prosecuting that opportunity they followed him with 300 bowmen, conducted by the King of *Pamunkey,* who in divisions searching the turnings of the river, found Robinson and Emry by the fireside: those they shot full of arrows and slew. Then finding the Captain, as is said, [who] used the savage that was his guide as his shield (three of them being slain and divers other[s] so galled) all the rest would not come near him. Thinking thus to have returned to his boat, regarding them, as he marched, more than his way, [he] slipped up to the middle in an oozy creek and his savage with him; yet durst they not come to him till being near[ly] dead with cold, he threw away his arms. Then according to their composition they drew him forth and led him to the fire, where his men were slain. Diligently they chafed his benumbed limbs.

He demanding for their captain, they showed him Opechancanough, King of *Pamunkey,* to whom he gave a round, ivory double compass dial. Much they marveled at the playing of the fly [compass card] and needle, which they could see so plainly, and yet not touch it, because of the glass that covered them. But when he demonstrated by that globe-like jewel, the roundness of the earth, and skies, the sphere of the sun, moon, and stars, and how the sun did chase the night round about the world continually; the greatness of the land and sea, the diversity of nations, variety of complexions, and how we were to the antipodes, and many other such like matters, they all stood as amazed with admiration.

Notwithstanding, within an hour after they tied him to a tree, and as many as could stand about him prepared to shoot him: but the King holding up the compass in his hand, they all laid down their bows and arrows, and in a triumphant manner led him to *Orapaks,* where he was after their manner kindly feasted, and well used.

Their order in conducting him was thus; drawing themselves all in file, the King in the middle had all their pieces and swords borne before him. Captain Smith was led after him by three great savages, holding him fast by each arm; and on each side six went in file with their arrows nocked [ready to shoot]. But arriving at the town (which was but only thirty or forty hunting houses made of mats, which they remove as they please, as we our tents) all the women and children staring to behold him, the soldiers first all in file performed the form [ceremonial dance] of a *biscione* so well as could be; and on each flank, officers as sergeants to see them keep their orders. A good time they continued this exercise, and then cast themselves in a ring, dancing in such several postures, and singing and yelling out such hellish notes and screeches; being strangely painted, everyone his quiver of arrows, and at his back a club; on his arm a fox or an otter's skin, or some such matter for his vambrace [armor]; their heads and shoulders painted red, with oil and *puccoon* [bloodroot] mingled together, which scarlet-like color made an exceeding[ly] handsome show; his bow in his hand, and the skin of a bird with her wings abroad dried, tied on his head, a piece of copper, a white shell, a long feather, with a small rattle growing at the tails of their snakes tied to it, or some such like toy. All this while Smith and the King stood in the middle guarded, as before is said: and after three dances they all departed. Smith they conducted to a long house, where thirty or forty tall fellows did guard him; and ere long more bread and venison [were] brought him than would have served twenty men. I think his stomach at that time was not very good; what he left they put in baskets and tied over his head. About midnight they set the meat again before him, all this time not one of them would eat a bit with him, till the next morning they brought him as much more; and then did they eat all the old, and reserved the new as they had done the other, which made him think they would fat him to eat him. Yet in this desperate estate to defend him from the cold, one Maocassater brought him his gown, in requital of some beads and toys Smith had given him at his first arrival in Virginia.

Two days after a man would have slain him (but that the guard prevented it) for the death of his son, to whom they conducted him to recover [help] the poor man then breathing his last. Smith told them that at Jamestown he had a water [which] would do it, if they would let him fetch it, but they would not permit that: but made all the preparations they could to assault Jamestown, craving his advice; and for recompense he should have life, liberty, land, and women. In part of a table book he writ his mind to them at the fort, what was intended, how they should follow that direction to affright the messengers, and without fail send him such things as he writ for. And an inventory with them. The difficulty and danger, he told the savages, of the mines, great guns, and other engines exceedingly affrighted them, yet according to his request they went to Jamestown, in as bitter weather as could be of frost and snow, and within three days returned with an answer.

But when they came to Jamestown, seeing men sally out as he had told them they would, they fled; yet in the night they came again to the same place where he had told them they should receive an answer, and such things as he had promised them: which they found accordingly, and with which they returned with no small expedition, to the wonder of them all that heard it, that he could either divine, or the paper could speak.

Then they led him to the *Youghtanunds,* the *Mattapanients,* the *Piankatanks,* the *Nantaughtacunds,* and *Onawmanients* upon the rivers of Rappahannock, and Potomac; over all those rivers, and back again by divers other several nations, to the King's habitation at *Pamunkey:* where they entertained him with most strange and fearful conjurations. . . .

Not long after, early in a morning a great fire was made in a long house, and a mat spread on the one side, as on the other; on the one they caused him to sit, and all the guard went out of the house, and presently came skipping in a great grim fellow, all painted over with coal, mingled with oil; and many snakes and weasels' skins stuffed with moss, and all their tails tied together, so as they met on the crown of his head in a tassel; and round about the tassel was as a coronet of feathers, the skins hanging round about his head, back, and shoulders, and in a manner covered his face; with a hellish voice, and a rattle in his hand. With most strange gestures and passions he began his invocation, and environed the fire with a circle of meal; which done, three more such like devils came rushing in with the like antique tricks, painted half black, half red: but all their eyes were painted white, and some red strokes like mutches [ties on a bonnet], along their cheeks; round about him those fiends danced a pretty while, and then came in three more as ugly as the rest; with red eyes, and white strokes over their black faces, at last they all sat down right against him; three of them on the one hand of the chief priest, and three on the other. Then all with their rattles began a song, which ended, the chief priest laid down five wheat corns: then straining his arms and hands with such violence that he sweat, and his veins swelled, he began a short oration: at the conclusion they all gave a short groan; and then laid down three grains more. After that, began their song again, and then another oration, ever laying down so many corns as before, till they had twice encircled the fire; that done, they took a bunch of little sticks prepared for that purpose, continuing still their devotion, and at the end of every song and oration, they laid down a stick betwixt the divisions of corn. Till night, neither he nor they did either eat or drink; and then they feasted merrily, with the best provisions they could make. Three days they used this ceremony; the meaning whereof they told him, was to know if he intended them well or no. The circle of meal signified their country, the circles of corn the bounds of the sea, and the sticks his country. They imagined the world to be flat and round, like a trencher; and they in the middle.

After this they brought him a bag of gunpowder, which they carefully preserved till the next spring, to plant as they did their corn; because they would be acquainted with the nature of that seed.

Opitchapam the King's brother invited him [Smith] to his house, where, with as many platters of bread, fowl, and wild beasts, as did environ him, he bid him welcome; but not any of them would eat a bit with him, but put up all the remainder in baskets.

At his return to Opechancanough's, all the King's women, and their children, flocked about him for their parts; as a due by custom, to be merry with such fragments. . . .

At last they brought him to *Meronocomoco,* where was Powhatan their Emperor. Here more than two hundred of those grim courtiers stood wondering at him, as he had been a monster; till Powhatan and his train had put themselves in their greatest braveries. Before a fire upon a seat like a bedstead, he sat covered with a great robe, made of *rarowcun* [raccoon] skins, and all the tails hanging by. On either hand did sit a young wench of 16 or 18 years, and along on each side [of] the house, two rows of men, and behind them as many women, with all

their heads and shoulders painted red: many of their heads bedecked
with the white down of birds; but everyone with something: and a great
chain of white beads about their necks.

At his entrance before the King, all the people gave a great shout.
The Queen of *Appomattoc* was appointed to bring him water to wash
his hands, and another brought him a bunch of feathers, instead of a
towel to dry them: having feasted him after their best barbarous manner
they could, a long consultation was held, but the conclusion was, two
great stones were brought before Powhatan: then as many as could
laid hands on him, dragged him to them, and thereon laid his head, and
being ready with their clubs, to beat out his brains, Pocahontas the
King's dearest daughter, when no entreaty could prevail, got his head
in her arms, and laid her own upon his to save him from death:
whereat the Emperor was contented he should live to make him
hatchets, and her bells, beads, and copper; for they thought him as well
of all occupations as themselves. For the King himself will make his
own robes, shoes, bows, arrows, pots; plant, hunt, or do anything so
well as the rest. . . .

Two days after, Powhatan having disguised himself in the most fear-
fullest manner he could, caused Captain Smith to be brought forth to a
great house in the woods, and there upon a mat by the fire to be left
alone. Not long after from behind a mat that divided the house, was
made the most dolefullest noise he ever heard; then Powhatan more
like a devil than a man, with some two hundred more as black as
himself, came unto him and told him now they were friends, and
presently he should go to Jamestown, to send him two great guns, and
a grindstone, for which he would give him the country of *Capahowasick,*
and forever esteem him as his son Nantaquaus.

So to Jamestown with 12 guides Powhatan sent him. That night
they quartered in the woods, he still expecting (as he had done all
this long time of his imprisonment) every hour to be put to one death
or [an]other: for all their feasting. But almighty God (by his divine
providence) had mollified the hearts of those stern barbarians with
compassion. The next morning betimes they came to the fort, where
Smith having used the savages with what kindness he could, he showed
Rawhunt, Powhatan's trusty servant, two demi-culverings [cannons]
and a millstone to carry Powhatan: they found them somewhat too
heavy; but when they did see him discharge them, being loaded with
stones, among the boughs of a great tree loaded with icicles, the ice

and branches came so tumbling down, that the poor savages ran away half dead with fear. But at last we regained some conference with them, and gave them such toys; and sent to Powhatan, his women, and children such presents, as gave them in general full content.

Now in Jamestown they were all in combustion [confusion], the strongest preparing once more to run away with the pinnace; which with the hazard of his life, with saker, falcon [cannon] and musket shot, Smith forced now the third time to stay or sink.

Some no better than they should be, had plotted with the President [Ratcliffe], the next day to have put him to death by the Levitical law, for the lives of Robinson and Emry; pretending the fault was his that had led them to their ends: but he quickly took such order [gained control of the situation] with such lawyers, that he laid them by the heels till he sent some of them prisoners [to] England.

Now ever[y] once in four or five days, Pocahontas with her attendants, brought him so much provision, that saved many of their lives, that else for all this had starved with hunger. . . .

His relation of the plenty he had seen, especially at *Werowocómoco*, and of the state and bounty of Powhatan, (which till that time was unknown) so revived their dead spirits (especially the love of Pocahontas) as all men's fear was abandoned.

Thus you may see what difficulties still crossed any good endeavor; and the good success of the business being thus oft brought to the very period of destruction; yet you see by what strange means God hath still delivered it.

As for the insufficiency of them admitted in commission [those who governed], that error could not be prevented by the electors; there being no other choice, and all strangers to each other's education, qualities, or disposition.

And if any deem it a shame to our nation to have any mention made of those enormities, let him peruse the histories of the Spaniards' discoveries and plantations, where they may see how many mutinies, disorders, and dissensions have accompanied them, and crossed their attempts: which being known to be particular men's offenses; doth take away the general scorn and contempt, which malice, presumption, covetousness, or ignorance might produce; to the scandal and reproach of those, whose actions and valiant resolutions deserve a more worthy respect.

Now whether it had been better for Captain Smith, to have concluded with any of those several projects [for returning to England], to have abandoned the country, with some ten or twelve of them, who were called the better sort, and have left Master Hunt our preacher, Master Anthony Gosnoll, a most honest, worthy, and industrious gentleman, Master Thomas Wotton, and some 27 others of his countrymen to the fury of the savages, famine, and all manner of mischiefs, and inconveniences, (for they were but forty in all to keep possession of this large country;) or starve himself with them for company, for want of lodging: or but adventuring abroad to make them provision, or by his opposition to preserve the action, and save all their-lives; I leave to the censure of all honest men to consider. . . .

Written by Thomas Studley, the first cape merchant in Virginia, Robert Fenton, Edward Harrington, and J[ohn] S[mith].

CHAPTER III.

The arrival of the first supply, with their proceedings, and the ship's return.

All this time our care was not so much to abandon the country; but the treasurer and Council in England, were as diligent and careful to supply us. Two good ships they sent us, with near[ly] a hundred men, well furnished with all things [as] could be imagined necessary, both for them and us; the one commanded by Captain Newport: the other by Captain Francis Nelson, an honest man, and an expert mariner. But such was the leewardness [blown to leeward and out to sea] of his ship [the *Phoenix*] (that though he was within the sight of Cape Henry) by stormy, contrary winds was he forced so far to sea, that the West Indies was the next land, for the repair of his masts, and relief of wood and water.

But Newport got in and arrived at Jamestown, not long after the redemption of Captain Smith. To whom the savages, as is said, every other day repaired, with such provisions that sufficiently did serve them from hand to mouth: part always they brought him as presents from their Kings, or Pocahontas; the rest he as their market clerk set the price himself, how they should sell: so he had enchanted these poor souls being their prisoner; and now Newport, whom he called his father arriving, near[ly] as directly as he foretold, they esteemed him as an oracle, and [he] had them at that submission he might command them what he listed. That God that created all things they knew he adored for his God: they would also in their discourses term the God of Captain Smith. . . .

But the President and Council so much envied his estimation among the savages (though we all in general equally participated with him [in] the good thereof,) that they wrought it into the savages' understandings (by their great bounty in giving four times more for their commodities than Smith appointed) that their greatness and authority as much exceeded his, as their bounty and liberality.

Now the arrival of this first supply so overjoyed us, that we could not devise too much to please the mariners. We gave them liberty to truck or trade at their pleasures. But in a short time it followed, that could not be had for a pound of copper, which before was sold us for an ounce: thus ambition and sufferance cut the throat of our trade, but confirmed their opinion of the greatness of Captain Newport, (wherewith Smith had possessed Powhatan) especially by the great presents Newport often sent him, before he could prepare the pinnace to go and visit him: so that this great savage desired also to see him. A great coil [demand] there was to set him forward.

When he went he was accompanied [by] Captain Smith, and Master Scrivener, a very wise, understanding gentleman, newly arrived and admitted [to] the Council, with thirty or forty chosen men for their guard.

Arriving at *Werowocómoco,* Newport's conceit of this great savage bred many doubts and suspicions of treacheries, which Smith to make appear [were] needless, with twenty men well appointed, undertook to encounter the worst that could happen. . . .

These [men] . . . coming ashore, landed amongst a many of creeks, over which they were to pass [by] such poor bridges, only made of a few cratches thrust in the ooze, and three or four poles laid on them, and at the end of them the like, tied together only with barks of trees, that it made them much suspect those bridges were but traps. Which caused Smith to make divers savages go over first, keeping some of the chief as hostage[s] till half his men were passed, to make a guard for himself and the rest.

But finding all things well, by two or three hundred savages they

were kindly conducted to their town. Where Powhatan strained himself
to the utmost of his greatness to entertain them, with great shouts of
joy, orations of protestations; and with the most plenty of victuals he
could provide to feast them.

Sitting upon his bed of mats, his pillow of leather embroidered
(after their rude manner with pearl and white beads) his attire a fair
robe of skins as large as an Irish mantel: at his head and [at his] feet
a handsome young woman: on each side [of] his house sat twenty of
his concubines, their heads and shoulders painted red, with a great
chain of white beads about each of their necks. Before those sat his
chiefest men in like order in his arbor-like house, and more than
forty platters of fine bread stood as a guard in two files on each side
[of] the door. Four or five hundred people made a guard behind them
for our passage: and proclamation was made, none upon pain of death
to presume to do us any wrong or discourtesy.

With many pretty discourses to renew their old acquaintance, this
great King and our Captain spent the time, till the ebb [tide] left our
barge aground. Then renewing their feasts with fetes, dancing and
singing, and such like mirth, we quartered that night with Powhatan.

The next day Newport came ashore and received as much content
as those people could give him: a boy named Thomas Savage was
then given unto Powhatan, whom Newport called his son; for whom
Powhatan gave him Namontack his trusty servant, and one of a shrewd,
subtle capacity.

Three or four days more we spent in feasting, dancing, and trading,
wherein Powhatan carried himself so proudly, yet discreetly (in his
savage manner) as made us all admire his natural gifts, considering his
education.

As scorning to trade as his subjects did; he bespake Newport in this
manner.

Captain Newport it is not agreeable to my greatness, in this piddling
manner to trade for trifles; and I esteem you also a great Werowance.
Therefore lay me down all your commodities together; what I like
I will take, and in recompense give you what I think fitting their value.

Captain Smith being our interpreter, regarding Newport as his
father, knowing best the disposition of Powhatan, told us his intent
was but only to cheat us; yet Captain Newport thinking to outbrave
[defy] this savage in ostentation of greatness, and so to bewitch him
with [his] bounty, as to have what he listed, it so happened, that

Powhatan having his desire, valued his corn at such a rate, that I think it [were] better cheap in Spain: for we had not four bushels for that we expected to have twenty hogsheads.

This bred some unkindness between our two Captains; Newport seeking to please the insatiable desire of the savage, Smith to cause the savage to please him; but smothering his distaste to avoid the savage's suspicion, [Smith] glanced in [flashed before] the eyes of Powhatan many trifles, who fixed his humor upon a few blue beads. A long time he importunately desired them, but Smith seemed so much the more to affect them, as being composed of a most rare substance of the color of the skies, and not to be worn but by the greatest kings in the world. This made him half mad to be the owner of such strange jewels; so that ere we departed, for a pound or two of blue beads, he brought over my King for 2 or 300 bushels of corn; yet parted good friends.

The like entertainment we found of Opechancanough King of Pamunkey, whom also he [Smith] in like manner fitted (at the like rates) with blue beads: which grew by this means, of that estimation, that none durst wear any of them but their great kings, their wives and children.

And so we returned all well to Jamestown, where this new supply being lodged with the rest, [had] accidently fired their quarters, and so the town: which being but thatched with reeds, the fire was so fierce as it burnt their palisades, (though eight or ten yards distant) with their arms, bedding, apparel, and much private provision. Good Master Hunt our preacher lost all his library, and all he had but the clothes on his back: yet none never heard him repine at his loss. This happened in the winter in that extreme frost, 1607[-1608].

Now though we had victual sufficient I mean only of oatmeal, meal and corn: yet the ship staying 14 weeks when she might as well have been gone in 14 days, spent a great part of that, and near[ly] all the rest that was sent to be landed.

When they departed what their discretion could spare us, to make a little poor meal or two, we called feasts, to relish our mouths: of each somewhat they left us, yet I must confess, those that had either money, spare clothes, credit to give bills of payment, gold rings, furs, or any such commodities, were ever welcome to this removing [remote] tavern, such was our patience to obey such vile commanders, and buy our own provisions at 15 times the value, suffering them feast (we bearing the charge) yet [we] must not repine, but fast, least we should incur the censure of [being] factious and seditious persons: and then leakage, ship rats, and other casualties occasioned them loss: but the vessels and remnants (for totals [as a full cargo]) we were glad to receive with all our hearts to make up the account, highly commending their providence for preserving that, least they should discourage any more to come to us.

Now for all this plenty our ordinary [staple food] was but meal and water, so that this great charge little relieved our wants, whereby with the extremity of the bitter cold frost and those defects, more than half of us died.

I cannot deny but both Smith and Scrivener did their best to amend what was amiss, but with the President went the major part, that their horns were too short [Smith and Scrivener lacked support].

But the worst [were] our gilded refiners with their golden promises [who] made all men their slaves in hope of recompenses; there was no talk, no hope, no work, but dig gold, wash gold, refine gold, load gold, such a bruit [rumor] of gold, that one mad fellow [a wag] desired to be buried in the sands least they should by their art make gold of his bones: little need there was and less reason, the ship should stay, their wages run on, our victuals consume 14 weeks, that the mariners might say, they did help to build such a golden church that we can say the rain washed near to nothing in 14 days.

Were it that Captain Smith would not applaud all those golden inventions, because they admitted him not to the sight of their trials [samples] nor golden consultations, I know not; but I have heard him oft question with Captain Martin and tell him, except he could show him a more substantial trial, he was not enamored with their dirty skill, breathing out these and many other passions, never anything did more torment him, than to see all necessary business neglected, to fraught such a drunken ship with so much gilded dirt.*

Till then we never accounted, Captain Newport a refiner, who being ready to set sail for England, and we not having any use of parliaments, plays, petitions, admirals, recorders, interpreters, chronologers, courts of plea, nor justices of peace, sent [10 April 1608] Master Wingfield and Captain Archer home with him, that had engrossed all those titles, to seek some better place of employment. . . .

---

* When tested in England, it proved to be fool's gold, as Smith foresaw.

CHAPTER IV.

The arrival of the Phoenix; *her return;*
and other accidents.

The authority now consisting in Captain Martin, and the still sickly President [Ratcliffe], the sale of the store's commodities maintained his estate, as an inheritable revenue.

The spring approaching, and the ship departing, Master Scrivener and Captain Smith divided betwixt them the rebuilding [of] Jamestown; the repairing [of] our palisades; the cutting down [of] trees, preparing our fields, planting our corn, and to rebuild our church, and recover our storehouse.

All men thus busy with their several labors, Master Nelson arrived with his lost *Phoenix;* lost (I say) for that we all deemed him lost. Landing safely all his men, (so well he had managed his ill hap,) causing the Indian Isles [Caribbean] to feed his company, that his victual to that we had gotten, as is said before, was near[ly], after our allowance, sufficient for half a year. He had not anything but he freely imparted it, which honest dealing (being a mariner) caused us [to] admire him: we would not have wished more than he did for us.

Now to relade this ship with some good tidings, the President (not holding it stood with the dignity of his place to leave the fort) gave order to Captain Smith to discover [explore] and search the commodities of the *Monacans'* country beyond the falls. Sixty able men [were] allotted them, the which within six days, Smith had so well trained to their arms and orders, that they little feared with whom they should encounter: yet so unseasonable was the time, and so opposite was Captain Martin to anything, but only to fraught this ship also with his fantastical gold, as Captain Smith rather desired to relade her with cedar [logs], (which was a present dispatch) than either with dirt, or the hopes and reports of an uncertain discovery, which he would perform when they had less charge and more leisure. . . .

Whilst the conclusion was a resolving, this happened.

Powhatan (to express his love to Newport) when he departed, presented him with twenty turkeys, conditionally to return him twenty swords, which immediately [were] sent him.

Now after his departure, he presented Captain Smith with the like luggage, but not finding his humor obeyed in not sending such weapons as he desired, he caused his people with twenty devices to obtain them. At last by ambushes at our very ports [gates] they would take them perforce, surprise us at work, or any way; which was so long permitted, they became so insolent there was no rule [control]: the command from England was so strait [clear] not to offend them, as our authority bearers [leaders] (keeping their houses) would rather be anything than peace-breakers.

This charitable humor prevailed, till well it chanced they meddled with Captain Smith, who without further deliberation gave them such an encounter, as some he so hunted up and down the isle, some he so terrified with whipping, beating, and imprisonment; as for revenge they surprised two of our foraging disorderly soldiers, and having assembled their forces, boldly threatened at our ports to force Smith to redeliver seven savages, which for their villainies he detained prisoners, or we were all but dead men. But to try their furies he sallied out amongst them, and in less than an hour, he so hampered their insolencies, [that] they brought them his two men, desiring peace without any further composition for their prisoners. Those he examined, and caused them all [to] believe, by several volleys of shot one of their companions was shot to death, because they would not confess their intents and plotters of those villainies.

And thus they all agreed in one point, they were directed only by Powhatan to obain [for] him our weapons, to cut our own throats; with the manner where, how, and when, which we plainly found most true and apparent: yet he sent his messengers, and his dearest daughter Pocahontas with presents to excuse him of the injuries done by some rash, untoward captains his subjects, desiring their liberties for this time, with the assurance of his love forever.

After Smith had given the prisoners what correction he thought fit, used them well a day or two after, and then delivered them [to] Pocahontas; for whose sake only he feigned to have saved their lives, and gave them liberty.

The patient Council that nothing would move to war with the savages, would gladly have wrangled with Captain Smith for his cruelty, yet none was slain to any man's knowledge: but it brought them in such fear and obedience, as his very name would sufficiently affright them; where before, we had sometime[s] peace and war twice in a day, and very seldom a week but we had some treacherous villainy or other.

The fraught of this ship being concluded to be cedar; by the diligence of the Master, and Captain Smith, she was quickly reladed: Master Scrivener was neither idle nor slow to follow all things at the fort; the ship being ready to set sail, Captain Martin being always very sickly, and unserviceable, and desirous to enjoy the credit of his supposed art of finding the golden mine, was most willingly admitted to return [to] England. . . .

From the writings of Thomas Studley and Anas Todkill.

Their names that were landed in this supply.

Matthew Scrivener appointed to be one of the Council.

Gentlemen
Michael Phittiplace
William Phittiplace
Ralph Morton
Richard Wiffin
John Taverner
William Cantrell
Robert Barnes
Richard Fetherstone
George Hill
George Pretty
Nathaniel Causey
Peter Pory
Robert Cutler
Michael Sicklemore
William Bentley
Thomas Coe
Doctor Russell
Jeffrey Abbot
Edward Gurgana
Richard Worley
Timothy Leeds
Richard Killingbeck
William Spence

Richard Prodger
Richard Potts
Richard Mullinax
William Bayley
Francis Perkins
John Harper
George Forest
John Nichols
William Grivell

Laborers
Raymond Goodison
William Simons
John Spearman
Richard Bristow
William Perce
James Watkins
John Bouth
Christopher Rods
Richard Burket
James Burre

Nicholas Ven
Francis Perkins
Richard Gradon
Rawland Nelstrop
Richard Savage
Thomas Savage
Richard Milmer
William May
Vere
Michael
Bishop Wiles

Apothecaries
Thomas Field
John Harford

Daniel Stallings, jeweler
William Dawson, a refiner
Abram Ransack, a refiner
William Johnson, a goldsmith
Peter Keffer, a gunsmith
Robert Alberton, a perfumer
Richard Belfield, a goldsmith
Post Ginnat, a surgeon
John Lewes, a cooper
Robert Cotton, a tobacco pipe maker
Richard Dole, a blacksmith

Tailors
Thomas Hope
William Ward
John Powell
William Yong
William Beckwith
Lawrence Towtales

And divers others to the number
of 120.

CHAPTER V.

The accidents that happened in the discovery of the Bay of Chesapeake.

The prodigality of the President's [Ratcliffe] state went so deep into our small store, that Smith and Scrivener tied him and his parasites to the rules of proportion. But now Smith being [ready] to depart, the President's authority so overswayed the discretion of Master Scrivener, that our store, our time, our strength and labors were idly consumed to fulfill his fantasies.

The second of June 1608, Smith left the fort to perform his discovery. . . .

[He sailed in] . . . an open barge near[ly] three tons burden.

Leaving the *Phoenix* at Cape Henry, they crossed the bay to the Eastern Shore, and fell with the isles called Smiths Isles, after our Captain's name.

The first people we saw were two grim and stout savages upon Cape Charles, with long poles like javelins, headed with bone, they boldly demanded what we were, and what we would; but after many circumstances they seemed very kind, and directed us to *Accomac,* the habitation of their *Werowance,* where we were kindly entreated.

This King was the comeliest, proper, civil savage we encountered. His country is a pleasant fertile clay soil, some small creeks; good harbors for small barks, but not for ships. He told us of a strange accident lately happened [to] him, and it was, two children being dead; some extreme passions, or dreaming visions, fantasies, or affection moved their parents again to revisit their dead carcasses, whose benumbed bodies reflected to the eyes of the beholders such delightful countenances, as though they had regained their vital spirits. This as a miracle drew many to behold them, all which, being a great part of his people, not long after died, and but few escaped.

They spake the language of Powhatan, wherein they made such descriptions of the bay, isles, and rivers, that often [gave] us exceeding pleasure.

Passing along the coast, searching every inlet, and bay, fit for harbors and habitations. Seeing many isles in the midst of the bay we bore up for them, but ere we could obtain them, such an extreme gust of wind, rain, thunder and lightning happened, that with great danger we escaped the unmerciful raging of that ocean-like water. The highest land on the main[land], yet it was but low, we called Keales Hill, and these uninhabited isles, Russells Isles.

The next day searching them for fresh water, we could find none, the defect whereof forced us to follow the next eastern channel, which brought us to the river of Pocomoke.

The people at first with great fury seemed to assault us, yet at last with songs and dances and much mirth became very tractable: but searching their habitations for water, we could fill but three barricoes [kegs], and that such puddle, that never till then we ever knew the want of good water. We digged and searched in many places, but before two days were expired, we would have refused two barricoes of gold for one of that puddle water of Pocomoke.

Being past these isles which are many in number, but all naught for habitation, falling with a high land upon the main, we found a great pond of fresh water, but so exceeding[ly] hot we supposed it some bath; that place we called Ployer Point, in honor of that most honorable House of Moussaye in Brittany, that in an extreme extremity once relieved our Captain.

From *Wighcocomoco* to this place, all the coast is low, broken isles of morass [marsh], grown a mile or two in breadth, and ten or twelve in length, good to cut for hay in summer, and to catch fish and fowl in winter: but the land beyond them is all covered over with wood, as is the rest of the country.

Being thus refreshed, in crossing over from the main[land] to other isles we discovered, the wind and waters so much increased, with thunder, lightning, and rain, that our mast and sail blew overboard and such mighty waves overracked us in that small barge, that with great labor we kept her from sinking by freeing [baling] out the water.

Two days we were enforced to inhabit these uninhabited isles; which for the extremity of gusts, thunder, rain, storms, and ill weather we called Limbo.

Repairing our sail with our shirts, we set sail for the main[land] and fell with a pretty convenient river on the east called [the] Nanticoke [*Kuskarawaock*]; the people ran as amazed in troupes from place to place, and divers got into the tops of trees. They were not sparing of their arrows, nor [of] the greatest passion they could express of their anger. Long they shot, we still riding at an anchor without their reach making all the signs of friendship we could.

The next day they came unarmed, with every one a basket, dancing in a ring, to draw us on shore: but seeing there was nothing in them but villainy, we discharged a volley of muskets charged with pistol shot; whereat they all lay tumbling on the ground, creeping some one way, some another into a great cluster of reeds hard by; where their companies lay in ambush. Towards the evening we weighed [anchor], and approaching the shore, discharging five or six shot among the reeds. We landed where there lay a many of baskets and much blood, but saw not a savage. A smoke appearing on the other side [of] the river, we rowed thither, where we found two or three little houses, in each a fire; there we left some pieces of copper, beads, bells, and looking glasses, and then went into the bay: but when it was dark we came back again.

Early in the morning four savages came to us in their canoe, whom we used with such courtesy, not knowing what we were, nor had done, [they] having been in the bay afishing; [who] bade us stay and ere long they would return, which they did and some twenty more with them: with whom after a little conference, two or three thousand men, women, and children came clustering about us, everyone presenting us with something, which a little bead would so well requite, that we became such friends they would contend who should fetch us water, stay with us for hostage, conduct our men any whither, and give us the best content.

Here doth inhabit the people of *Sarapinagh, Nause, Arseek,* and *Nanticoke* the best merchants of all other savages.

They much extolled a great nation called *Massawomekes,* in search of whom we returned by Limbo: this river but only at the entrance is very narrow, and the people of small stature as them of *Wighcocomoco,* the land but low, yet it may prove very commodious, because it is but a ridge of land betwixt the bay and the main ocean. Finding this eastern shore, [to be] shallow broken isles, and for [the] most part without fresh water; we passed by the straits of Limbo for the western shore: so broad is the bay here, we could scarce[ly] perceive the great high cliffs on the other side: by them we anchored that night and called them Rocky Point [Rickards Cliffs].

30 leagues we sailed more northwards not finding any inhabitants, leaving all the eastern shore, low islands, but overgrown with wood, as all the coast beyond them so far as we could see: the western shore by which we sailed we found all along well watered, but very mountainous and barren, the valleys very fertile, but extreme[ly] thick [with] small wood [as] well as trees, and much frequented with wolves, bears, deer and other wild beasts.

We passed many shallow creeks, but the first we found navigable for a ship, we called [the] Patapsco, for that the clay in many places under the cliffs by the high water mark, did grow up in red and white knots as gum out of trees; and in some places so participated together as though they were all of one nature, excepting the color, the rest of the earth on both sides being hard, sandy gravel which made us think it bole armeniac. . . .

When we first set sail some of our gallants doubted nothing but that our Captain would make too much haste home, but having lain in this small barge not above 12 or 14 days, oft tired at the oars, our bread spoiled with wet so much that it was rotten (yet so good were their stomachs that they could digest it) they did with continual complaints so importune him now [to] return, as caused him bespeak them in this manner [about 14 June 1608].

Gentlemen if you would remember the memorable history of Sir Ralph Lane, how his company importuned him to proceed in the discovery of Morattico, alleging they had yet a dog, that being boiled with sassafras leaves, would richly feed them in their returns; then what a shame would it be for you (that have been so suspicious of my tenderness) to force me return, with so much provision as we have, and scarce[ly] able to say where we have been, nor yet heard-of that we were sent to seek? You cannot say but I have shared with you in the worst which is past; and for what is to come, of lodging, diet, or whatsoever, I am contented you allot the worst part to myself. As for your fears that I will lose myself in these unknown large waters, or be swallowed up in some stormy gust; abandon these childish fears, for worse than is past is not likely to happen: and there is as much danger to return as to proceed. Regain therefore your old spirits, for return I will not (if God please) till I have seen the Massawomekes, found Patawomeke, or the head of this water you conceit [imagine] to be endless.

Two or 3 days we expected [experienced] wind and weather, whose adverse extremities added such discouragement, that three or four fell sick, whose pitiful complaints caused us to return, leaving the bay some nine miles broad, at nine and ten fathom water.

The 16 of June [1608], we fell with the river Potomac: fear being gone, and our men recovered, we were all content to take some pains, to know the name of that seven mile broad river. For thirty miles' sail, we could see no inhabitants: then we were conducted by two savages up a little bayed creek, towards *Onawmanient,* where all the woods were laid with ambushes to the number of three or four thousand savages, so strangely painted, grimed and disguised, shouting, yelling and crying as so many spirits from hell could not have showed more terrible.

Many bravados they made, but to appease their fury, our Captain prepared with as seeming a willingness (as they) to encounter them. But the grazing of our bullets upon the water (many being shot on purpose they might see them) with the echo of the woods so amazed them, as down went their bows and arrows; (and exchanging hostage)

James Watkins was sent six miles up the woods to their King's habitation. We were kindly used of those savages, of whom we understood, they were commanded to betray us, by the direction of Powhatan; and he so directed from the discontents [malcontents] at Jamestown, because our Captain did cause them stay in their country [Virginia] against their wills.

The like encounters we found at *Patawomeke, Cecocawonee,* and divers other places: but at *Moyaons, Nacotchtanke,* and *Toags* the people did their best to content us.

Having gone so high as we could with the boat, we met divers savages in canoes, well loade[d] with the flesh of bears, deer and other beasts; whereof we had part. Here we found mighty rocks, growing in some places above the ground as high as the shrubby trees, and divers other solid quarries of divers tinctures: and divers places where the waters had fallen from the high mountains they had left a tinctured, spangled scurf [deposits], that made many bare places seem as gilded. Digging the ground above in the highest cliffs of rocks, we saw it was a clay sand so mingled with yellow spangles as if it had been half pindust [brass filings].

In our return inquiring still for this *Matchqueon,* the King of *Patawomeke* gave us guides to conduct us up a little river called Aquia Creek, up which we rowed so high as we could. Leaving the boat; with six shot and divers savages, he marched seven or eight mile[s] before they came to the mine: leading his hostages in a small chain they were to have for their pains, being proud so richly to be adorned.

The mine is a great rocky mountain like antimony; wherein they digged a great hole with shells and hatchets: and hard by it, runneth a fair brook of crystal-like water, where they wash away the dross and keep the remainder, which they put in little bags and sell it all over the country to paint their bodies, faces, or idols; which makes them look like blackamoors dusted over with silver. With so much as we could carry we returned to our boat, kindly requiting this kind King and all his kind people.

The cause of this discovery was to search [for] this mine, of which Newport did assure us that those small bags (we had given him), in England he had tried to hold half silver; but all we got proved of no value: also to search what furs, the best whereof is at *Kuskarawaock,* where is made so much *rawranoke* or white beads that occasion as much dissention among the savages, as gold and silver amongst Christians;

and what other minerals, rivers, rocks, nations, woods, fishings, fruits, victual, and what other commodities the land afforded: and whether the bay were endless or how far it extended.

Of mines we were all ignorant, but a few beavers, otters, bears, martins and minks [skins] we found, and in divers places that abundance of fish, lying so thick with their heads above the water, as for want of nets (our barge driving amongst them) we attempted to catch them with a frying pan: but we found it a bad instrument to catch fish with: neither better fish, more plenty, nor more variety for small fish, had any of us ever seen in any place so swimming in the water, but they are not to be caught with frying pans. Some small cod also we did see swim close by the shore by Smiths Isles, and some as high as Rocky Point. And some we have found dead upon the shore.

To express all our quarrels, treacheries, and encounters amongst those savages I should be too tedious: but in brief, at all times we so encountered them, and curbed their insolencies, that they concluded with presents to purchase peace; yet we lost not a man: at our first meeting our Captain ever observed this order, to demand their bows and arrows, swords, mantels and furs, with some child or two for hostage, whereby we could quickly perceive, when they intended any villainy.

Having finished this discovery (though our victual was near[ly] spent) he intended to see his imprisonment-acquaintances upon the river of Rappahannock, . . . but our boat by reason of the ebb, chancing to ground upon a many shoals lying in the entrances, we spied many fishes lurking in the reeds: our Captain sporting himself by nailing them to the ground with his sword, set us all afishing in that manner: thus we took more in one hour than we could eat in a day.

But it chanced our Captain taking a fish from his sword (not knowing her condition) being much of the fashion of a thornback, but a long tail like a riding rod, whereon the middest is a most poisoned sting, of two or three inches long, bearded like a saw on each side, which she struck into the wrist of his arm near[ly] an inch and a half: no blood nor wound was seen, but a little blue spot, but the torment was instantly so extreme, that in four hours had so swollen his hand, arm and shoulder, we all with much sorrow concluded [anticipated] his funeral, and prepared his grave in an island by, as himself directed: yet it pleased God by a precious oil Doctor Russell at the first applied to it when he sounded it with probe, (ere night) his tormenting pain was so well assuaged that he [ate] of the fish [for] his supper, which gave no less joy and content to us than ease to himself. For which we called the island Stingray Isle [Stingray Point] after the name of the fish.

Having neither surgeon nor surgery [medical supplies] but that preservative oil, we presently set sails for Jamestown, passing the mouths of the rivers of Piankatank, and Pamunkey, the next day we safely arrived at *Kecoughtan.*

The simple savages seeing our Captain hurt, and another bloody by breaking his shin, our numbers of bows, arrows, swords, mantels, and furs, would needs imagine we had been at wars (the truth of these accidents would not satisfy them) but impatiently importuned us to know with whom. Finding their aptness to believe, we failed not (as a great secret) to tell them anything that might affright them, what spoil we had got and made of the *Massawomekes.* This rumor went faster up the river than our barge, that arrived at *Warraskoyack* the 20 of July; where trimming her with painted streamers, and such devices as we could, we made them at Jamestown jealous of [afraid the barge was] a Spanish frigate, where we all, God be thanked, safely arrived the 21 of July.

There we found the last supply were all sick; the rest some lame, some bruised: all unable to do anything but complain of the pride and unreasonable, needless cruelty of the silly President, that had riotously consumed the store: and to fulfill his follies about building him an unnecessary building for his pleasure in the woods, had brought them all to that misery; that had we not arrived, they had as strangely tormented him with revenge.

But the good news of our discovery, and the good hope we had by the savages' relation, that our bay had stretched into the South Sea, or somewhat near it, appeased their fury; but conditionally that Ratcliffe should be deposed, and that Captain Smith would take upon him the government, as by course it did belong.

Their request being effected, he substituted Master Scrivener his dear friend in the presidency, equally distributing those private provisions the other [Ratcliffe] had engrossed, appointing more honest officers to assist Master Scrivener (who then lay exceeding[ly] sick of a callenture [sunstroke]): and in regard of the weakness of the company, and heat of the year, they being unable to work, he left them to live at ease, to recover their healths; but embarked himself to finish his discovery. . . .

Written by Walter Russell, Anas Todkill, and Thomas Mumford.

CHAPTER VI.

The government surrendered to Master Scrivener.
What happened the second voyage in discovering the bay.

The 24 of July [1608], Captain Smith set forward to finish the discovery with twelve men. . . .

The wind being contrary, caused our stay two or three days at *Kecoughtan:* the King feasted us with much mirth, his people were persuaded we went purposely to be revenged of the *Massawomekes.* In the evening we fired a few rockets, which flying in the air so terrified the poor savages, they supposed nothing impossible we attempted; and desired to assist us.

The first night we anchored at Stingray Point. The next day [we] crossed [the] Potomac River, and hasted to the river Patapsco.

We went not much further before we might see the bay to divide in two heads, and arriving there we found it divided in four [the Susquehanna, the Northeast, the Elk, and the Sassafras], all [of] which we searched so far as we could sail them.

Two of them we found [un]inhabited, but in crossing the bay, we encountered 7 or 8 canoes full of *Massawomekes.*

We seeing them prepare to assault us, left our oars and made way with our sail to encounter them, yet were we but five with our Captain that could stand, for within 2 days after we left *Kecoughtan,* the rest (being all of the last supply) were sick almost to death, until they were seasoned to the country. Having shut them under our tarpaulin, we put their hats upon sticks by the barge's side, and betwixt two hats a man with two pieces, to make us seem many: and so we think the Indians supposed those hats to be men, for they fled with all possible speed to the shore, and there stayed, staring at the sailing of our barge till we anchored right against them.

Long it was ere we could draw them to come unto us. At last they sent two of their company unarmed in a canoe, the rest all followed to second them if need required. These two being but each presented with a bell, brought aboard all their fellows, presenting our Captain with venison, bears' flesh, fish, bows, arrows, clubs, targets, and bearskins.

We understood them nothing at all, but by signs, whereby they signified unto us they had been at wars with the *Tockwoughs,* the which they confirmed by showing us their green wounds.

But the night parting us, we imagined they appointed the next morning to meet; but after that we never saw them.

Entering the river of Sassafras, the savages all armed, in a fleet of boats, after their barbarous manner, round environed us; so it chanced one of them could speak the language of Powhatan, who persuaded the rest to a friendly parley. But when they saw us furnished with the *Massawomekes'* weapons, and we feigning the invention [fabrication] [at] *Kecoughtan,* to have taken them perforce; they conducted us to their palisaded town, mantelled with the barks of trees, with scaffolds like mounts, breasted about with breast[work]s very formally. Their men, women, and children with dances, songs, fruits, furs, and what they had, kindly welcomed us, spreading mats for us to sit on, [and] stretching their best abilities to express their loves.

Many hatchets, knives, pieces of iron, and brass, we saw amongst them, which they reported to have from the *Susquehannocks,* a mighty people and mortal enemies with the *Massawomekes.*

The *Susquehannocks* inhabit upon the chief spring of these four branches of the bay's head, two days' journey higher than our barge could pass for rocks; yet we prevailed with the interpreter to take with him another interpreter, to persuade the *Susquehannocks* to come visit us, for their language[s] are different.

Three or four days we expected their return, then sixty of those giant-like people came down, with presents of venison, tobacco pipes three feet in length, baskets, targets, bows and arrows. Five of their chief *Werowances* came boldly aboard us to cross the bay for *Tockwough,* leaving their men and canoes; the wind being so high they durst not pass.

Our order was daily to have prayer, with a psalm; at which solemnity the poor savages much wondered, our prayers being done, a while they were busied with a consultation till they had contrived their business. Then they began in a most passionate manner to hold up their hands to the sun, with a most fearful song, then embracing our Captain, they began to adore him in like manner; though he rebuked them, yet they proceeded till their song was finished: which done [one] with a most strange, furious action, and a hellish voice, began an oration of their loves.

That ended, with a great painted bearskin they covered him: then one ready with a great chain of white beads, weighing at least six or seven pound[s], hung it about his neck, the others had 18 mantels, made of divers sorts of skins sewed together; all these with many other toys they laid at his feet, stroking their ceremonious hands about his neck for his creation to be their governor and protector, promising their aids, victuals, or what they had to be his, if he would stay with them, to defend and revenge them of the *Massawomekes*.

But we left them at *Tockwough,* sorrowing for our departure; yet we promised the next year again to visit them.

Many descriptions and discourses they made us, of *Atquanachuke, Massawomeke,* and other people, signifying they inhabit upon a great water beyond the mountains, which we understood to be some great lake, or the river of Canada: and from the French to have their hatchets and commodities by trade. These know no more of the territories of Powhatan, than his name, and he as little of them: but the *Atquanachukes* are on the ocean sea. . . .

In all those places and the furthest we came up the rivers, we cut in trees so many crosses as we would, and in many places made holes in trees, wherein we writ notes: and in some places crosses of brass, to signify to any, Englishmen had been there.

Thus having sought all the inlets and rivers worth noting, we returned to discover the river of Patuxent; these people we found very tractable, and more civil than any: we promised them, as also the *Patawomekes* to revenge them of the *Massawomekes,* but our purposes were crossed.

In the discovery of this river . . . we were kindly entertained by the people of *Moraughtacund*.

Here we encountered our old friend Mosco, a lusty savage of *Wighcocomoco* upon the river of Potomac. We supposed him some Frenchman's son, because he had a thick black bush beard, and the savages seldom have any at all; of which he was not a little proud, to see so many of his countrymen. Wood and water he would fetch us, guide us any whither, nay, cause divers of his countrymen help us [to] tow against wind or tide from place to place till we came to *Patawomeke:* there he rested till we returned from the head of the river, and occasioned our conduct to the mine we supposed antimony.

And in the place he failed not to do us all the good he could, persuading us in any case not to go to the *Rappahannocks,* for they would kill us for being friends with the *Moraughtacunds* that but lately had stolen three of the King's women.

This we did think was but that his friends might only have our trade: so we crossed the river to the *Rappahannocks*. There some 12 or 16 standing on the shore, directed us [to] a little creek where was good landing, and commodities for us in three or four canoes we saw lie there: but according to our custom, we demanded to exchange a man in sign of love; which after they had a little consulted, four or five came up to the middles, to fetch our man, and leave us one of them, showing we need not fear them, for they had neither clubs, bows, nor arrows. Notwithstanding, Anas Todkill, being sent on shore to see if he could discover any ambushes, or what they had, desired to go over the plain to fetch some wood; but they were unwilling, except we would come into the creek, where the boat might come close ashore. Todkill by degrees having got some two stones' throws up the plain, perceived two or three hundred men (as he thought) behind the trees; so that offering to return to the boat, the savages assayed to carry him away perforce, that he called to us we were betrayed: and by that he had spoke[n] the word, our hostage was overboard, but Watkins his keeper slew him in the water. Immediately we let fly amongst them, so that they fled, and Todkill escaped; yet they shot so fast that he fell flat on the ground ere he could recover the boat.

Here the *Massawomeke* targets stood us in good stead, for upon Mosco's words, we had set them about the forepart of our boat like a forecastle; from whence we securely beat the savages from off the plain without any hurt: yet they shot more than a thousand arrows, and then fled into the woods. Arming ourselves with these light targets (which are made of little small sticks woven betwixt strings of their hemp and silk grass, as is our cloth, but so firmly that no arrow can possibly pierce them:) we rescued Todkill; who was all bloody [from] some of them who were shot by us that held him, but as God pleased he had no hurt: and following them up to the woods, we found some slain, and in divers places much blood. It seems all their arrows were spent, for we heard no more of them.

Their canoes we took; the arrows we found we broke, save them we kept for Mosco, to whom we gave the canoes for his kindness, that entertained us in the best triumphing manner, and warlike order in arms of conquest he could procure of the *Moraughtacunds*. The rest of the day we spent in accommodating [fitting out] our boat, instead of thoules [oar locks] we made sticks like bedstaves, to which we fastened so many of our *Massawomeke* targets, that environed her as waist clothes.

The next morning we went up the river, and our friend Mosco followed us along the shore, and at last desired to go with us in our boat. But as we passed by *Pissaseck, Matchopeak,* and *Mecuppom,* three towns situated upon high, white clay cliffs; the other side all a low plain marsh, and the river there but narrow. Thirty or forty of the *Rappahannocks* had so accommodated [camouflaged] themselves with branches, [that] we took them for little bushes growing among the sedge, till seeing their arrows strike the targets, and dropped in the river: whereat Mosco fell flat in the boat on his face, crying the *Rappahannocks,* which presently we espied to be the bushes, which at our first volley fell down in the sedge: when we were near[ly] half a mile from them, they showed themselves dancing and singing very merrily.

The Kings of *Pissaseck, Nantaughtacund,* and *Cuttatawomen,* used us kindly, and all their people neglected not anything to Mosco to bring us to them.

Betwixt *Secobeck* and *Massawteck* is a small isle or two, which causeth the river to be broader than ordinary; there it pleased God to take one of our company called Master Fetherstone, that all the time he had been in this country, had behaved himself, honestly, valiantly, and industriously; where in a little bay we called Fetherstone's Bay we buried him with a volley of shot: the rest notwithstanding their ill diet, and bad lodging, crowded in so small a barge, in so many dangers, never resting, but always tossed to and again, had all well recovered their healths.

The next day we sailed [as] high as our boat would float; there setting up crosses, and [en]graving our names in the trees. Our sentinel saw an arrow fall by him; though we had ranged up and down more than an hour, in digging in the earth, looking [at] stones, herbs, and springs, not seeing where a savage could well hide himself.

Upon the alarm, by that we had recovered our arms, there [were] about a hundred nimble Indians skipping from tree to tree, letting fly their arrows [as] fast as they could: the trees here served us for barricades as well as they. But Mosco did us more service than we expected; for having shot away his quiver of arrows, he ran to the boat for more. The arrows of Mosco at the first made them pause upon the matter, thinking by his bruit [noise] and skipping, there were many savages. About half an hour this continued, then they all vanished as suddenly as they approached. Mosco followed them [as] far as he could see us, till they were out of sight. As we returned there lay a savage as dead, shot in the knee; but taking him up we found he had life: which Mosco seeing, never was dog more furious against a bear, than Mosco was to have beat out his brains. So we had him to our boat, where our surgeon who went with us to cure our Captain's hurt of the stingray, so dressed this savage that within an hour after he looked somewhat cheerfully, and did eat and speak. In the meantime we contented Mosco in helping him to gather up their arrows, which were an armful; whereof he gloried not a little.

Then we desired Mosco to know what he was, and what countries were beyond the mountains; the poor savage mildly answered, he and all with him were of *Hassinunga,* where there are three Kings more, like unto them, namely the King of *Stegara,* the King of *Tanxsnitania,* and the King of *Shackakonia,* that were come to *Mohaskahod,* which is only a hunting town, and the bounds betwixt the kingdom of the *Manahoacs* and the *Nantaughtacunds,* but hard by where we were.

We demanded why they came in that manner to betray us, that came to them in peace, and to seek their loves; he answered, they heard we were a people come from under the world, to take their world from them.

We asked him how many worlds he did know, he replied, he knew no more but that which was under the sky that covered him, which were the *Powhatans,* with the *Monacans* and the *Massawomekes* that were higher up in the mountains.

Then we asked him what was beyond the mountains, he answered the sun: but of anything else he knew nothing; because the woods were not burnt [not cleared, so that travel was almost impossible].

These and many such questions we demanded, concerning the *Massawomekes,* the *Monacans,* their own country, and where were the Kings of *Stegara, Tanxsnitania,* and the rest. The *Monacans* he said were their neighbors and friends, and did dwell as they in the hilly countries by small rivers, living upon roots and fruits, but chiefly by hunting. The *Massawomekes* did dwell upon a great water, and had many boats, and so many men that they made war with all the world. For their Kings, they were gone every one a several way with their men on hunting. But those with him came thither afishing till they saw us, notwithstanding they would be all together at night at *Mohaskahod*.

For his relation we gave him many toys, with persuasions to go with us: and he as earnestly desired us to stay the coming of those Kings that for his good usage should be friends with us, for he was brother to Hassinunga. But Mosco advised us presently to be gone, for they were all naught; yet we told him we would not till it was night. All things we made ready to entertain what came, and Mosco was as diligent in trimming his arrows.

The night being come we all embarked; for the river was so narrow, had it been light the land on the one side was so high, they might have done us exceeding[ly] much mischief. All this while the K[ing] of *Hassinunga* was seeking the rest, and had consultation a good time what to do. But by their espies seeing we were gone, it was not long before we heard their arrows dropping on every side [of] the boat; we caused our savages to call unto them, but such a yelling and hallowing they made that they heard nothing, but now and then [we shot off] a piece, aiming [as] near as we could [to] where we heard the most voices. More than 12 miles they followed us in this manner; then the day appearing, we found ourselves in a broad bay, out of danger of their shot, where we came to an anchor, and fell to breakfast. Not so much as speaking to them till the sun was risen.

Being well refreshed, we untied our targets that covered us as a deck, and all showed ourselves with those shields on our arms, and swords in our hands, and also our prisoner Amoroleck. A long discourse there was betwixt his countrymen and him, how good we were, how well we used him, how we had a *Patawomeke* with us, [who] loved us as his life, that would have slain him had we not preserved him, and that he should have his liberty would they be but friends; and to do us any hurt it was impossible.

Upon this they all hung their bows and quivers upon the trees, and one came swimming aboard us with a bow tied on his head, and another with a quiver of arrows, which they delivered our Captain as a present: the Captain having used them [as] kindly as he could, told them the other three Kings should do the like, and then the great King of our world should be their friend; whose men we were. It was no sooner demanded but performed, so upon a low, moorish [swampy] point of land we went to the shore, where those four Kings came and received Amoroleck: nothing they had but bows, arrows, tobacco bags, and pipes: what we desired, none refused to give us, wondering at everything we had, and heard we had done: our pistols they took for pipes, which they much desired, but we did content them with other commodities. And so we left four or five hundred of our merry *Manahoacs*, singing, dancing, and making merry, and set sail for *Moraughtacund*.

In our returns we visited all our friends, [who] rejoiced much at our victory against the *Manahoacs*, who many times had wars also with them, but now they were friends; and desired we would be friends with the *Rappahannocks*, as we were with the *Manahoacs*. Our Captain told them, they had twice assaulted him that came only in love to do them good, and therefore he would now burn all their houses, destroy their corn, and forever hold them his enemies, till they made him satisfaction. They desired to know what that should be. He told them they should present him the King's bow and arrows, and not offer to come armed where he was; that they should be friends with the *Moraughtacunds* his friends and give him their King's son in pledge to perform it; and then all King James' . . . men should be their friends. Upon this they presently sent to the *Rappahannocks* to meet him at the place where they first fought, where would be the Kings of *Nantaughtacund* and *Pissaseck*: which according to their promise were there [as] soon as we; where *Rappahannock* presented his bow and arrows, and confirmed all we desired, except his son, having no more but him he could not live without him, but instead of his son he would give him the three women Moraughtacund had stolen. This was accepted: and so in three or four canoes, so many as could went with us to *Moraughtacund*, where Mosco made them such relations, and gave to his friends so many bows and arrows, that they no less loved him than admired us. The 3 women were brought our Captain, to each he gave a chain of beads: and then causing Moraughtacund, Mosco, and Rappahannock stand before him, bid Rappahannock take her he loved best, and Moraughtacund choose next, and to Mosco he gave the third. Upon this, away went their canoes over the water, to fetch their venison, and all the provision they could; and they that wanted boats swam over the river. The dark[ness] commanded us then to rest.

The next day there [were] of men, women, and children, as we conjectured, six or seven hundred, dancing, and singing; and not a

bow nor arrow seen amongst them. Mosco changed his name [to]
Uttasantasough, which we interpret Stranger, for so they call us. All
promising ever to be our friends, and to plant corn purposely for
us; and we to provide hatchets, beads, and copper for them, we
departed: giving them a volley of shot, and they us as 'loud shouts
and cries as their strengths could utter.

That night we anchored in the river of Piankatank, and discovered
it so high as it was navigable; but the people were most[ly] ahunting,
save a few old men, women, and children, that were tending their
corn: of which they promised us part·when we would fetch it, as had
done all the nations where ever we had yet been.

In a fair calm, rowing towards Point Comfort, we anchored in
Gosnold's Bay, but such a sudden gust surprised us in the night with
thunder and rain, that we never thought more to have seen Jamestown.
Yet running before the wind, we sometimes saw the land by the
flashes of fire from heaven, by which light only we kept from the
splitting shore, until it pleased God in that black darkness to preserve
us by that light to find Point Comfort.

There refreshing ourselves, because we had only but heard of the
Chesapeakes and *Nansemonds,* we thought it as fit to know all our
neighbors near home, as so many nations abroad. So setting sail for
the southern shore, we sailed up a narrow river up the country of
Chesapeake; it hath a good channel, but many shoals about the
entrance. By that we had sailed six or seven miles, we saw two or three
little garden plots with their houses, the shores overgrown with the
greatest pine and fir trees we ever saw in the country. But not seeing
nor hearing any people, and the river very narrow, we returned to the
great river, to see if we could find any of them. Coasting the shore
towards *Nansemond,* which is most[ly] oyster banks; at the mouth of
that river, we espied six or seven savages making their weirs, who
presently fled: ashore we went, and where they wrought we threw
divers toys, and so departed. Far we were not gone ere they came
again, and began to sing, and dance, and recall us: and thus we began
our first acquaintance. At last one of them desired us to go to his
house up that river; into our boat voluntarily he came, the rest ran
after us by the shore with all show of love that could be. Seven or
eight miles we sailed up this narrow river: at last on the western shore
we saw large cornfields, in the midst a little isle, and in it was abundance
of corn. The people he told us were all ahunting, but in the isle was his

house, to which he invited us with much kindness: to him, his wife, and children, we gave such things as they seemed much contented them. The others being come, desired us also to go but a little higher to see their houses: here our host left us, the rest rowed by us in a canoe, till we were so far past the isle the river became very narrow.

Here we desired some of them to come aboard us, whereat pausing a little, they told us they would but fetch their bows and arrows and go all with us: but being ashore and thus armed, they persuaded us to go forward, but we could neither persuade them into their canoe, nor into our boat. This gave us cause to provide for the worst. Far we went not ere seven or eight canoes full of men armed appeared following us, staying to see the conclusion. Presently from each side [of] the river came arrows so fast as two or three hundred could shoot them, whereat we returned to get the open [down river]. They in the canoes let fly also as fast; but amongst them we bestowed so many shot; the most of them leaped overboard and swam ashore, but two or three escaped by rowing. Being against their plans: our muskets they found shot further than their bows, for we made not twenty shot ere they all retired behind the next trees. Being thus got out of their trap, we seized on all their canoes, and moored them in the midst of the open. More than a hundred arrows struck in our targets, and about the boat; yet none [was] hurt, only Anthony Bagnall was shot in his hat, and another in his sleeve. But seeing their multitudes, and suspecting as it was, that both the *Nansemonds,* and the *Chesapeakes* were together; we thought it best to ride by their canoes a while, to bethink if it were better to burn all in the isle, or draw them to composition [reach an agreement] till we were provided to take all they had, which was sufficient to feed all our colony: but to burn the isle at night it was concluded.

In the interim we began to cut in pieces their canoes, and they presently to lay down their bows, making signs of peace. Peace we told them we would accept it, would they bring us their King's bows and arrows, with a chain of pearl; and when we came again give us four hundred baskets full of corn: otherwise we would break all their boats, and burn their houses, and corn, and all they had. To perform all this they alleged only the want of a canoe; so we put one adrift and bade them swim to fetch her: and till they performed their promise, we would but only break their canoes. They cried to us to do no more, all should be as we would: which presently they performed.

Away went their bows and arrows, and tag and rag [all the Indians] came with their baskets: so much as we could carry we took, and so departing good friends, we returned to Jamestown, where we safely arrived the 7 of September, 1608.

There we found Master Scrivener, and divers others well recovered: many dead; some sick: the late President [Ratcliffe] [a] prisoner for mutiny: by the honest diligence of Master Scrivener, the harvest gathered; but the provision in the store much spoiled with rain.

Thus was that summer (when little wanted) consumed and spent, and nothing done (such was the government of Captain Ratcliffe) but only this discovery; wherein to express all the dangers, accidents, and encounters this small number passed in that small barge, by the scale of proportion, about three thousand miles, with such watery diet in those great waters and barbarous countries (till then to any Christian utterly unknown) I rather refer their merit to the censure of the courteous and experienced reader, than I would be tedious or partial being a party. . . .

Written by Anthony Bagnall, Nathaniel Powell, and Anas Todkill.

CHAPTER VII.

The Presidency surrendered to Captain Smith: the arrival and return of the second supply. And what happened.

The tenth of September, by the election of the Council, and request of the company, Captain Smith received the letters patent: which till then by no means he would accept, though he was often importuned thereunto.

Now the building of Ratcliffe's palace stayed, as a thing needless; the church was repaired; the storehouse recovered; buildings prepared for the supplies we expected; the fort reduced to a five-square form; the order of the watch renewed; the squadrons (each setting of the watch) trained; the whole company every Saturday exercised, in the plain by the west bulwark, prepared for that purpose, we called Smithfield:

where sometimes more than a hundred savages would stand in an amazement to behold, how a file [of soldiers] would batter a tree, where he would make them a mark to shoot at; the boats trimmed for trade, which being sent out with Lieutenant Percy, in their journey encountered the second supply, that brought them back to discover the country of *Monacan*.

How or why Captain Newport obtained such a private commission, as not to return without a lump of gold, a certainty of the South Sea, or one of the lost company sent out by Sir Walter Raleigh, I know not; nor why he brought such a five pieced barge, not to bear us to that South Sea, till we had borne her over the mountains, which how far they extend is yet unknown.

As for the coronation of Powhatan, and his presents of basin and ewer, bed, bedstead, clothes, and such costly novelties, they had been much better well spared than so ill spent, for we had his favor much better only for a plain piece of copper, till this stately kind of soliciting, made him so much overvalue himself, that he respected us as much as nothing at all.

As for the hiring of the Poles and Dutchmen, to make pitch, tar, glass, mills, and soap ashes, when the country is replenished with people, and necessaries, would have done well: but to send them and seventy more without victuals to work, was not so well advised nor considered of, as it should have been. Yet this could not have hurt us had they been 200, though then we were 130 that wanted for ourselves. For we had the savages in that decorum (their harvest being newly gathered) that we feared not to get victuals for 500.

Now was there no way to make us miserable, but to neglect that time to make provision whilst it was to be had, the which was done by the direction from England to perform this strange discovery, but a more strange coronation, to lose that time, spend that victuals we had, tire and starve our men, having no means to carry victuals, munition, the hurt or sick, but on their own backs. How or by whom they were invented I know not.

But Captain Newport we only accounted the author, who to effect these projects, had so gilded men's hopes with great promises, that both company and Council concluded his resolution for the most part. God doth know they little knew what they did, nor understood their own estates to conclude his [Newport's] conclusions, against all the inconveniences the foreseeing President [Smith] alleged [pointed out].

Of this supply there was added to the Council, one Captain Richard Waldo, and Captain [Peter] Winne, two ancient soldiers, and valiant gentlemen; but yet ignorant of the business, (being but newly arrived.) Ratcliffe was also permitted to have his voice, and Master Scrivener, desirous to see strange countries: so that although Smith was President, yet the major part of the Council had the authority, and ruled it as they listed.

As for clearing Smith's objections, how pitch and tar, wainscot, clapboard, glass, and soap ashes, could be provided, to relade the ship: or provision got to live withal [at the same time], when none was in the country; and that [provisions] we had, spent, before the ship departed to effect these projects. The answer was, Captain Newport undertook to fraught the pinnace of twenty tons with corn in going and returning in his discovery, and to refraught her again from *Werowocómoco* of Powhatan. Also promising a great proportion of victuals from the ship; inferring that Smith's propositions were only devices to hinder his journey, to effect it himself; and that the cruelty he [Smith] had used to the savages might well be the occasion to hinder these designs, and seek revenge on him. For which taxation, all works were left, and 120 chosen men were appointed for Newport's guard in this discovery.

But Captain Smith to make clear all those seeming suspicions, that the savages were not so desperate as was pretended by Captain Newport, and how willing (since by their authority they would have it so) he was to assist them what he could, because the coronation would consume much time, he undertook himself their message to Powhatan, to entreat him to come to Jamestown to receive his presents.

And where Newport durst not go with less than 120, he only took with him Captain Waldo, Master Andrew Buckler, Edward Brinton, and Samuel Collier: with these four he went overland to *Werowocómoco*, some 12 miles; there he passed the river of Pamunkey in a savage canoe.

Powhatan being 30 miles of[f], was presently sent for: in the meantime, Pocahontas and her women entertained Captain Smith in this manner.

In a fair plain field they made a fire, before which, he sitting upon a mat, suddenly amongst the woods was heard such a hideous noise and shrieking, that the [five] English betook themselves to their arms, and seized on two or three old men by them, supposing Powhatan with all his power was come to surprise them. But presently Pocahontas came, willing him to kill her if any hurt were intended; and the beholders, which were men, women, and children, satisfied the Captain there was no such matter.

Then presently they were presented with this antic; thirty young women came naked out of the woods, only covered behind and before with a few green leaves, their bodies all painted, some of one color, some of another, but all differing, their leader [Pocahontas?] had a fair pair of buck's horns on her head, and an otter's skin at her girdle, and another at her arm, a quiver of arrows at her back, a bow and arrows in her hand; the next had in her hand a sword, another a club, another a pot-stick; all horned alike: the rest every one with their several devices.

These fiends with most hellish shouts and cries, rushing from among the trees, cast themselves in a ring about the fire, singing and dancing with most excellent ill variety, oft falling into their infernal passions, and solemnly again to sing and dance; having spent near[ly] an hour in this masquerade, as they entered, in like manner they departed.

Having reaccommodated themselves, they solemnly invited him to their lodgings, where he was no sooner within the house, but all these nymphs more tormented him than ever, with crowding, pressing, and hanging about him, most tediously crying, Love you not me? Love you not me?

This salutation ended, the feast was set, consisting of all the savage dainties they could devise: some attending, others singing and dancing about them; which mirth being ended, with fire-brands instead of torches they conducted him to his lodging. . . .

The next day came Powhatan. Smith delivered his message of the presents sent him, and redelivered him Namontack he had sent [to] England; desiring him to come to his Father Newport, to accept those presents, and conclude their revenge against the *Monacans*.

Whereunto this subtle savage thus replied.

If your King have sent me presents, I also am a King, and this is my land: eight days I will stay to receive them. Your Father is to come to me, not I to him, nor yet to your fort, neither will I bite at such a bait: as for the Monacans *I can revenge my own injuries, and as for* Atquanachuke, *where you say your brother was slain, it is a contrary way from those parts you suppose it; but for any salt water beyond the mountains, the relations you have had from my people are false.*

Whereupon he began to draw plots upon the ground (according to his discourse) of all those regions.

Many other discourses they had (yet both content to give each other content in complimental courtesies) and so Captain Smith returned with this answer.

Upon this, the presents were sent by water which is near[ly] a hundred miles, and the Captains went by land with fifty good shot.

All being met at *Werowocómoco,* the next day was appointed for his coronation, then the presents were brought him, his basin and ewer, bed and furniture set up, his scarlet cloak and apparel with much ado put on him, being persuaded by Namontack they would not hurt him: but a foul trouble there was to make him kneel to receive his crown, he neither knowing the majesty nor meaning of a crown, nor bending of the knee, endured so many persuasions, examples, and instructions, as tired them all; at last by leaning hard on his shoulders, he a little stooped, and three having the crown in their hands put it on his head, when by the warning of a pistol the boats were prepared with such a volley of shot, that the King start[ed] up in a horrible fear, till he saw all was well. Then remembering himself, to congratulate their kindness, he gave his old shoes and his mantel to Captain Newport.

But perceiving his purpose was to discover the *Monacans,* he labored to divert his resolution, refusing to lend him either men or guides more than Namontack; and so after some small complimental kindness on both sides, in requital of his presents he presented Newport with a heap of wheat [corn] ears that might contain some 7 or 8 bushels, and as much more we bought in the town: wherewith we returned to the fort.

The ship having disburdened herself of 70 persons, with the first gentlewoman and woman servant that arrived in our colony. Captain Newport with 120 chosen men, led by Captain Waldo, Lieutenant Percy, Captain Winne, Master West, and Master Scrivener, set forward for the discovery of *Monacan,* leaving the President at the fort with about 80 or 90 (such as they were) to relade the ship.

Arriving at the falls [the site of present-day Richmond], we marched by land some forty miles in two days and a half; and so returned down the same path we went. Two towns we discovered of the *Monacans',* called *Massinacack* and *Mowhemenchugh;* the people neither used us well nor ill, yet for our security we took one of their petty Kings, and led him bound to conduct us the way.

And in our returns [we] searched many places we supposed mines, about which we spent some time in refining, having one William Callicut, a refiner fitted for that purpose. From that crust of earth we digged, he persuaded us to believe he extracted some small quantity of silver; and (not unlikely) better stuff might be had for the digging.

With this poor trial, being contented to leave this fair, fertile, well-watered country; and coming to the falls, the savages feigned there were divers ships come into the bay, to kill them at Jamestown. Trade they would not, and find their corn we could not; for they had hid[den] it in the woods: and being thus deluded, we arrived at Jamestown, half sick, all complaining, and tired with toil, famine, and discontent, to have only but discovered our gilded hopes, and such fruitless certainties, as Captain Smith foretold us. . . .

No sooner were we landed, but the President dispersed so many as were able, some for glass, others for tar, pitch, and soap ashes, leaving them with the fort to the Council's oversight.

But 30 of us he conducted down the river some 5 miles from Jamestown, to learn to make clapboard, cut down trees, and [to make] lye in [the] woods. Amongst the rest he had chosen Gabriel Beadle, and John Russell, the only two gallants of this last supply, and both proper gentlemen. Strange were these pleasures to their conditions; yet lodging, eating, and drinking, working or playing, they but doing as the President did himself. All these things were carried so pleasantly as within a week they became masters: making it their delight to hear the trees thunder as they fell; but the axes so oft blistered their tender fingers, that many times every third blow had a loud oath to drown the echo; for remedy of which sin, the President devised how to have every man's oaths numbered, and at night for every oath to have a can of water poured down his sleeve, with which every offender was so washed (himself and all) that a man should scarce hear an oath in a week. . . .

By this, let no man think that the President and these gentlemen spent their times as common wood haggers [cutters] at felling of trees, or such other like labors; or that they were pressed to it as hirelings, or common slaves; for what they did, after they were but once a little inured, it seemed and some conceited it, only as a pleasure and recreation: yet 30 or 40 of such voluntary gentlemen would do more in a day than 100 of the rest that must be pressed to it by compulsion; but twenty good workmen had been better than them all.

Master Scrivener, Captain Waldo, and Captain Winne at the fort, every one in like manner carefully regarded their charge. The President returning from amongst the woods, seeing the time consumed and no provision gotten, (and the ship lay idle at a great charge and did nothing) presently embarked himself in the discovery barge, giving order to the Council to send Lieutenant Percy after him with the next barge that arrived at the fort; two barges he had himself and 18 men, but arriving at *Chickahominy,* that dogged nation was too well acquainted with our wants, refusing to trade, with as much scorn and insolency as they could express. The President perceiving it was Powhatan's policy to starve us, told them he came not so much for their corn, as to revenge his imprisonment, and the death of his men murdered by them; and so landing his men and ready to charge them, they immediately fled: and presently after sent their ambassadors with corn, fish, fowl, and what they had to make their peace; (their corn being that year but bad) they complained extremely of their own wants, yet fraughted our boats with a hundred bushels of corn, and in like manner Lieutenant Percy's that not long after arrived, and having done the best they could to content us, we parted good friends, and returned to Jamestown.

Though this much contented the company (that feared nothing more than starving), yet some so envied his good success, that they rather desired to hazard a starving, than his pains should prove so much more effectual than theirs. Some projects there were invented by Newport and Ratcliffe, not only to have deposed him, but to have kept him out of the fort; for that being President, he would leave his place and the fort without their consents: but their horns were so much too short to effect it, as they themselves more narrowly escaped a greater mischief.

All this time our old tavern made as much of all them that had either money or ware as could be desired: by this time they were become so perfect on all sides (I mean the soldiers, sailors, and savages) as there was ten times more care to maintain their damnable and private trade, than to provide for the colony things that were necessary. Neither was it a small policy in Newport and the mariners to report in England we had such plenty, and bring us so many men without victuals, when they had so many private factors in the fort, that within six or seven weeks, of two or three hundred axes, chisels, hoes, and pick-axes, scarce[ly] twenty could be found: and for pike-heads, shot, powder, or anything they could steal from their fellows, [which] was vendible; they knew as well (and as secretly) how to convey them to trade with the savages for furs, baskets, *mussaneeks,* young beasts, or such like commodities, as exchange them with the sailors for butter, cheese, beef, pork, aqua vitae, beer, biscuit, oatmeal, and oil: and then feign all was sent them from their friends. And though Virginia afforded no furs for the store, yet one master in one voyage hath got so many by this indirect means, as he confessed to have sold in England for £30.

Those are the saint-seeming worthies of Virginia (that have notwithstanding all this, meat, drink, and wages); but now they begin to grow weary, their trade being both perceived and prevented.

None hath been in Virginia, that hath observed anything, [who] knows not this to be true: and yet the loss, the scorn, the misery, and shame, was the poor officers', gentlemen's, and careless governors', who were all thus bought and sold; the adventurers cozened, and the action overthrown by their false excuses, informations, and directions. By this let all men judge, how this business could prosper, being thus abused by such pilfering occasions. And had not Captain Newport cried *peccavi* [admitted his mistake], the President would have discharged the ship, and caused him to have stayed one year in Virginia, to learn to speak of his own experience.

Master Scrivener was sent with the barges and pinnace to *Werowocómoco,* where he found the savages more ready to fight than trade: but his vigilancy was such as prevented their projects, and by the means of Namontack, [he] got three or four hogsheads of corn; and as much *puccoon,* which is a red root, which then was esteemed an excellent dye.

Captain Newport being dispatched, with the trials [samples] of pitch, tar, glass, frankincense, soap ashes; with that clapboard and wainscot that could be provided met with Master Scrivener at Point Comfort, and so returned [to] England. We remaining were about two hundred.

> *The copy of a letter sent to the treasurer*
> *and Council of [the] Virginia [Company]*
> *from Captain Smith, then President in Virginia.*

Right Honorable, &c.
   I received your letter, wherein you write, that our minds are so set upon faction, and idle conceits in dividing the country without your

consents, and that we feed you but with ifs and ands, hopes, and some few proofs; as if we would keep the mystery of the business to ourselves: and that we must expressly follow your instructions sent by Captain Newport: the charge of whose voyage amounts to near[ly] two thousand pounds, the which if we cannot defray by the ships' return, we are like to remain as banished men. To these particulars I humbly entreat your pardons if I offend you with my rude answer.

For our factions, unless you would have me run away and leave the country, I cannot prevent them: because I do make many stay that would else fly any whither. For the idle letter sent [by Captain Newport's ship in April 1608?] to my Lord of Salisbury, by the President [Ratcliffe] and his confederates, for dividing the country &c. What it was I know not, for you saw no hand of mine to it; nor ever dreamed I of any such matter. That we feed you with hopes, &c. Though I be no scholar, I am past a school-boy; and I desire but to know, what either you, and these here, do know but that I have learned to tell you by the continual hazard of my life. I have not concealed from you anything I know; but I fear some cause you to believe much more than is true.

Expressly to follow your directions by Captain Newport, though they be performed, I was directly against it; but according to our commission, I was content to be overruled by the major part of the Council, I fear to the hazard of us all; which now is generally confessed when it is too late. Only Captain Winne and Captain Waldo I have sworn of the Council, and crowned Powhatan according to your instructions.

For the charge of this voyage of two or three thousand pounds, we have not received the value of a hundred pounds. And for the quartered boat to be borne by the soldiers over the falls, Newport had 120 of the best men he could choose. If he had burnt her to ashes, one might have carried her in a bag; but as she is, five hundred cannot, to a navigable place above the falls. And for him at that time to find in the South Sea, a mine of gold, or any of them sent by Sir Walter Raleigh: at our consultation I told them was as likely as the rest. But during this great discovery of thirty miles, (which might as well have been done by one man, and much more, for the value of a pound of copper at a seasonable time) they had the pinnace and all the boats with them, but one that remained with me to serve the fort.

In their absence I followed the new[ly] begun works of pitch and tar, glass, soap ashes, and clapboard; whereof some small quantities we have sent you. But if you rightly consider, what an infinite toil it is in Russia and Swethland [Sweden], where the woods are proper for naught else, and though there by the help both of man and beast in those ancient commonwealths, which many a hundred years have used it; yet thousands of those poor people can scarce[ly] get necessaries to live, but from hand to mouth. And though your factors there can buy as much in a week as will fraught you a ship, or as much as you please; you must not expect from us any such matter, which are but a many [group] of ignorant, miserable souls, that are scarce[ly] able to get wherewith to live, and defend ourselves against the inconstant savages: finding but here and there a tree fit for the purpose, and want all things else the Russians have.

For the coronation of Powhatan, by whose advice you sent him such presents, I know not; but this give me leave to tell you, I fear they will be the confusion of us all ere we hear from you again. At your ship's arrival, the savages' harvest was newly gathered, and we going to buy it; our own not being half sufficient for so great a number. As for the two ships' loading of corn Newport promised to provide [for] us from Powhatan, he brought us but fourteen bushels; and from the Monacans nothing, but the most of the men sick and near[ly] famished. From your ship we had not provision in victuals worth twenty pound[s], and we are more than two hundred to live upon this: the one half sick, the other little better. For the sailors (I confess) they daily make good cheer, but our diet is a little meal and water, and not sufficient of that. Though there be fish in the sea, fowls in the air, and beasts in the woods, their bounds are so large, they so wild, and we so weak and ignorant, we cannot much trouble them. Captain Newport we much suspect to be the author of those inventions.

Now that you should know, I have made you as great a discovery as he, for less charge than he spendeth you every meal; I have sent you this map of the bay and rivers, with an annexed relation of the countries and nations that inhabit them, as you may see at large. Also two barrels of stones, and such as I take to be good iron ore at the least; so divided, as by their notes you may see in what places I found them.

The soldiers say many of your officers maintain their families out of that you send us: and that Newport hath a hundred pounds a year for carrying news. For every master you have yet sent can find the way as well as he, so that a hundred pounds might be spared, which is more than we have all, that helps to pay him wages.

Captain Ratcliffe is now called Sicklemore, a poor counterfeited imposture. I have sent you him home, least the company should cut his throat. What he is, now everyone can tell you: if he and Archer return again, they are sufficient to keep us always in factions.

When you send again I entreat you rather send but thirty carpenters, husbandmen, gardners, fishermen, blacksmiths, masons, and diggers up of trees, roots, well provided; than a thousand of such as we have: for except we be able both to lodge them, and feed them, the most will consume with want of necessaries before they can be made good for anything.

Thus if you please to consider this account, and of the unnecessary wages to Captain Newport, or his ships so long lingering and staying here (for notwithstanding his boasting to leave us victuals for 12 months; though we had 89 by this discovery lame and sick, and but a pint of corn a day for a man, we were constrained to give him three hogsheads of that to victual him homeward) or yet to send into Germany or Poland for glass-men and the rest, till we be able to sustain ourselves and relieve them when they come. It were better to give five hundred pound[s] a ton for those gross commodities in Denmark, than send for them hither, till more necessary things be provided. For in over-toiling our weak and unskillful bodies, to satisfy this desire of present profit, we can scarce[ly] ever recover ourselves from one supply to another.

And I humbly entreat you hereafter, let us know what we should receive, and not stand to the sailors' courtesy to leave us what they please; else you may charge us with what you will, but we not you with anything.

These are the causes that have kept us in Virginia, from laying such a foundation, that ere this might have given much better content and satisfaction; but as yet you must not look for any profitable returns: so I humbly rest.

The names of those in this supply, were these:
with their proceedings and accidents.

Captain Peter Winne, Captain Richard Waldo, were appointed to be of the Council.

Master Francis West, brother to the Lord De La Warr.

Gentlemen
Thomas Graves
Raleigh Chroshaw
Gabriel Beadle
John Beadle
John Russell
William Russell
John Cuderington
William Sambage
Henry Leigh
Henry Philpot
Harmon Harrison
Daniel Tucker
Henry Collings
Hugh Wolleston
John Hoult
Thomas Norton
George Yarington
George Burton
Thomas Abbay
William Dowman
Thomas Maxes
Michael Lowick
Master Hunt
Thomas Forrest
John Dauxe

Tradesmen [Artisans]
Thomas Phelps
John Prat
John Clarke
Jeffrey Shortridge
Dionis Oconor
Hugh Winne
David ap Hugh

Thomas Bradley
John Burras
Thomas Lavander
Henry Bell
Master Powell
David Ellis
Thomas Gibson

Laborers
Thomas Dawse
Thomas Mallard
William Tayler
Thomas Fox
Nicholas Hancock
Walker
Williams
Floud
Morley
Rose
Scot
Hardwyn

Boys
Milman
Hilliard

Mistress Forrest, and Anne Burras her maid; eight Dutchmen and Poles, with some others, to the number of seventy persons, &c.

These poor conclusions so affrighted us all with famine, that the President provided for *Nansemond,* and took with him Captain Winne, and Master Scrivener, then returning from Captain Newport.

These people also long denied him not only the 400 baskets of corn they promised, but any trade at all; (excusing themselves they had spent most they had; and were commanded by Powhatan to keep that they had, and not to let us come into their river) till we were constrained to begin with them perforce.

Upon the discharging of our muskets they all fled and shot not an arrow; the first house we came to we set on fire, which when they perceived, they desired we would make no more spoil, and they would give us half they had: how they collected it I know not, but before night they loaded our three boats.

And so we returned to our quarter some four miles down the river, which was only the open woods under the lee of a hill, where all the ground was covered with snow, and hard frozen; the snow we digged away and made a great fire in the place; when the ground was well dried, we turned away [pushed back] the fire; and covering the place with a mat, there we lay very warm. To keep us from the wind we made a shade of another mat; as the wind turned we turned our shade: and when the ground grew cold we removed the fire [to another spot and started the process again]. And thus many a cold winter night have we lain in this miserable manner, yet those that most commonly went upon all those occasions, were always in health, lusty, and fat.

For sparing them this year, the next year they promised to plant purposely for us; and so we returned to Jamestown.

About this time there was a marriage betwixt John Laydon and Anne Burras; which was the first marriage we had in Virginia.

Long he stayed not, but fitting himself and Captain Waldo with two barges. From *Chawopoweanock,* and all parts thereabouts, all the people were fled, as being jealous of our intents; till we discovered the river and people of *Appomattoc;* where we found not much: that they had we equally divided; but gave them copper and such things as contented them in consideration.

Master Scrivener and Lieutenant Percy went also abroad, but could find nothing.

The President seeing the procrastinating of time, was no course to live, resolved with Captain Waldo (whom he knew to be sure in time of need) to surprise Powhatan, and all his provision, but the unwillingness of Captain Winne, and Master Scrivener (for some private respect, plotted in England to ruin Captain Smith), did their best to hinder their project.

But the President whom no persuasions could persuade to starve, being invited by Powhatan to come unto him: and if he would send him but men to build him a house, give him a grindstone, fifty swords, some pieces, a cock and a hen, with much copper and beads, he would load his ship with corn.

The President not ignorant of his devises and subtlety, yet unwilling to neglect any opportunity, presently sent three Dutchmen and two English; having so small allowance, [that] few were able to do anything to purpose: knowing there needed no better a castle to effect this project, took order with Captain Waldo to second him, if need required. Scrivener he left his substitute, and set forth with the pinnace, two barges, and forty-six men, which only were such as voluntarily offered themselves for his journey, the which by reason of Master Scrivener's ill success, was censured [as] very desperate: they all knowing Smith would not return empty, if it were to be had; howsoever, it caused many of those that he had appointed, to find excuses to stay behind.

CHAPTER VIII.

Captain Smith's journey to Pamunkey.

The twenty-nin[th] of December [1608] he set forward for *Werowocómoco* . . . [with two boats, while others] were sent by land before, to build the house for Powhatan against our arrival.

This company being victualled but for three or four days, lodged the first night at *Warraskoyack,* where the President took sufficient provision.

This kind King did his best to divert him from seeing Powhatan; but perceiving he could not prevail, he advised in this manner.

Captain Smith, you shall find Powhatan to use you kindly: but trust him not, and be sure he have no opportunity to seize on your arms; for he hath sent for you only to cut your throats.

The Captain thanking him for his good counsel: yet the better to try his love, desired guides to *Chawanoac;* for he would send a present to that King, to bind him his friend. To perform this journey was sent Master Sicklemore, a very valiant, honest, and a painful soldier: with him two guides, and directions how to seek for the lost company of Sir Walter Raleigh's, and silk grass.

Then we departed thence, the President assuring the King [of his] perpetual love; and left with him Samuel Collier his page to learn the language. . . .

The next night, being lodged at *Kecoughtan;* six or seven days the extreme wind, rain, frost, and snow caused us to keep Christmas [31 December 1608 — 6 January 1609] among the savages, where we were never more merry, nor fed on more plenty of good oysters, fish, flesh, wild fowl, and good bread; nor never had better fires in England, than in the dry, smoky houses of *Kecoughtan.*

But departing thence, when we found no houses we were not curious in any weather to lie three or four nights together under the trees by a fire. . . . A hundred [and] forty-eight fowls the President, Anthony Bagnall, and Sergeant Pising did kill at three shoots.

At *Kiskiack* the frost and contrary winds forced us three or four days also (to suppress the insolency of those proud savages) to quarter in their houses, yet guard our barge, and cause them [to] give us what we wanted; though we were but twelve and himself, yet we never wanted shelter where we found any houses.

The 12 of January we arrived at *Werowocómoco,* where the river was frozen near[ly] half a mile from the shore; but to neglect no time, the President with his barge so far had approached by breaking the ice, as the ebb left him amongst those oozy shoals, yet rather than to lie there frozen to death, by his own example he taught them to march near middle deep, a flight shot through this muddy, frozen ooze. When the barge floated, he appointed two or three to return her aboard the pinnace. Where for want of water, in melting the ice, they made fresh water, for the river there was salt. But in this march Master Russell, (whom none could persuade to stay behind) being somewhat ill, and exceeding[ly] heavy, so overtoiled himself as the rest had much ado (ere he got ashore) to regain life into his dead, benumbed spirits.

Quartering in the next houses we found, we sent to Powhatan for provision; who sent us plenty of bread, turkeys, and venison.

The next day having feasted us after his ordinary manner, he began to ask us when we would be gone: feigning he sent not for us, neither had he any corn; and his people much less: yet for forty swords he would procure us forty baskets.

The President showing him the men there present that brought him the message and conditions, asked Powhatan how it chanced he became so forgetful; thereat the King concluded the matter with a merry laughter, asking for our commodities, but none he liked without guns and swords, valueing a basket of corn more precious than a basket of copper; saying he could rate [eat] his corn, but not the copper.

Captain Smith seeing the intent of this subtle savage, began to deal with him after this manner.

Powhatan, though I had many courses to have made my provision, yet believing your promises to supply my wants, I neglected all to satisfy your desire: and to testify my love, I sent you my men for your building, neglecting mine own. What your people had, you have engrossed, forbidding them our trade: and now you think by consuming the time, we shall consume for want, not having to fulfill your strange demands. As for swords and guns, I told you long ago I had none to spare; and you must know those I have can keep me from want: yet steal or wrong you I will not, nor dissolve that friendship we have mutually promised, except you constrain me by our bad usage.

The King having attentively listened to this discourse, promised that both he and his country would spare him what he could, the which within two days they should receive. *Yet Captain Smith,* saith the King, *some doubt I have of your coming hither, that makes me not so kindly seek to relieve you as I would: for many do inform me, your coming hither is not for trade, but to invade my people, and possess my country, who dare not come to bring you corn, seeing you thus armed with your men. To free us of this fear, leave aboard your weapons, for here they are needless, we being all friends, and forever Powhatans.*

With many such discourses, they spent the day; quartering that night in the King's houses.

The next day he renewed his building, which he little intended should proceed. For the Dutchmen finding his plenty, and knowing our want; and perceiving his preparations to surprise us, little thinking we could escape both him and famine; (to obtain his favor) revealed to him so much as they knew of our estates and projects, and how to prevent them. One of them being of so great a spirit, judgment, and resolution; and a hireling that was certain of his wages for his labor, and ever well used both he and his countrymen; that the President knew not whom better to trust: and not knowing any fitter for that employment, he sent him as a spy to discover Powhatan's intent, then little doubting his honesty, nor could ever be certain of his villainy till near[ly] half a year after.

Whilst we expected the coming in of the country, we wrangled out of the King ten quarters of corn for a copper kettle, the which the President perceiving him much to affect, valued it at a much greater rate; but in regard of his scarcity he would accept it, provided we should have as much more the next year, or else the country of *Monacan*. Wherewith each seemed well contented, and Powhatan began to expostulate the difference of peace and war after this manner.

Captain Smith, you may understand that I having seen the death of all my people thrice, and not anyone living of those three generations but myself; I know the difference of peace and war better than any in my country. But now I am old and ere long must die, my brethren, namely Opitchapam, Opechancanough, and Kekataugh, my two sisters, and their two daughters, are distinctly each others' successors. I wish their experience no less than mine, and your love to them no less than mine to you. But this bruit from Nansemond, *that you are come to destroy my country, so much affrighteth all my people as they dare not visit you. What will it avail you to take that by force you may quickly have by love, or to destroy them that provide you food. What can you get by war, when we can hide our provisions and fly to the woods? whereby you must famish by wronging us your friends. And why are you thus jealous of our loves seeing us unarmed, and both do, and and are willing still to feed you, with that you cannot get but by our labors? Think you I am so simple, not to know it is better to eat good meat, lie well, and sleep quietly with my women and children, laugh and be merry with you, have copper, hatchets, or what I want being your friend: than be forced to fly from all, to lie cold in the woods, feed upon acorns, roots, and such trash; and be so hunted by you, that I can neither rest, eat, nor sleep; but my tired men must watch, and if a twig but break, every one crieth there cometh Captain Smith: then must I fly I know not whither: and thus with miserable fear, end my miserable life, leaving my pleasures to such youths as you, [who] through your rash unadvisedness may quickly as miserably end, for want of that, you never know where to find. Let this therefore assure you of our loves, and every year our friendly trade shall furnish*

*you with corn; and now also, if you would come in friendly manner
to see us, and not thus with your guns and swords as to invade your
foes.*

To this subtle discourse, the President thus replied.

*Seeing you will not rightly conceive of our words, we strive to
make you know our thoughts by our deeds; the vow I made you of
my love, both myself and my men have kept. As for your promise
I find it every day violated by some of your subjects: yet we finding
your love and kindness, our custom is so far from being ungrateful, that
for your sake only, we have curbed our thirsting desire of revenge; else
had they known as well the cruelty we use to our enemies, as our true
love and courtesy to our friends. And I think your judgment sufficient
to conceive, as well by the adventures we have undertaken, as by the
advantage we have (by our arms) of yours: that had we intended you
any hurt, long ere this we could have effected it. Your people coming
to Jamestown are entertained with their bows and arrows without any
exceptions; we esteeming it with you as it is with us, to wear our
arms as our apparel. As for the danger of our enemies, in such wars
consist our chiefest pleasure: for your riches we have no use: as for
the hiding your provision, or by your flying to the woods, we shall not
so unadvisedly starve as you conclude, your friendly care in that behalf
is needless, for we have a rule to find beyond your knowledge.*

Many other discourses they had, till at last they began to trade. But
the King seeing his will would not be admitted as a law, our guard
[not] dispersed, nor our men disarmed, he (sighing) breathed his
mind once more in this manner.

Captain Smith, I never use any Werowance *so kindly as yourself,
yet from you I receive the least kindness of any. Captain Newport gave
me swords, copper, clothes, a bed, towels, or what I desired; ever
taking what I offered him, and would send away his guns when I
entreated him: none doth deny to [lay] at my feet, or refuse to do,
what I desire, but only you; of whom I can have nothing but what
you regard not, and yet you will have whatsoever you demand. Captain
Newport you call father, and so you call me; but I see for all us both
you will do what you list, and we must both seek to content you. But
if you intend so friendly as you say, send hence your arms, that I may
believe you; for you see the love I bear you, doth cause me thus nakedly
to forget myself.*

Smith seeing this savage but trifle the time to cut his throat, procured the savages to break the ice, that his boat might come to fetch his corn and him; and gave order for more men to come on shore, to surprise the King, with whom also he but trifled the time till his' men were landed: and to keep him from suspicion, entertained the time with this reply.

Powhatan, you must know, as I have but one God, I honor but one King; and I live not here as your subject, but as your friend to pleasure you with what I can. By the gifts you bestow on me, you gain more than by trade: yet would you visit me as I do you, you should know it is not our custom, to sell our courtesies as a vendible commodity. Bring all your country with you for your guard, I will not dislike it as being over jealous. But to content you, tomororw I will leave my arms, and trust to your promise. I call you father indeed, and as a father you shall see I will love you: but the small care you have of such a child caused my men to persuade me to look to myself.

By this time Powhatan having knowledge his men were ready; whilst the ice was abreaking, with his luggage, women and children, fled. Yet to avoid suspicion, left two or three of the women talking with the Captain, whilst he secretly ran away, and that his men secretly beset the house. Which being presently discovered to Captain Smith, with his pistol, sword, and target he made such a passage among these naked devils; that at his first shot, they next [to] him tumbled one over another, and the rest quickly fled some one way, some another: so that without any hurt, only accompanied [by] John Russell, he obtained the *corps du guard.*

When they perceived him so well escaped, and with his eighteen men (for he had no more with him ashore), to the uttermost of their skill they sought excuses to dissemble the matter: and Powhatan to excuse his flight and the sudden coming of this multitude, sent our Captain a great bracelet and a chain of pearl, by an ancient orator that bespoke us to this purpose; perceiving even then from our pinnace, a barge and men departing and coming unto us.

Captain Smith, our Werowance *is fled, fearing your guns, and knowing when the ice was broken there would come more men, sent these numbers but to guard his corn from stealing, that might happen without your knowledge: now though some be hurt by your misprison, yet Powhatan is your friend and so will forever continue. Now since the ice is open, he would have you send away your corn; and if you would have his company, send away also your guns, which so affrighteth his people, that they dare not come to you as he promised they should.*

Then having provided baskets for our men to carry our corn to the boats, they kindly offered their service to guard our arms, that none should steal them. A great many they were of goodly well proportioned fellows, as grim as devils; yet [at] the very sight of cocking our matches, and being [about to] let fly, a few words caused them to leave their bows and arrows to our guard, and bear down our corn on their backs; we needed not importune them to make dispatch.

But our barges being left on the ooze by the ebb, caused us stay till the next high water; so that we returned again to our old quarter.

Powhatan and his Dutchmen bursting with desire to have the head of Captain Smith; for if they could but kill him, they thought all was theirs, neglected not any opportunity to effect his purpose. The Indians with all the merry sports they could devise, spent the time till night: then they all returned to Powhatan, who all this time was making ready his forces to surprise the house and him at supper.

Notwithstanding the eternal all-seeing God did prevent him, and by a strange means. For Pocahontas his dearest jewel and daughter, in that dark night came through the irksome woods, and told our Captain great cheer should be sent us by and by: but Powhatan and all the power he could make, would after come kill us all, if they that brought it could not kill us with our own weapons when we were at supper. Therefore if we would live, she wished us presently to be gone. Such things as she delighted in, he would have given her: but with the tears running down her cheeks, she said she durst not be seen to have any: for if Powhatan should know it, she were but dead, and so she ran away by herself as she came.

Within less than an hour came eight or ten lusty fellows, with great platters of venison and other victual, very importunate to have us put out our matches (whose smoke made them sick) and sit down to our victual. But the Captain made them taste every dish, which done he sent some of them back to Powhatan, to bid him make haste for he was prepared for his coming. As for them he knew they came to betray him at his supper: but he would prevent them and all their other intended villainies: so that they might be gone. Not long after came more messengers, to see what news; not long after them, others.

Thus we spent the night as vigilantly as they, till it was high water, yet seemed to the savages as friendly as they to us: and that we were so desirous to give Powhatan content, as he requested, we did leave him Edward Brinton to kill him fowl, and the Dutchmen to finish his house; thinking at our return from *Pamunkey* the frost would be gone, and then we might find a better opportunity if necessity did occasion it, little dreaming yet of the Dutchmen's treachery. . . .

CHAPTER IX.

How we escaped surprising at Pamunkey.

We had no sooner set sail but Powhatan returned, and sent Adam and Francis (two stout Dutchmen) to Jamestown: who feigning to Captain Winne that all things were well, and that Captain Smith had use of their arms, wherefore they requested new (the which were given them). They told him their coming was for some extraordinary tools, and shift of apparel; by which colorable [plausible] excuse they obtained six or seven more to their confederacy, such expert thieves, that presently furnished them with a great many swords, pikeheads, pieces, shot, powder and such like: savages they had at hand to carry it away; and the next day they returned unsuspected, leaving their confederates to follow, and in the interim to convey them such things as they could: for which service they should live with Powhatan as his chief affected, free from those miseries that would happen [to] the colony.

Samuel their other consort Powhatan kept for their pledge, whose diligence had provided them three hundred of their kind of hatchets; the rest fifty swords, eight pieces, and eight pikes.

Brinton and Richard Savage seeing the Dutchmen so diligent to accommodate the savages with weapons, attempted to have gotten to Jamestown; but they were apprehended, and expected ever when to be put to death.

Within two or three days, we arrived at *Pamunkey,* the King as many days entertained us with feasting and much mirth.

And the day appointed to begin our trade, the President . . . and some others to the number of fifteen, went up to Opechancanough's house a quarter of a mile from the river; where we found nothing but a lame fellow and a boy: and all the houses round about of all things abandoned.

Not long we stayed ere the King arrived, and after him came divers of his people loade[d] with bows and arrows: but such pinching [cheap] commodities, and those esteemed at such a value, as our Captain began with the King after this manner.

Opechancanough, the great love you profess with your tongue, seems mere deceit by your actions. Last year you kindly fraughted our ship: but now you have invited me to starve with hunger: you know my want, and I your plenty; of which by some means I must have part: remember it is fit for Kings to keep their promise. Here are my commodities, whereof take your choice; the rest I will proportion fit bargains for your people.

The King seemed kindly to accept his offer, and the better to color his project, sold us what they had to our own content; promising the next day, more company, better provided.

The barges and pinnace being committed to the charge of Master Fettiplace; the President [the next day] . . . marched up to the King's house: where we found four or five men newly arrived, each with a great basket.

Not long after came the King, who with a strained cheerfulness held us with discourse what pains he had taken to keep his promise; till Master Russell brought us in news that we were all betrayed: for at least seven hundred savages well armed, had environed the house, and beset the fields.

The King conjecturing what Russell related, we could well perceive how the extremity of his fear bewrayed his intent: whereat some of our company seeming[ly] dismayed with the thought of such a multitude; the Captain encouraged us to this effect.

Worthy countrymen, were the mischiefs of my seeming friends no more than the danger of these enemies, I little cared were they as many more: if you dare do, but as I. But this is my torment, that if I escape them, our malicious Council with their open mouthed minions, will make me such a peace breaker (in their opinions in England) as will break my neck. I could wish those here, that make these seem saints, and me an oppressor. But this is the worst of all, wherein I pray you aid me with your opinions. Should we begin with them and surprise the King, we cannot keep him and defend well ourselves. If we should each kill our man, and so proceed with all

in the house; the rest will all fly: then shall we get no more than the
bodies that are slain, and so starve for victual. As for their fury it is
the least danger; for well you know, being alone assaulted with two or
three hundred of them, I made them by the help of God compound to
save my life. And we are sixteen, and they but seven hundred at the
most; and assure yourselves, God will so assist us, that if you dare
stand but to discharge your pieces, the very smoke will be sufficient to
affright them. Yet howsoever, let us fight like men, and not die like
sheep: for by that means you know God hath oft delivered me, and
so I trust will now. But first, I will deal with them, to bring it to pass
we may fight for something, and draw them to it by conditions. If you
like this motion, promise me you will be valiant.

The time not permitting any argument, all vowed to execute whatsoever he attempted or die: whereupon the Captain in plain terms
told the King this.

I see Opechancanough your plot to murder me, but I fear it not. As
yet your men and mine have done no harm, but by our direction. Take
therefore your arms, you see mine, my body shall be as naked as yours:
the isle in your river is a fit place, if you be contented: and the conqueror
(of us two)shall be lord and master over all our men. If you have not
enough, take time to fetch more, and bring what number you will;
so everyone bring a basket of corn, against all which I will stake the
value in copper: you see I have but fifteen, and our game shall be, the
conqueror take all.

The King being guarded with forty or fifty of his chief men, seemed
kindly to appease Smith's suspicion of unkindness, by a great present
at the door, they entreated him to receive. This was to draw him out
of the door, where the bait was guarded with at least two hundred men,
and thirty lying under a great tree (that lay thwart as a barricade) each
his arrow nocked ready to shoot.

The President commanded one to go see what kind of deceit this
was, and to receive the present; but he refused to do it; yet the gentlemen and all the rest were importunate to go, but he would not permit
them, being vexed at that coward: and commanded Lieutenant Percy,
Master West, and the rest to make good the house; Master Powell and
Master Beheathland he commanded to guard the door; and in such
a rage snatched the King by his long lock in the midst of his men, with
his pistol ready bent against his breast. Thus he led the trembling
King, near[ly] dead with fear amongst all his people: who delivering

the Captain his vambrace [armor for the forearm], bow, and arrows, all his men were easily entreated to cast down their arms, little dreaming any durst in that manner have used their King: who then to escape himself bestowed his presents in good sadness.

And causing a great many of them come before him unarmed, holding the King by the hair (as is said), he spake to them to this effect.

I see (you Pamunkeys) the great desire you have to kill me, and my long suffering your injuries hath emboldened you to this presumption. The cause I have forborne your insolencies, is the promise I made you (before the God I serve) to be your friend, till you give me just cause to be your enemy. If I keep this vow, my God will keep me, you cannot hurt me; if I break it, he will destroy me. But if you shoot but one arrow to shed one drop of blood of any of my men, or steal the least of these beads, or copper, I spurn here before you with my foot; you shall see I will not cease revenge (if once I begin) so long as I can hear where to find one of your nation that will not deny the name of Pamunkey. I am not now at Rassawek half drowned with mire, where you took me prisoner; yet then for keeping your promise and your good usage and saving my life, I so affect you, that your denials of your treachery do half persuade me to mistake myself. But if I be the mark you aim at, here I stand, shoot he that dare. You promised to fraught my ship ere I departed, and so you shall; or I mean to load her with your dead carcasses: yet if as friends you will come and trade, I once more promise not to trouble you, except you give me the first occasion; and your King shall be free and be my friend, for I am not come to hurt him or any of you.

Upon this, away went their bows and arrows; and men, women, and children brought in their commodities: two or three hours they so thronged about the President and so overwearied him, [that] he retired himself to rest, leaving Master Beheathland and Master Powell to receive their presents.

But some savages perceiving him fast asleep, and the guard somewhat carelessly dispersed, forty or fifty of their choice men each with a club or an English sword in his hand, began to enter the house with two or hundred others, that pressed to second them. The noise and haste they made in, did so shake the house they awoke him from his sleep; and being half amazed with this sudden sight, [he] betook him straight to his sword and target; Master Crashaw and some others charged in like manner; whereat they quickly thronged faster back than before forward. The house thus cleansed, the King and some of his ancients we kept yet with him, who with a long oration, excused this intrusion.

The rest of the day was spent with much kindness, the company again renewing their presents with their best provisions, and whatsoever he gave them they seemed therewith well content.

Now in the meanwhile, since our departure, this happened at our fort.

Master Scrivener having received letters from England to make himself either Caesar or nothing, he began to decline in his affection to Captain Smith, that ever regarded him as himself; and was willing to cross the surprising of Powhatan. Some certain days after the President's departure, he would needs go visit the Isle of Hogs, and took with him Captain Waldo (though the President had appointed him to be ready to second his occasions) with Master Anthony Gosnoll and eight others; but so violent was the wind (that extreme frozen time) that the boat sunk, but where or how none doth know. The skiff was much over-loade[d], and would scarce[ly] have lived in that extreme tempest had she been empty: but by no persuasion he could be diverted, though both Waldo and a hundred others doubted as it happened.

The savages were the first that found their bodies, which so much the more encouraged them to effect their projects.

To advertise the President of this heavy news, none could be found [who] would undertake it, but the journey was often refused [by] all in the fort, until Master Richard Wiffin undertook alone the performance thereof. In this journey he was encountered with many dangers and difficulties in all parts as he passed. As for that night he lodged with Powhatan, [at *Werowocómoco*] perceiving such preparation for war, not finding the President there: he did assure himself some mischief was intended. Pocahontas hid him for a time, and sent them who pursued him the clean contrary way to seek him; but by her means and extraordinary bribes and much trouble in three days' travel, at length he found us in the midst of these turmoils.

This unhappy news the President swore him to conceal from the company, and so dissembling his sorrow with the best countenances he could, when the night approached [he] went safely aboard with all his soldiers; leaving Opechancanough at liberty, according to his promise, the better to have Powhatan in his return.

Now so extremely Powhatan had threatened the death of his men, if they did not by some means kill Captain Smith: that the next day, they appointed all the country should come to trade unarmed: yet unwilling to be treacherous, but that they were constrained, hating fighting with him almost as ill as hanging, such fear they had of bad success.

The next morning, the sun had not long appeared, but the fields appeared covered with people and baskets, to tempt us on shore: but nothing was to be had without his presence, nor they would not endure the sight of a gun.

When the President saw them begin to depart, being unwilling to lose such a booty, he so well contrived the pinnace and his barges with ambushes, as only with Lieutenant Percy, Master West, and Master Russell, with their arms [he] went on shore; others he appointed unarmed to receive what was brought. The savages flocked before him in heaps, and the bank serving as a trench for a retreat, he drew them fair[ly] open[ly] to his ambushes.

For he not being to be persuaded to go [and] visit their King, the King knowing the most of them [to be] unarmed, came to visit him with two or three hundred men, in the form of two half moons; and with some twenty men, and many women loade[d] with painted baskets. But when they approached somewhat near us, their women and children fled. For when they had environed and beset the fields in this manner, they thought their purpose sure, yet so trembled with fear as they were scarce[ly] able to nock their arrows: Smith standing, with his three men ready bent, beholding them till they were within danger of our ambushes; who upon the word discovered [showed] themselves, and he retired to the barge. Which the savages no sooner perceived, than away they fled, esteeming their heels for their best advantage.

That night we sent Master Crashaw, and Master Ford [evidently in a barge], to Jamestown to Captain Winne. In the way between *Werowocómoco* and the fort, they met four or five of the Dutchmen's confederates going to Powhatan: the which to excuse those gentlemen's suspicion of their running to the savages, returned to the fort and there continued.

The savages hearing our barge go down the river in the night, were so terribly afraid, that we sent for more men (we having so much threatened their ruin, and the razing of their houses, boats, and weirs), that the next day the King sent our Captain a chain of pearl, to alter his purpose and stay his men: promising though they wanted themselves, to fraught our ship and bring it aboard to avoid suspicion: so that, five or six days after, from all parts of the country within ten or twelve miles, in the extreme frost and snow, they brought us provision on their naked backs.

Yet notwithstanding this kindness and trade; had their art and poison been sufficient, the President, with Master West, and some others had been poisoned; it made them sick, but expelled itself.

Wecuttanow, a stout young fellow, knowing he was suspected for bringing this present of poison, with forty or fifty of his chief companions (seeing the President but with a few men at *Potauncack*) so proudly braved it, as though he expected to encounter a revenge. Which the President perceiving, in the midst of his company, did not only beat, but spurned him like a dog, as scorning to do him any worse mischief. Whereupon all of them fled into the woods, thinking they had done a great matter to have so well escaped: and the townsmen remaining presently fraughted our barge to be rid of our companies, framing many excuses to excuse Wecuttanow, (being son to their chief King, but [excepting] Powhatan) and told us if we would show them him that brought the poison, they would deliver him to us to punish as we pleased.

Men may think it strange there should be such a stir for a little corn, but had it been gold with more ease we might have got it; and had it wanted, the whole colony had starved. We may be thought very patient to endure all those injuries, yet only with fearing them we got what they had. Whereas if we had taken revenge; then by their loss, we should have lost ourselves.

We searched also the countries of *Youghtanund* and *Mattapanient,* where the people imparted that little they had, with such complaints and tears from the eyes of women and children, as he had been too cruel to have been a Christian, that would not have been satisfied and moved with compassion.

But had this happened in October, November, and December, when that unhappy discovery of *Monacan* was made, we might have fraughted a ship of forty tons, and twice as much might have been had from the rivers of Rappahannock, Potomac, and Patuxent.

The main occasion of our thus temporizing with them was, to part friends as we did, to give the less cause of supicion to Powhatan to fly [from *Werowocómoco*]; by whom we now returned with a purpose to have surprised him and his provision. For effecting whereof (when we came against the town) the President sent Master Wiffin and Master Coe ashore to discover and make way for his intended project.

But they found that those damned Dutchmen had caused Powhatan to abandon his new house and *Werowocómoco,* and to carry away all his corn and provision: and the people they found so ill affected, that they were in great doubt how to escape with their lives.

So the President finding his intent frustrated, and that there was nothing now to be had, and therefore an unfit time to revenge their abuses, sent Master Michael Fettiplace by land to Jamestown, whither we sailed with all the speed we could; we having in this journey (for 25 l[bs.] of copper, and 50 l[bs.] of iron and beads) enough to keep 46 men six weeks, and every man for his reward a month's provision extraordinary (no trade being allowed but for the store). We got near[ly] 200 l[bs.] weight of deer suet, and delivered to the cape merchant [officer in charge of the commissary at Jamestown] 479 bushels of corn.

Those temporizing proceedings to some may seem too charitable, to such a daily daring treacherous people: to others not pleasing, that we washed not the ground with their bloods, nor showed such strange inventions in mangling, murdering, ransacking, and destroying (as did the Spaniards) the simple bodies of such ignorant souls; nor delightful, because not stuffed with relations of heaps and mines of gold and silver, nor such rare commodities, as the Portuguese and Spaniards found in the East and West Indies. The want whereof hath begot us (that were the first undertakers) no less scorn and contempt, than the noble conquests and valiant adventures beautified with it, praise and honor. Too much I confess the world cannot attribute to their ever memorable merit: and to clear us from the blind world's ignorant censure, these few words may suffice any reasonable understanding.

It was the Spaniards' good hap to happen in those parts where were infinite numbers of people, who had manured the ground with that providence, it afforded victuals at all times. And time had brought them to that perfection, they had the use of gold and silver, and the most of such commodities as those countries afforded: so that, what the Spaniard got was chiefly the spoil and pillage of those country people, and not the labors of their own hands. But had those fruitful countries been as savage, as barbarous, as ill peopled, as little planted, labored, and manured, as Virginia: their proper labors it is likely would have produced as small profit as ours.

But had Virginia been peopled, planted, manured, and adorned with such store of precious jewels, and rich commodities as was the Indies: then had we not gotten and done as much as by their examples might be expected from us, the world might then have traduced us and our merits, and have made shame and infamy our recompense and reward.

But we chanced in a land even as God made it, where we found only an idle, improvident, scattered people, ignorant of the knowledge of gold and silver, or any commodities, and careless of anything but from hand to mouth, except baubles of no worth; nothing to encourage us, but what accidentally we found nature afforded. Which ere we could bring to recompense our pains, defray our charges, and satisfy our adventurers; we were to discover [explore] the country, subdue the people, bring them to be tractable, civil, and industrious, and teach them trades, that the fruits of their labors might make us some recompense; or plant such colonies of our own, that must first make provision how to live of themselves, ere they can bring to perfection the commodities of the country: which doubtless will be as commodious for England as the West Indies for Spain, if it be rightly managed: notwithstanding all our home-bred opinions, that will argue the contrary, as formerly some have done against the Spaniards and Portuguese.

But to conclude, against all rumor of opinion, I only say this, for those that the three first years began this plantation; notwithstanding all their factions, mutinies, and miseries, so gently corrected, and well prevented: peruse the *Spanish Decades;* the relations of Master Hakluyt, and tell me how many ever with such small means as a barge of 22 [in fact, two] tons, sometimes with seven, eight, or nine, or but at most, twelve or sixteen men, did ever discover so many fair and navigable rivers, subject so many several Kings, people, and nations, to obedience and contribution, with so little bloodshed.

And if in the search of those countries we had happened where wealth had been we had as surely had it as obedience and contribution; but if we have overskipped it, we will not envy them that shall find it: yet can we not but lament, it was our fortunes to end when we had but only learned how to begin, and found the right course how to proceed. . . .

By Richard Wiffin, William Phittiplace, Jeffrey Abbot,
and Anas Todkill.

CHAPTER X.

How the savages became subject to the English.

When the ships departed, all the provision of the store (but that the President had gotten) was so rotten with the last summer's rain, and eaten with rats and worms, as the hogs would scarcely eat it. Yet it was the soldiers' diet till our returns, so that we found nothing done, but our victuals spent; and the most part of our tools, and a good part of our arms conveyed to the savages.

But now casting up the store, and finding sufficient till the next harvest, the fear of starving was abandoned, and the company divided into tens, fifteens, or as the business required; six hours each day was spent in work, the rest in pastime and merry exercises.

But the untowardness of the greatest number caused the President [to] advise as followeth.

Countrymen, the long experience of our late miseries, I hope is sufficient to persuade every one to a present correction of himself, and think not that either my pains, nor the adventurers purses, will ever maintain you in idleness and sloth. I speak not this to you all, for divers of you I know deserve both honor and reward, better than is yet here to be had: but the greater part must be more industrious, or starve, however you have been heretofore tolerated by the authority of the Council, from that I have often commanded you. You see now that power resteth wholly in myself: you must obey this now for a law, that he that will not work shall not eat (except by sickness he be disabled:) for the labors of thirty or forty honest and industrious men shall not be consumed to maintain a hundred and fifty idle loiterers. And though you presume the authority here is but a shadow, and that I dare not touch the lives of any but my own must answer it: the letters patent shall each week be read to you, whose contents will tell you the contrary. I would wish you therefore without contempt seek to observe these orders set down, for there are now no more Councillors to protect you, nor curb my endeavors. Therefore he that offendeth, let him assuredly expect his due punishment.

He made also a table [notice board], as a public memorial of every man's deserts, to encourage the good, and with shame to spur on the rest to amendment. By this many became very industrious, yet more by punishment performed their business; for all were so tasked, that there was no excuse could prevail to deceive him.

Yet the Dutchmen's consorts so closely conveyed them powder, shot, swords, and tools, that though we could find the defect, we could not find by whom, till it was too late.

All this time [February–March 1609] the Dutchmen remaining with Powhatan (who kindly entertained them to instruct the savages [in] the use of our arms), and their consorts not following them as they expected; to know the cause, they sent Francis their companion, a stout young fellow, disguised like a savage, to the glass house, a place in the woods near[ly] a mile from Jamestown; where was their rendezvous for all their unsuspected villainy.

Forty men they procured to lie in ambush for Captain Smith, who no sooner heard of this Dutchman, but he sent to apprehend him (but he was gone): yet to cross his return to Powhatan, the Captain presently dispatched 20 shot after him; himself returning from the glass house alone.

By the way he encountered the king of *Paspahegh,* a most strong, stout savage, whose persuasions not being able to persuade him to his ambush, seeing him only armed but with a falchion [sword], attempted to have shot him, but the President prevented his shot by grappling with him, and the savage as well prevented him [from] drawing his falchion, and perforce bore him into the river to have drowned him. Long they struggled in the water, till the President got such hold on his throat, he had near[ly] strangled the King; but having drawn his falchion to cut off his head, seeing how pitifully he begged [for] his life, he led him prisoner to Jamestown, and put him in chains.

The Dutchman ere long was also brought in, whose villainy though all this time it was suspected, yet he feigned such a formal excuse, that for want of language Captain Winne understood him not rightly, and for their dealings with Powhatan, that to save their lives they were constrained to accommodate [him with] his arms, of whom he extremely complained to have detained them perforce, and that he made this escape with the hazard of his life, and meant not to have returned, but was only walking in the woods to gather walnuts.

Yet for all this fair tale, there was so small appearance of truth, and [also] the plain confession of Paspahegh of his treachery, [that] he went by the heels: Smith purposing to regain the Dutchmen, by the saving of his [Paspahegh's] life.

The poor savage did his best by his daily messengers to Powhatan, but all returned that the Dutchmen would not return, neither did Powhatan stay them; and to bring them fifty miles [from *Orapaks*] on his men's backs they were not able. Daily this King's wives, children, and people came to visit him with presents, which he liberally bestowed to make his peace. Much trust they had in the President's promise: but the King finding his guard negligent, though fettered yet escaped. Captain Winne thinking to pursue him found such troupes of savages to hinder his passage, as they exchanged many volleys of shot for flights of arrows.

Captain Smith hearing of this, in returning to the fort took two savages prisoners, called Kemps and Tassore, the two most exact villains in all the country.

With these he sent Captain Winne and fifty choice men, and Lieutenant Percy, to have regained the King, and revenged this injury.

And so [he] had done, if they had followed his directions, or been advised with those two villains, that would have betrayed both King and kindred for a piece of copper: but he trifled away the night, the savages the next morning by the raising of the sun, braved him to come ashore to fight. A good time both sides let fly at [each] other, but we heard of no hurt; only they took two canoes, burnt the King's house, and so returned to Jamestown.

The President fearing those bravadoes would but encourage the savages, began again himself to try his conclusions [plans]; whereby six or seven were slain, [and] as many made prisoners. He burnt their houses, took their boats, with all their fishing weirs, and planted some of them at Jamestown for his own use, and now resolved not to cease till he had revenged himself of all them [that] had injured him.

But in his journey passing by *Paspahegh* towards *Chickahominy,* the savages did their best to draw him to their ambushes; but seeing him regardlessly pass their country, all showed themselves in their bravest manner. To try their valors he could not but let fly; and ere he could land, they no sooner knew him, but they threw down their arms and desired peace. Their orator was a lusty young fellow called Okanindge, whose worthy discourse deserveth to be remembered. And thus it was:

Captain Smith, my master is here present in the company, thinking it Captain Winne, and not you, (of him he intended to have been revenged) having never offended him. If he hath offended you in escap-

*ing your imprisonment, the fishes swim, the fowls fly, and the very
beasts strive to escape the snare and live. Then blame not him being a
man. He would entreat you remember, you being a prisoner, what
pains he took to save your life. If since he hath injured you, he was
compelled to it: but howsoever, you have revenged it with our too great
loss. We perceive and well know you intend to destroy us, that are
here to entreat and desire your friendship; and to enjoy our houses and
plant our fields, of whose fruit you shall participate: otherwise you will
have the worse by our absence; for we can plant anywhere, though with
more labor, and we know you cannot live if you want our harvest, and
that relief we bring you. If you promise us peace, we will believe you;
if you proceed in revenge, we will abandon the country.*

Upon these terms, the President promised them peace, till they did us
injury, upon condition they should bring in provision. Thus all departed good friends, and so continued till Smith left the country.

Arriving at Jamestown, complaint was made to the President, that
the *Chickahominies,* who all this while continued trade and seemed our
friends, by color thereof were the only thieves. And amongst other
things a pistol being stolen and the thief fled, there was apprehended
two proper young fellows, that were brothers, known to be his confederates.

Now to regain this pistol, the one was imprisoned, the other was sent
to return the pistol again within twelve hours, or his brother to be
hanged. Yet the President pitying the poor naked savage in the dungeon,
sent him victual and some charcoal for a fire.

Ere midnight his brother returned with the pistol, but the poor savage
in the dungeon was so smothered with the smoke he had made, and
so piteously burnt, that we found him dead. The other most lamentably
bewailed his death, and broke forth into such bitter agonies, that the
President to quiet him, told him that if hereafter they would not steal,
he would make him alive again: but he little thought he could be recovered. Yet we doing our best with aqua vitae and vinegar, it pleased
God to restore him again to life; but so drunk and affrighted, that he
seemed lunatic: the which as much tormented and grieved the other
[his brother], as before to see him dead. Of which malady upon promise of their good behavior, the President promised to recover him: and
so causing him to be laid by a fire to sleep; who in the morning having
well slept, had recovered his perfect senses, and then being dressed of
his burning, and each a piece of copper given them, they went away so

well contented, that this was spread among all the savages for a miracle, that Captain Smith could make a man alive that was dead.

Another ingenuous savage of Powhatan's, having gotten a great bag of powder, and the back of an armor, at *Werowocómoco* amongst a many of his companions, to show his extraordinary skill, he did dry it on the back as he had seen the soldiers at Jamestown. But he dried it so long, they peeping over it to see his skill, it took fire, and blew him to death, and one or two more; and the rest [were] so scorched, they had little pleasure to meddle anymore with powder.

These and many other such pretty accidents, so amazed and affrighted both Powhatan, and all his people, that from all parts with presents they desired peace; returning many stolen things which we never demanded nor thought of: and after that, those that were taken stealing, both Powhatan and his people have sent them back to Jamestown, to receive their punishment; and all the country became absolute[ly] as free for us, as for themselves.

CHAPTER XI.

What was done in three months having victuals.
The store devoured by rats, how we lived three months
of such natural fruits as the country afforded.

Now we so quietly followed our business, that in three months [February–April 1609] we made three or four lasts [one last is 4000 pounds] of tar, pitch, and soap ashes; produced a trial of glass; made a well in the fort of excellent sweet water, which till then was wanting; built some twenty houses; recovered our church: provided nets and weirs for fishing; and to stop the disorders of our disorderly thieves, and the savages, built a blockhouse in the neck of our isle, kept by a garrison to entertain the savages' trade, and none to pass nor repass savage nor Christian without the President's order. Thirty or forty acres of ground we digged and planted. Of three sows in eighteen months, increased 60 and odd pigs. And near[ly] 500 chickens brought up themselves without having any meat [food] given them: but the hogs were transported to Hog Isle: where also we built a blockhouse with a garrison to give us notice of any shipping, and for their exercise they made clapboard and wainscot, and cut down trees.

We built also a fort for a retreat near a convenient river upon a high commanding hill, very hard to be assaulted and easy to be defended; but ere it was finished this defect caused a stay.

In searching our casked corn [April 1609], we found it half rotten, and the rest so consumed with so many thousands of rats that increased so fast, but their original was from the ships, as we knew not how to keep that little we had. This did drive us all to our wits' end, for there was nothing in the country but what nature afforded.

Until this time Kemps and Tassore were fettered prisoners, and did double task and taught us how to order and plant our fields: whom now for want of victual we set at liberty, but so well they liked our companies they did not desire to go from us.

And to express their loves, for 16 days' continuance, the country people brought us (when least) 100 a day, of squirrels, turkeys, deer and other wild beasts.

But this want of corn occasioned the end of all our works, it being work sufficient to provide victual. 60 or 80 with Ensign Laxon [were] sent down the river to live upon oysters, and 20 with Lieutenant Percy to try for fishing at Point Comfort: but in six weeks they would not agree once to cast out the net, he being sick and burnt sore with gunpowder. Master West with as many went up to the falls, but nothing could be found but a few acorns; of that in store every man had [his] equal proportion.

Till this present, by the hazard and endeavors of some thirty or forty, this whole colony had ever been fed. We had more sturgeon, than could be devoured by dog and man, of which the industrious by drying and pounding, mingled with caviar, sorrel and other wholesome herbs would make bread and good meat: others would gather as much *tuckahoe* roots in a day as would make them bread [for] a week, so that of those wild fruits, and what we caught, we lived very well in regard of such a diet.

But such was the strange condition of some 150, that had they not been forced *nolens volens* [willing or unwilling], perforce to gather and prepare their victual they would all have starved or have eaten one another. Of those wild fruits the savages often brought us, and for that the President would not fulfill the unreasonable desire of those distracted gluttonous loiterers, to sell not only our kettles, hoes, tools, and iron, nay swords, pieces, and the very ordnance and houses, might they have prevailed to have been but idle: for those savage fruits, they would have had imparted all to the savages, especially for one basket of corn they heard of to be at Powhatan's [his house at *Orapaks*], fifty miles from our fort. Though he bought near[ly] half of it to satisfy their humors; yet to have had the other half, they would have sold their souls, though not sufficient to have kept them a week. Thousands were their exclamations, suggestions and devices, to force him [Smith] to those base inventions to have made it an occasion to abandon the country.

Want perforce constrained him to endure their exclaiming follies, till he found out the author, one Dyer, a most crafty fellow and his ancient maligner, whom he worthily punished, and with the rest he argued the case in this manner.

Fellow soldiers, I did little think any so false to report, or so many to be so simple to be persuaded, that I either intend to starve you, or that Powhatan at this present hath corn for himself, much less for you; or that I would not have it, if I knew where it were to be had. Neither did I think any so malicious as now I see a great many; yet it shall not so passionate [enrage] me, but I will do my best for my most maligner. But dream no longer of this vain hope from Powhatan, [nor] that I will longer forbear to force you from your idleness, and punish you if you rail. But if I find any more runners for Newfoundland with the pinnace, let him assuredly look to arrive at the gallows. You cannot deny but that by the hazard of my life many a time I have saved yours, when (might your own wills have prevailed) you would have starved; and will do still whether I will or no; but I protest by that God that made me, since necessity hath not power to force you to gather for yourselves those fruits the earth doth yield, you shall not only gather for yourselves, but those that are sick. As yet I never had more from the store than the worst of you: and all my English extraordinary provision that I have, you shall see me divide it amongst the sick.

And this savage trash you so scornfully repine at; being put in your mouths your stomachs can digest: if you would have better, you should have brought it; and therefore I will take a course you shall provide what is to be had. The sick shall not starve, but equally share of all our labors; and he that gathereth not every day as much as I do, the next day shall be set beyond the river, and be banished from the fort as a drone, till he amend his conditions or starve. . . .

This order many murmured was very cruel, but it caused the most part so well [to] bestir themselves, that of 200 (except they were drowned) there died not past seven.

As for Captain Winne and Master Leigh they were dead ere this want happened, and the rest died not for want of such as preserved the rest.

Many were billetted amongst the savages, whereby we knew all their passages, fields and habitations, how to gather and use their fruits as well as themselves; for they did know we had such a commanding power at Jamestown they durst not wrong us of a pin.

So well those poor savages used us that were thus billeted, that divers of the soldiers ran away to search Kemps and Tassore our old prisoners. Glad were these savages to have such an opportunity to testify their love unto us, for instead of entertaining them [the deserters], and such things as they had stolen, with all their great offers, and promises they made them how to revenge their injuries upon Captain Smith; Kemps first made himself sport, in showing his countrymen [by them] how he was used, feeding them with this law, who would not work must not eat, till they were near[ly] starved indeed, continually threatening to beat them to death: neither could they get from him, till he and his consorts brought them perforce to our Captain, that so well contented him and punished them, as many others that intended also to follow them, were rather contented to labor at home, than adventure to live idly amongst the savages; (of whom there was more hope to make better Christians and good subjects, than the one half of those that counterfeited themselves both.)

For so afraid [were] all those Kings and the better sort of the people to displease us, that some of the baser sort that we have extremely hurt and punished for their villainies would hire [bribe] us, [that] we should not tell it to their Kings, or countrymen; who would also repunish them, and yet return them to Jamestown to content the President, for a testimony of their loves.

Master Sicklemore well returned from *Chawanoac;* but found little hope and less certainty of them [that] were left by Sir Walter Raleigh. The river, he saw was not great, the people few, the country most[ly] overgrown with pines, where there did grow here and there stragglingly *pemminaw,* we call silk grass. But by the river the ground was good, and exceeding[ly] fertile.

Master Nathaniel Powell and Anas Todkill were also by the *Qui-*

youghcohannocks conducted to the *Mangoaks* to search [for] them there: but nothing could they learn but [that] they were all dead.

This honest, proper, good, promise keeping King, of all the rest did ever best affect us, and though to his false gods he was very zealous, yet he would confess our God as much exceeded his as our guns did his bow and arrows, often sending our President many presents, to pray to his God for rain or his corn would perish, for his gods were angry.

Three days' journey they conducted them through the woods, into a high country towards the southwest: where they saw here and there a little cornfield, by some little spring or small brook, but no river they could see: the people in all respects like the rest, except their language; they live most[ly] upon roots, fruits and wild beasts; and trade with them towards the sea and the fatter countries for dried fish and corn, [with] skins.

All this time to recover the Dutchmen and one Bentley another fugitive, we employed one William Volda, a Zwitzar [Swiss] by birth, with pardons and promises to regain them. Little we then suspected this double villain of any villainy; who plainly taught us, in the most trust was the greatest treason; for this wicked hypocrite, by the seeming hate he bore to the lewd conditions of his cursed countrymen, (having this opportunity by his employment to regain them) conveyed them everything they desired to effect their projects, to destroy the colony.

With much devotion they expected the Spaniard, to whom they intended good service, or any other that would but carry them from us. But to begin with the first opportunity; they seeing necessity thus enforced us to disperse ourselves, importuned Powhatan to lend them but his forces, and they would not only destroy our hogs, fire our town, and betray our pinnace; but bring to his service and subjection the most of our company. With this plot they had acquainted many discontents, and many were agreed to their devilish practice. But one Thomas Dowse, and Thomas Mallard (whose Christian hearts relented at such an unchristian act) voluntarily revealed it to Captain Smith, who caused them to conceal it, persuading Dowse and Mallard to proceed in their confederacy: only to bring the irreclaimable Dutchmen and the inconstant savages in such a manner amongst such ambushes as he had prepared, that not many of them should return from our peninsula [Jamestown].

But this bruit coming to the ears of the impatient multitude they so importuned the President to cut off those Dutchmen, as amongst many that offered to cut their throats before the face of Powhatan, the first was Lieutenant Percy, and Master John Cuderington, two gentlemen of as bold, resolute spirits as could possibly be found. But the President had occasion of other employment for them, and gave way to Master Wiffin and Sergeant Jeffrey Abbot, to go and stab them or shoot them.

But the Dutchmen made such excuses, accusing Volda whom they supposed had revealed their project, as Abbot would not; yet Wiffin would, perceiving it but deceit.

The King understanding of this their employment, sent presently his messengers to Captain Smith to signify it was not his fault to detain them, nor hinder his men from executing his command: nor did he nor would he maintain them or any, to occasion his displeasure.

But whilst this business was in hand, arrived [10 July 1609] one Captain Argall, and Master Thomas Sedan, sent by Master Cornelius to truck with the colony, and fish for sturgeon, with a ship well furnished with wine and much other good provision. Though it was not sent us, our necessities [were] such as enforced us to take it. He brought us news of a great supply and preparation for the Lord De La Warr, with letters that much taxed our President for his hard dealing with the savages, and not returning the ships fraughted. Notwithstanding we kept this ship till the fleet arrived [11 August 1609].

True it is Argall lost his voyage, but we revictualled him, and sent him [to] England, with a true relation of the causes of our defailments, and how impossible it was to return that wealth they expected, or observe their instructions to endure the savages' insolencies, or do anything to any purpose, except they would send us men and means that could produce that [which] they so much desired: otherwise all they did was lost, and could not but come to confusion.

The villainy of Volda we still dissembled. Adam upon his pardon came home, but Samuel still stayed with Powhatan to hear further of their estates by this supply. Now all their plots Smith so well understood, they were his best advantages to secure us from any treachery, [that] could be done by them or the savages: which with facility he could revenge when he would, because all those countries more feared him than Powhatan, and he had such parties with all his bordering neighbors: and many of the rest for love or fear would have done anything he would have them, upon any commotion, though these fugitives had done all they could to persuade Powhatan, [that] King James would kill Smith, for using him and his people so unkindly.

By this you may see for all those crosses, treacheries, and dissensions, how he wrestled and overcame (without bloodshed) all that happened: also what good was done; how few died; what food the country naturally affordeth; what small cause there is men should starve, or be murdered by the savages, that have discretion to manage them with courage and industry.

The two first years, though by his adventures, he had oft brought the savages to a tractable trade; yet you see how the envious authority ever crossed him, and frustrated his best endeavors. But it wrought in him that experience and estimation amongst the savages, as otherwise it had been impossible, he had ever effected that he did.

Notwithstanding the many miserable, yet generous and worthy adventures, he had oft and long endured in the wide world; yet in this case he was again to learn his lecture [lesson] by experience. Which with thus much ado having obtained, it was his ill chance to end, when he had but only learned how to begin.

And though he left those unknown difficulties (made easy and familiar) to his unlawful successors (who only by living in Jamestown, presumed to know more than all the world could direct them.) Now though they had all his soldiers, with a triple power, and twice triple better means; by what they have done in his absence, the world may see what they would have done in his presence, had he not prevented their indiscretions: it doth justly prove, what cause he had to send them [to] England and that he was neither factious, mutinous, nor dishonest.

But they have made it more plain since his return [to] England; having his absolute authority freely in their power, with all the advantages and opportunity that his labors had effected. As I am sorry their actions have made it so manifest, so I am unwilling to say what reason doth compel me, but only to make apparent the truth, least I should seem partial, reasonless, and malicious.

CHAPTER XII.

The arrival of the third supply.

To redress those jars [disputes] and ill proceedings, the treasurer, Council, and company of Virginia, not finding that return and profit they expected; and them engaged there, not having means to subsist of themselves; made means to His Majesty, to call in their commission [charter], and take a new in their own names, as in their own publication, 1610, you may read at large.*

Having thus annihilated the old by virtue of a [new] commission made to the Right Honorable, Sir Thomas West, Lord De La Warr, to be General of Virginia; Sir Thomas Gates, his Lieutenant; Sir George Somers, Admiral; Sir Thomas Dale, High Marshall; Sir Fardinando Wainman, General of the Horse; and so all other offices to many other worthy gentlemen, for their lives: (though not any of them had ever been in Virginia, except Captain Newport, who was also by patent made vice-admiral:) those noble gentlemen drew in such great sums of money, that they sent Sir Thomas Gates, Sir George Somers, and Captain Newport with nine ships, and five hundred people: who [Gates, Somers, and Newport] had each of them a commission [new instructions], who first arrived to call in the old [government of John Smith], without the knowledge or consent of them that had endured all those former dangers to beat the path, not any regard [being] had at all of them.

All things being ready, because those three Captains could not agree for place, it was concluded they should go all in one ship, so all their three commissions [letters of instruction] were in that ship with them, call the *Sea Venture.*

They set sail from England in May 1609.

A small catch perished at sea in a hurricane: the admiral [flag-ship] with a hundred and fifty men, with the two knights, and their new commission, their bills of loading, with all manner of directions, and the most part of their provision, arrived not.

With the other seven ships as Captains arrived Ratcliffe, whose right name (as is said) was Sicklemore, Martin, and Archer, with Captain Wood, Captain Webb, Captain Moone, Captain King, Captain Davis, and divers gentlemen of good means, and great parentage. But the first [Ratcliffe, Martin, and Archer] as they had been troublesome at sea, began again to mar all ashore: for though (as is said) they were formerly sent [to] England, yet now returning again, graced by the titles of Captains of the passengers, seeing the admiral wanting, and

* This refers to the Royal Charter of 1609 which made the London Company into a joint stock company. The government in Virginia was taken out of the hands of the Council and given to a governor. Smith seems to have felt as if he had been cheated by this move.

great probability of her loss, strengthened themselves with those new companies, so exclaiming against Captain Smith, that they mortally hated him ere ever they saw him.

Who understanding by his scouts [of] the arrival of such a fleet, little dreaming of any such supply, supposed them Spaniards. But he quickly so determined and ordered our affairs, as we little feared their arrival, nor the success of our encounter; nor were the savages any way negligent for the most part, to aid and assist us with their best power.

Had it so been we had been happy; for we would not have trusted them but as our foes, where[as] receiving them as our countrymen and friends, they did what they could to murder our President, to surprise the store, the fort, and our lodgings, to usurp the government, and make us all their servants and slaves, till they could consume us and our remembrance; and rather indeed to supplant us than supply us, as Master William Box an honest gentleman in this voyage thus relateth.

In the tail of a hurricane we were separated from the admiral, which although it was but the remainder of that storm, there is seldom any such in England, or those northern parts of Europe. Some lost their masts, some their sails blown from their yards; the seas so over-raking our ships, much of our provision was spoiled, our fleet separated, and our men sick, and many died: and in this miserable estate we arrived in Virginia. . . .

To a thousand mischiefs those lewd Captains [Ratcliffe, &c.] led this lewd company, wherein were many unruly gallants packed thither by their friends to escape ill destinies, and those would dispose and determine of the government, sometimes to one, the next day to another; today the old commission must rule, tomorrow the new, the next day neither; in fine they would rule all, or ruin all: yet in charity we must endure them thus to destroy us; or by correcting their follies, have brought the world's censure upon us to be guilty of their bloods. Happy had we been had they never arrived, and we forever abandoned, and as we were left to our fortunes: for on earth, for the number, was never more confusion, or misery, than their factions occasioned.

The President seeing the desire those braves had to rule; seeing how his authority was so unexpectedly changed, would willingly have left all, and have returned [to] England. But seeing there was small hope this new commission would arrive, longer he would not suffer those factious spirits to proceed.

It would be too tedious, too strange, and almost incredible; should I particularly relate the infinite dangers, plots, and practices, he daily escaped amongst this factious crew; the chief whereof he quickly laid by the heels, till his leisure better served to do them justice: and to take away all occasions of further mischief, Master Percy had his request granted to return [to] England, being very sick; and Master West with a hundred and twenty of the best he could choose, he sent to the falls; Martin with near[ly] as many to *Nansemond,* with their due proportions of all provisions according to their numbers.

Now the President's year [term of office] being near[ly] expired, he made Captain Martin President, to follow the order for the election of a President every year: but he knowing his own insufficiency, and the company's untowardness and little regard of him within three hours after resigned it again to Captain Smith; and [to] *Nansemond* thus proceeded.

The people being contributors used him kindly; yet such was his jealous fear, in the midst of their mirth, he did surprise this poor naked King, with his monuments, houses, and the isle he inhabited, and there fortified himself; but so apparently distracted with fear, as emboldened the savages to assault him, kill his men, release their King, gather and carry away a thousand bushels of corn, he not once offering to intercept them; but sent to the President, then at the falls, for thirty good shot; which from Jamestown immediately was sent him. But he so well employed them they did just nothing, but returned complaining of his tenderness: yet he came away with them to Jamestown, leaving his company to their fortunes.

Here I cannot omit the courage of George Forrest, [who] had seventeen arrows sticking in him, and one shot through him, yet lived six or seven days, as if he had small hurt; then for want of surgery died.

Master West having seated his men by the falls, presently returned to revisit Jamestown: the President followed him to see that company seated; met him by the way, wondering at his so quick return; and found his company planted [located] so inconsiderately [badly], in a place not only subject to the river's inundation, but round environed with many intolerable inconveniences.

For remedy whereof he [Smith] presently sent to [Little Powhatan, brother of the chief] to sell him the place called *Powhatan,* promising to defend him against the *Monacans.* And these should be his conditions:

[Powhatan's brother] (with his people) to resign him the fort and houses, and all that country for a proportion of copper; that all stealing offenders should be sent him, there to receive their punishment; that every house as a custom should pay him a bushel of corn for an inch square of copper, and a proportion of *puccoons,* as a yearly tribute to King James for their protection, as a duty; what else they could spare to barter at their best discretions.

But both this excellent place and those good conditions did those furies [the men sent to live at the falls] refuse; condemning both him, his kind care and authority. So much they depended on the Lord General's new commission, as they regarded none: the worst they could do to show their spites they did; supposing all the *Monacans'* country, gold; and none should come there but whom they pleased. I do more than wonder to think how only with five men, he [Smith] either durst or would adventure as he did, (knowing how greedy they were of his blood) to land amongst them, and commit to imprisonment all the chieftains [colonists] of those mutinies, till by their multitudes being a hundred and twenty they forced him to retire: yet in that interim he surprised one of their boats, wherewith he returned to their ship, where indeed was their provision; which also he took, and well it chanced he found the mariners so tractable and constant, or there had been small possibility he had ever escaped.

There were divers other[s] of better reason and experience, that from their first landing, hearing the general good reports of his old soldiers, and seeing with their eyes his actions so well managed with discretion, as Captain Wood, Captain Webb, Captain Moone, Captain Fitz James, Master William Powell, Master Partridge, Master White, and divers others, when they perceived the malice of Ratcliffe and Archer, and their faction, left their companies, and ever rested his faithful friends.

But the worst was that the poor savages, that daily brought in their contribution to the President, that disorderly company so tormented those poor souls, by stealing their corn, robbing their gardens, beating them, breaking their houses and keeping some prisoners; that they daily complained to Captain Smith, he had brought them for protectors, worse enemies than the *Monacans* themselves: which though till then, for his love they had endured, they desired pardon if hereafter they defended themselves; since he would not correct them, as they had long expected he would. So much they [the Indians] importuned him to punish their [the English] misdemeanors, [that] they offered (if he would lead them) to fight for him against them.

But having spent nine days [August–September 1609] in seeking to reclaim them; showing them how much they did abuse themselves with these great gilded hopes of the South Sea mines, commodities, or victories, they so madly conceived; then seeing nothing would prevail, he set sail for Jamestown. . . .

Now no sooner was the ship under sail, but the savages assaulted those hundred and twenty in their fort [at the falls], finding some straggling abroad in the woods: they slew many, and so affrighted the rest, as their prisoners escaped, and they safely retired, with the swords and cloaks of those they had slain.

But ere we had sailed half a league, our ship grounding, gave us once more liberty to summon them to a parley; where we found them all so strangely amazed with this poor silly assault of twelve savages, that they submitted themselves upon any terms to the President's mercy; who presently put by the heels six or seven of the chief offenders.

The rest he seated gallantly at *Powhatan,* in that savage fort, ready built, and prettily fortified with poles and barks of trees, sufficient to have defended them from all the savages in Virginia, dry houses for lodgings, and near[ly] two hundred acres of ground ready to be planted, and no place we knew so strong, so pleasant and delightful in Virginia for which we called it Nonsuch.

The savages also he presently appeased, redelivering to either party their former losses.

Thus all were friends. New officers [were] appointed to command, and the President again ready to depart.

At that instant arrived Captain West, whose gentle nature, by the persuasions and compassion of those mutinous prisoners (alleging they had only done this for his honor) was so much abused, that to regain their old hopes, new turmoils did arise. For they ashore being possessed of all their victual, munition, and everything, grew to that height in their former factions, as the President left them to their fortunes: they returning again to the open air at West's Fort, abandoning Nonsuch, and he to Jamestown with his best expedition.

But this happened [to] him in that journey. Sleeping in his boat, (for the ship was returned two days before) accidentally, one fired his powder-bag, which tore the flesh from his body and thighs, nine or ten inches square in a most pitiful manner; but to quench the tormenting fire, frying him in his clothes he leaped overboard into the deep river, where ere they could recover him he was near[ly] drowned. In this estate without either surgeon, or surgery he was to go near[ly] a hundred miles.

Arriving at Jamestown, causing all things to be prepared for peace or wars [and] to obtain provision.

Whilst those things were providing, Ratcliffe, Archer, and the rest of their confederates, being to come to their trials; their guilty consciences fearing a just reward for their deserts, seeing the President unable to stand, and near[ly] bereft of his senses by reason of his torment, they had plotted to have murdered him in his bed. But his heart did fail him that should have given fire to that merciless pistol.

So not finding that course to be the best, they joined together to usurp the government, thereby to escape their punishment.

The President had notice of their projects, the which to withstand, though his old soldiers importuned him but permit them to take their heads that would resist his command, yet he would not suffer them; but sent for the Masters of the ships, and took order with them for his return [to] England.

Seeing there was neither surgeon, nor surgery in the fort to cure his hurt, and the ship to depart the next day [about 13 September 1609], his commission to be suppressed he knew not why, himself and soldiers to be rewarded he knew not how, and a new commission granted they knew not to whom (the which disabled that authority he had, as made them presume so oft to those mutinies as they did:) besides so grievous were his wounds, and so cruel his torments (few expecting he could live) nor was he able to follow his business to regain what they had lost, suppress those factions, and range the countries for provision as he intended; and well he knew in those affairs his own actions and presence [were] as requisite as his directions, which now could not be: he went presently abroad, resolving there to appoint them governors, and to take order for the mutineers; but he could find none he thought fit for it, [who] would accept it. In the meantime, seeing him gone, they persuaded Master Percy to stay, who was then to go [to] England, and be their President.

Within less than an hour was this mutation [change] begun and concluded.

For when the company understood Smith would leave them, and saw the rest in arms called Presidents and Councillors, divers began to fawn on those new commanders, that now bent all their wits to get him [to] resign them his commission: who after much ado and many bitter repulses; that their confusion [ruin] (which he told them was at their elbows [very near]) should not be attributed to him, for leaving the colony without a commission, he was not unwilling they should steal it, but never would he give it to such as they. . . .

But had that unhappy blast not happened, he would quickly have qualified the heat of those humors and factions, had the ships but once left them and us to our fortunes; and have made that provision from among the savages, as we neither feared Spaniard, savage, nor famine; nor would have left Virginia, nor our lawful authority, but at as dear a price as we had bought it, and paid for it.

What shall I say, but thus we left [lost] him, that in all his proceedings, made justice his first guide, and experience his second, even hating baseness, sloth, pride, and indignity, more than any dangers; that never allowed more for himself, than his soldiers with him; that upon no danger would send them where he would not lead them himself; that would never see us want, what he either had, or could by any means get us; that would rather want than borrow, or starve than not pay; that loved action more than words, and hated falsehood and covetousness worse than death; whose adventures were our lives, and whose loss our deaths.

Leaving us thus with three ships, seven boats, commodities ready to trade, the harvest newly gathered, ten weeks' provision in the store, four hundred ninety and odd persons, twenty-four pieces of ordnance, three hundred muskets, snaphances [flint-locks] and firelocks; shot, powder, and match sufficient; curats [armor], pikes, swords, and morions [helmets] more than men; the savages, their language, and habitations well known to a hundred well trained and expert soldiers; nets for fishing; tools of all sorts to work; apparel to supply our wants; six mares and a horse; five or six hundred swine; as many hens and chickens; some goats; some sheep. What was brought or bred there, remained.

But they, regarding nothing but from hand to mouth, did consume that we had, took care for nothing but to perfect some colorable complaints against Captain Smith. For effecting whereof three weeks longer [from about 13 September to 4 October 1609] they stayed the ships, till they could produce them. That time and charge might much better have been spent, but it suited well with the rest of their discretions.

Besides Jamestown that was strongly palisaded, containing some fifty or sixty houses, he left five or six other several forts and plantations: though they were not so sumptuous as our successors expected, they were better than they provided any for us. All this time we had but one carpenter in the country, and three others that could do little, but desired to be learners; two blacksmiths; two sailors; and those we writ [list as] laborers were for [the] most part footmen, and such as they that were [by] adventurers brought to attend them, or such as they could persuade to go with them, that never did know what a day's work was: except the Dutchmen and Poles, and some dozen other. For all the rest were poor gentlemen, tradesmen, serving men, libertines, and such like, ten times more fit to spoil a commonwealth, than either begin one, or but help to maintain one. For when neither the fear of God, nor the law, nor shame, nor displeasure of their friends could rule them here [in England], there is small hope ever to bring one in twenty of them ever to be good there [in Virginia]. Notwithstanding, I confess divers amongst them, had better minds and grew much more industrious than was expected: yet ten good workmen would have done more substantial work in a day, than ten of them in a week. Therefore men may rather wonder how we could do so much, than use us so badly because we did no more, but leave those examples to make others beware; and the fruits of all, we know not for whom.

But to see the justice of God upon these Dutchmen; Volda before spoke[n] of, made a shift [effort] to get [to] England, where persuading the merchants what rich mines he had found, and great service he would do them, was very well rewarded, and returned with the Lord De La Warr [June 1610]: but being found a mere imposter, he died most miserably.

Adam and Francis his two consorts were fled again [in the winter of 1609–1610] to Powhatan, to whom they promised at the arrival of my Lord [June 1610], what wonders they would do, would he suffer them but to go to him. But the King seeing they would be gone, replied; *You that would have betrayed Captain Smith to me, will certainly betray me to this great Lord for your peace:* so [he] caused his men to beat out their brains. . . .

Now this our young commonwealth in Virginia, as you have read once consisted but of 38 persons and in two years increased but to 200, yet by this small means so highly was approved the plantation in Virginia, as how many Lords, with worthy knights, and brave gentlemen pretended [intended] to see it, and some did; and now after the expense of fifteen years more [1609–1624], and such massy sums of men and money, grow they disanimated [discouraged]? If we truly consider our proceedings with the Spaniards, and the rest, we have no reason to despair, for with so small charge, they never had either greater discoveries, with such certain trials of more several commodities, than in this short time hath been returned from Virginia, and by much less means. New England was brought out of obscurity, and afforded fraught for near[ly] 200 sail of ships, where there is now erected a brave plantation [the settlement of the Pilgrims at Plymouth]. For the happiness of [the] Summer Isles, they are no less than either, and yet those have had a far less, and a more difficult beginning, than either Rome, Carthage, or Venice.

Written by Richard Potts, Clerk of the Council,
William Tankard, and G. P.

3. John Smith and the Promise
of New England

Selections from Book IV of
*The Generall Historie of Virginia,
New England, and the Summer Isles*

The Description of New England.

That part we call New England, is betwixt the degrees of forty-one
and forty-five, the very mean betwixt the North Pole and the line; but
that part this discourse speaketh of, stretcheth but from *Penobscot* to
Cape Cod, some seventy-five leagues by a right line distant each from
[the] other; within which bounds I have seen at least forty several
habitations upon the seacoast, and sounded about five and twenty excellent good harbors, in many whereof there is anchorage for five hun-
red sail of ships of any burden; in some of them for one thousand, and
more than two hundred isles overgrown with good timber of divers
sorts of wood, which do make so many harbors, as required a longer
time than I had to be well observed.

The principal habitation northward we were at, was *Penobscot.* Southward along the coast and up the rivers, we found *Mecaddacut* [Cam-
den, Maine], *Segocket, Pemaquid, Nuscoucus, Sagadahoc, Anmoughcawgin,* and *Kennebec;* and to those countries belong the people of
Segotago, Paghhuntanuck, Pocopassum, Taughtanakagnet, Warbig-

ganus, Nassaque, Masherosqueck, Wawrigweck, Moshoquen, Wakcogo, Pasharanack, &c. To these are allied in confederacy, the countries of *Ancocisco, Accomynticus, Passataquack, Agawam* [Ipswich, Massachusetts], and *Naemkeck:* all these for anything I could perceive, differ little in language, fashion, or government: though most of them be lords of themselves, yet they hold the *Bashabes* of *Penobscot,* the chief and greatest amongst them.

The next I can remember by name, are *Mattahunts,* two pleasant isles of groves, gardens, and cornfields a league in the sea from the main-[land]: then *Totant, Massachusett, Topent, Secassaw, Totheet, Nasnocomacack, Accomac* [Plymouth County, Massachusetts], *Chawum* [Barnstable County, Massachusetts], *Patuxet* [Plymouth, Massachusetts], *Massasoyts, Pakanokick:* then Cape Cod, by which is *Pawmet* [Barnstable County, Massachusetts] and the Isle [of] *Nauset* [near Eastman, Massachusetts], of the language and alliance of them at *Chawum;* the others are called *Massachusetts,* and differ somewhat in language, custom, and condition.

For their trade and merchandise, to each of their principal families or habitations, they have divers towns and people belonging, and by their relations and descriptions, more than twenty several habitations and rivers that stretch themselves far into the country, even to the borders of divers great lakes, where they kill and take most of their otters.

From *Penobscot* to *Kennebec.* This coast is mountainous, and isles of huge rocks, but overgrown for [the] most part, with most sorts of excellent good woods, for building houses, boats, barks or ships, with an incredible abundance of most sorts of fish, much fowl, and sundry sorts of good fruits for man's use.

Betwixt *Kennebec* and *Sowocatuck* [the coast south of Portland] there [are] but two or three sandy bays, but betwixt that and Cape Cod very many: especially the coast of the *Massachusetts* is so indifferently mixed with high clay or sandy cliffs in one place, and the tracts of large long ledges of divers sorts, and quarries of stones in other places, so strangely divided with tinctured veins of divers colors: as freestone for building, slate for tiling, smooth stone to make furnaces and forges for glass and iron, and iron ore sufficient conveniently to melt in them; but the most part so resembleth the coast of Devonshire, I think most of the cliffs would make such limestone: if they be not of these qualities, they are so like they may deceive a better judgment than mine: all which are so near adjoining to those other advantages I observed in these parts, that if the ore prove as good iron and steel in those parts as I know it is within the bounds of the country, I dare engage my head (having but men skillful to work the simples [raw materials] there growing) to have all things belonging to the building and rigging of ships of any proportion, and good merchandise for their fraught, within a square of ten or fourteen leagues, and it were no hard matter to prove it within a less limitation.

And surely by reason of those sandy cliffs, and cliffs of rocks, both which we saw so planted with gardens and cornfields, and so well inhabited with a goodly, strong, and well proportioned people, besides the greatness of the timber growing on them, the greatness of the fish, and the moderate temper of the air (for of five and forty not a man was sick, but two that were many years diseased before they went, notwithstanding our bad lodging and accidental [haphazard] diet) who can but approve this a most excellent place, both for health and fertility: and of all the four parts of the world I have yet seen not inhabited, could I have but means to transport a colony, I would rather live here than anywhere; and if it did not maintain itself, were we but once indifferently well fitted, let us starve.

The main staple from hence to be extracted for the present, to produce the rest, is fish, which howbeit may seem a mean and a base commodity; yet who will but truly take the pains and consider the sequel [result], I think will allow it well worth the labor. It is strange to see, what great adventures the hopes of setting forth men of war to rob the industrious innocent would procure, or such massy promises in gross [by the dozens], though more are choked than well fed with such hasty hopes. But who doth not know that the poor Hollanders chiefly by fishing at a great charge [trouble] and labor in all weathers in the open sea, are made a people so hardy and industrious, and by the venting [selling] this poor commodity to the Easterlings [Hanse merchants] for as mean, which is wood, flax, pitch, tar, rosin, cordage, and such like; which they exchange again to the French, Spaniards, Portuguese, and English, &c. for what they want, are made so mighty, strong, and rich, as no state but Venice of twice their magnitude is so well furnished, with so many fair cities, goodly towns, strong fortresses, and that abundance of shipping, and all sorts of merchandise, as well of gold, silver, pearls, diamonds, precious stones, silks, velvets, and cloth of gold; as fish, pitch, wood, or such gross commodities? What voyages and discoveries, east

and west, north and south, yea about the world, make they? What an
army by sea and land have they long maintained, in despite of one of
the greatest Princes of the world, and never could the Spaniard with
all his mines of gold and silver, pay his debts, his friends, and army,
half so truly as the Hollanders still have done by this contemptible trade
of fish. Divers (I know) may allege many other assistances; but this is
the chiefest mine, and the sea the source of those silver streams of all
their virtue, which hath made them now the very miracle of industry,
the only pattern of perfection for these affairs: and the benefit of fishing
is that *primum mobile* that turns all their spheres to this height, of
plenty, strength, honor, and exceeding[ly] great admiration.

Herring, cod, and ling, is that triplicity, that makes their wealth
and shippings' multiplicity such as it is: and from which (few would
think it) they should draw so many millions yearly as they do, . . . and
such an incredible number of ships, that breeds them so many sailors,
mariners, soldiers, and merchants, never to be wrought out of that
trade, and fit for any other. I will not deny but others may gain as well
as they that will use it, though not so certainly, nor so much in quantity,
for want of experience: and this herring they take upon the coast
of England and Scotland, their cod and ling upon the coast of Iceland,
and in the north seas, if we consider what gains the Hamburgans
[merchants of Hamburg], the Biskinners [fishermen from the Bay
of Biscay], and French make by fishing; nay, but how many thousands
this [last] fifty or sixty years have been maintained by Newfoundland,
where they take nothing but small cod, whereof the greatest they make
cor-fish [salted fish], and the rest is hard dried, which we call Poor-John,
would amaze a man with wonder.

If then from all those parts such pains [are] taken for this poor gains
of fish, especially by the Hollanders, that hath but little of their own,
for building of ships and setting them to sea; but at the second, third,
fourth, or fifth hand, drawn from so many parts of the world ere
they come together to be used in those voyages: if these (I say)
can gain, why should we more doubt than they; but do much better,
that may have most of all those things at our doors for taking and
making, and here are no hard landlords to rack us with high rents, or
extorting fines, nor tedious pleas in law to consume us with their many
years' disputation for justice; nor multitudes to occasion such impediments to good orders as in popular states: so freely hath God and
His Majesty bestowed those blessings on them [that] will attempt to

obtain them, as here every man may be master of his own labor and
land, or the greatest part (if His Majesty's royal meaning be not
abused) and if he have nothing but his hands, he may set up his
trade; and by industry quickly grow rich, spending but half that time
well, which in England we abuse in idleness, worse, or as ill.

Here is ground as good as any [which] lieth in the height of
forty-one, forty-two, forty-three, &c. [degrees of north latitude] which
is as temperate, and as fruitful as any other parallel in the world. . . .

Therefore I conclude, if the heart and entrails of those regions
were sought, if their land were cultured, planted, and manured
[worked] by men of industry, judgment, and experience; what hope
is there, or what need they doubt, having the advantages of the sea,
but it might equalize any of these famous kingdoms in all commodities,
pleasures, and conditions: seeing even the very hedges do naturally
afford us such plenty, as no ship need return away empty, and only
use but the season of the sea, fish will return an honest gain, besides
all other advantages; her treasures having yet never been opened, nor
her originals wasted, consumed, nor abused.

And whereas it is said the Hollanders serve the Easterlings themselves, and other parts that want with herring, ling, and wet cod: the
Easterlings [supply] a great part of Europe, with sturgeon and caviar.
. . . Newfoundland [provides] the most part of the chief southern
ports in Europe, with a thin Poor-John; which hath been so long, so
much overlaid with fishers [fished out] as the fishing decayeth, so that
many oft times are constrained to return with a small fraught. Norway
and Poland afford pitch and tar, masts and yards. Sweden and Russia,
iron and ropes. France and Spain, canvas, wine, steel, iron, and oil.
Italy and Greece, silks and fruits. I dare boldly say, because I have
seen naturally growing or breeding in those parts, the same materials
that all these are made of, they may as well be had here, or the most
part of them within the distance of seventy leagues for some few
ages, as from all those parts, using but the same means to have them
that they do; but surely in Virginia, their most tender and daintiest
fruits or commodities, would be as perfect as theirs, by reason of the
heat, if not in New England, and with all those advantages.

First, the ground is so fertile, that questionless [undoubtedly] it is
capable of producing any grain, fruits, or seeds, you will sow or
plant, growing in the regions aforenamed. But it may . . . not [grow]
to that perfection of delicacy, because the summer is not so hot, and

the winter is more cold in those parts we have yet tried near the sea side, than we find in the same height [latitude] in Europe or Asia: yet I made a garden upon the top of a rocky isle in three and forty degrees and a half, four leagues from the main[land] in May, that grew so well, as it served us for salads in June and July.

All sorts of cattle may here be bred and fed in the isles or peninsulas securely for nothing. In the interim, till they increase (if need be) observing the seasons, I durst undertake to have corn enough from the savages for three hundred men, for a few trifles; and if they should be untowards, as it is most certain they will, thirty or forty good men will be sufficient to bring them all in subjection, and make this provision, if they understand what to do: two hundred whereof may eight or nine months in the year be employed in helping the fishermen, till the rest provide other necessaries, fit to furnish us with other commodities.

In March, April, May, and half [of] June, here is cod in abundance; in May, June, July, and August, mullet and sturgeon, whose roes do make caviar and botargo; herring, if any desire them: I have taken many out of the bellies of cods, some in nets; but the savages compare the store in the sea with the hairs of their heads: and surely there are an incredible abundance upon this coast. In the end of August, September, October, and November, you may have cod again to make cor-fish or Poor-John: hake you may have when the cod fails in summer, if you will fish in the night, which is better than cod. Now each hundred you take here, is as good as two or three hundred in Newfoundland; so that half the labor in hooking, splitting and touring [transportation], is saved: and you may have your fish at what market you will, before they have any in Newfoundland, where their fishing is chiefly but in June and July; where[as] it is here in March, April, May, September, October and November, as is said: so that by reason of this plantation, the merchants may have their fraught [vessels laded] both out and home, which yields an advantage worth consideration.

Your cor-fish you may in like manner transport as you see cause, to serve the ports in Portugal, as Lisbon . . . and divers others, (or what market you please) before your islanders [Icelanders] return. They being tied to the season in the open sea, and you having a double season, and fishing before your doors, may every night sleep quietly ashore with good cheer, and what fires you will, or when you please with your wives and family: they only and their ships in the main ocean, that must carry and contain all they use, besides their fraught.

The mullets here are in that abundance, you may take them with nets sometimes by hundreds, where at Cap Blanc they hook them: yet those are but a foot and a half in length; these two, three, or four, as oft I have measured, which makes me suspect they are some other kind of fish, though they seem the same, both in fashion and goodness. Much salmon some have found up the rivers as they have passed; and here the air is so temperate, as all these at any time may be preserved.

Now, young boys and girls, savages, or any other be they never such idlers, may turn, carry or return a fish, without either shame or any great pain. He is very idle that is past twelve years of age and cannot do so much; and she is very old that cannot spin a thread to make engines [lines] to catch a fish.

For their transportation, the ships that go there to fish may transport the first: who for their passage will spare the charge of double manning their ships, which they must do in Newfoundland to get their fraught; but one third part of that company are only proper to serve a stage [platform for drying fish], carry a barrow, and turn Poor-John; notwithstanding, they must have meat, drink, clothes, and passage [as] well as the rest.

Now all I desire is but this, that those that voluntarily will send shipping, should make here the best choice they can, or accept such as shall be presented them to serve them at that rate: and their ships returning leave such with me, with the value of that they should receive coming home, in such provisions and necessary tools, arms, bedding, apparel, salt, nets, hooks, lines, and such like, as they spare of the remainings; who till the next return may keep their boats, and do them many other profitable offices. Provided, I have men of ability to teach them their functions, and a company fit for soldiers to be ready upon any occasion, because of the abuses that have been offered the poor savages, and the liberty that both French and English, or any that will, have to deal with them as they please; whose disorders will be hard to reform, and the longer the worse.

Now such order with facility might be taken, with every port, town, or city, with free power to convert the benefit of their fraughts to what advantage they please, and increase their numbers as they see occasion, who ever as they are able to subsist of themselves, may begin

the new towns in New England, in memory of their old: which freedom
being confined but to the necessity of the general good, the event
(with God's help) might produce an honest, a noble, and a profitable
emulation.

Salt upon salt may assuredly be made, if not at the first in ponds, yet
till they be provided this may be used: then the ships may transport
kine, horse[s], goats, coarse cloth, and such commodities as we want;
by whose arrival may be made that provision of fish to fraught the
ships that they stay not; and then if the sailors go for wages it matters
not, it is hard if this return defray not the charge: but care must be
had they arrive in the spring, or else that provision be made for them
against winter. . . .

Of the muskrat may be well raised gains worth their labor, that
will endeavor to make trial of their goodness.

Of beavers, otters and martens, black foxes, and furs of price, may
yearly be had six or seven thousand, and if the trade of the French
were prevented, many more: 25,000 this year [1614] were brought
from those northern parts into France, of which trade we may have
as good part as the French if we take good courses.

Of mines of gold and silver, copper, and probabilities of lead,
crystal and alum, I could say much if relations were good assurances;
it is true indeed, I made many trials according to the instructions I had,
which doth persuade me I need not despair but that there are metals
in the country: but I am no alchemist, nor will promise more than
I know: which is, who will undertake the rectifying [operation] of
an iron forge, if those that buy meat and drink, coals, ore, and all
necessaries at a dear rate, gain; where all the settings [materials] are
to be had for taking up, in my opinion cannot lose.

Of woods, seeing there is such plenty of all sorts, if those that build
ships and boats, buy wood at so great a price as it is in England, Spain,
France and Holland, and all other provisions for the nourishment of
man's life, live well by their trade; when labor is all [that is] required
to take these necessaries without any other tax, what hazard will be
here but to do much better, and what commodity in Europe doth more
decay than wood? For the goodness of the ground, let us take it fertile
or barren, or as it is, seeing it is certain it bears fruits to nourish and
feed man and beast as well as England, and the sea those several sorts
of fishes I have related.

Thus seeing all good things for man's sustenance may with this

facility be had by a little extraordinary labor, till that transported
be increased, and all necessaries for shipping only for labor, to which
may [be] added the assistance of the savages which may easily be
had, if they be discreetly handled in their kinds, towards fishing,
planting, and destroying woods.

What gains might be raised if this were followed (when there are
but once men to fill your storehouses dwelling there, you may serve
all Europe better and far cheaper than can the Iceland fishers, or the
Hollanders, Cap Blanc, or Newfoundland, who must be at much more
charge than you) may easily be conjectured by this example.

Two thousand [pounds] will fit out a ship of 200 tons, and one
[ship] of 100 tons. If of the dry fish they both make, [they] fraught
that of 200 and go for Spain, sell it but at ten shillings a quintal, but
commonly it gives fifteen or twenty, especially when it cometh first,
which amounts to 3 or 400 pound[s], but say but ten, which is the
lowest, allowing the rest for waste, it amounts at that rate to 2000
[pounds] which is the whole charge of your two ships and the
equipage: then the return [by exchange] of the money and the fraught
of the ship for the vintage [season?] or any other voyage is clear gain;
with your ship of one hundred tons of train [fish] oil and cor-fish,
besides the beavers and other commodities, and that you may have
at home within six months if God please to send but an ordinary
passage.

Then saving half this charge by the not staying of your ships, your
victual, overplus [excess] of men and wages, with her fraught thither
with necessaries for the planters, the salt being there made, as also
may the nets and lines within a short time; if nothing may be expected
but this, it might in time equalize your Hollanders' gains, if not exceed
them: having their fraughts always ready against the arrival of the ships.

This would so increase our shipping and sailors, and so encourage
and employ a great part of our idlers and others that want employment
fitting their qualities at home, where they shame to do that they would
do abroad, that could they but once taste the sweet fruits of their own
labors, doubtless many thousands would be advised by good discipline
to take more pleasure in honest industry, than in their humors of
dissolute idleness.

But to return a little more to the particulars of this country, which
I intermingle thus with my projects and reasons, not being so sufficiently
yet acquainted in those parts, to write fully the estate of the sea, the

air, the land, the fruits, their rocks, the people, the government, religion, territories, limitations, friends and foes: but as I gathered from their niggardly relations in a broken language, during the time I ranged those countries, &c.

The most northern part I was at, was the Bay of Penobscot, which is east and west, north and south, more than ten leagues: but such were my occasions, I was constrained to be satisfied of them I found in the bay, that the river ran far up into the land, and was well inhabited with many people; but they were from their habitations, either fishing amongst the isles, or hunting the lakes and woods for deer and beavers. The bay is full of great isles of one, two, six or eight miles in length, which divides it into many fair and excellent good harbors.

On the east of it are the *Tarrentines,* their mortal enemies, where inhabit the French, as they report, that live with those people as one nation or family. And northwest of *Penobscot* is *Mecaddacut,* at the foot of a high mountain, a kind of fortress against the *Tarrentines,* adjoining to the high mountains of *Penobscot,* against whose feet doth beat the sea; but over all the land, isles, or other impediments, you may well see them fourteen or eighteen leagues from their situation. *Segocket* is the next, then *Nuskoucus, Pemaquid,* and *Kennebec.*

Up this river [the Kennebec], where was the western plantation, are *Anmoughcawgin, Kennebec,* and divers others, where are planted some cornfields. Along this river thirty or forty miles, I saw nothing but great high cliffs of barren rocks overgrown with wood, but where the savages dwell there the ground is excellent[ly] salt [rich] and fertile.

Westward of this river is the country of *Ancocisco* [Casco Bay], in the bottom of a large deep bay, full of many great isles, which divides it into many good harbors.

Sawocotuck [the coast south of Portland] is the next, in the edge of a large sandy bay, which hath many rocks and isles, but few good harbors but for barks I yet know.

But all this coast to *Penobscot,* and as far as I could see eastward of it, is nothing but such high, craggy, cliffy rocks and stony isles, that I wonder such great trees could grow upon so hard foundations. It is a country rather to affright than delight one, and how to describe a more plain spectacle of desolation, or more barren, I know not; yet are those rocky isles so furnished with good woods, springs, fruits, fish

and fowl, and the sea the strangest fish pond I ever saw, that it makes
me think, though the coast be rocky and thus affrightable, the valleys
and plains and interior parts may well notwithstanding be very fertile.
But there is no country so fertile [that] hath not some part barren,
and New England is great enough to make many kingdoms and
countries, were it all inhabited.

As you pass the coast still westward, *Accomynticus* and *Passataquack*
[at the mouth of the Piscataqua] are two convenient harbors for small
barks; and a good country within their craggy cliffs.

Augoan [south of Odiornes Point] is the next: this place might
content a right curious judgment, but there are many sands at the
entrance of the harbor, and the worst is, it is embayed too far from
the deep sea; here are many rising hills, and on their tops and descents
are many cornfields and delightful groves. On the east is an isle of
two or three leagues in length, the one half plain marshy ground, fit
for pasture or salt ponds, with many fair, high groves of mulberry
trees and gardens; there [are] also oaks, pines, walnuts, and other
wood[s] to make this place an excellent habitation, being a good and
safe harbor.

Naemkeck [Cape Ann coast], though it be more rocky ground,
for *Augoan* is sandy, [is] not much inferior neither for the harbor, nor
anything I could perceive but the multitude of people.

From hence doth stretch into the sea the fair headland *Trabigzanda*,
now called Cape Ann, fronted with the three isles we called the three
Turks' heads; to the north of this doth enter a great bay, where we
found some habitations and cornfields, they report a fair river [the
Merrimack] and at least 30 habitations doth possess this country. But
because the French had got their trade, I had no leisure to discover it.

The isles of *Mattahunts* are on the west side of this bay, where are
many isles and some rocks that appear a great height above the water
like the pyramids in Egypt, and amongst them many good harbors, and
then the country of the Massachusetts [Massachusetts Bay], which is
the paradise of all those parts; for here are many isles planted with
corn, groves, mulberries, savage gardens and good harbors, the coast
is for the most part high, clayie, sandy cliffs, the seacoast as you pass
shows you all along large cornfields, and great troupes of well proportioned people: but the French having remained here near[ly] six
weeks, left nothing for us to take occasion to examine the inhabitants'
relations, *viz.,* if there be three thousand people upon those isles, and

that the river doth pierce many days' journey the entrails of that country.

We found the people in those parts very kind, but in their fury no less valiant; for upon a quarrel we fought with forty or fifty of them, till they had spent all their arrows, and then we took six or seven of their canoes, which towards the evening they ransomed for beaver skins: and at *Quonahasset* [Cohasset] falling out there but with one of them, he with three others crossed the harbor in a canoe to certain rocks whereby we must pass, and there let fly their arrows for our shot, till we were out of danger; yet one of them was slain, and another shot through his thigh.

Then come you to *Accomac* [Plymouth] an excellent good harbor, good land, and no want of anything but industrious people: after much kindness, we fought also with them, though some were hurt, some slain, yet within an hour after they became friends.

Cape Cod is the next [that] presents itself, which is only a headland of high hills, overgrown with shrubby pines, hurts and such trash; but an excellent harbour for all weathers. This Cape is made by the main sea on the one side, and a great bay on the other in [the] form of a sickle; on it doth inhabit the people of *Pawmet,* and in the bottom of the bay them of *Chawum.*

Towards the south and southwest of this cape, is found a long and dangerous shoal of rocks and sand, but so far as I encircled it, I found thirty fathom water and a strong current, which makes me think there is a channel about this shoal, where is the best and greatest fish to be had winter and summer in all the country; but the savages say there is no channel, but that the shoals begin from the main[land] at *Pawmet* [Barnstable County, Massachusetts] to the Isle of *Nauset* [near Eastham], and so extends beyond their knowledge into the sea.

The next to this is *Capawucke,* and those abounding countries of copper, corn, people and minerals, which I went to discover this last year [1615]; but because I miscarried by the way, I will leave them till God please I have better acquaintance with them.

The *Massachusetts* they report sometimes have wars with the *Bashabes* of *Penobscot,* and are not always friends with them of *Chawum* and their alliance; but now they are all friends, and have each trade with other so far as they have society on each others' frontiers: for they [the *Bashabes*] make no such voyages as from *Penobscot* to Cape Cod, seldom to *Massachusett.*

In the north as I have said they have begun to plant corn, whereof

the south part hath such plenty as they have what they will from them
of the north, and in the winter much more plenty of fish and fowl;
but both winter and summer hath it in one part or other all the year,
being the mean and most indifferent temper betwixt heat and cold, of
all the regions betwixt the line and the pole: but the furs northward
are much better, and in much more plenty than southward. . . .

The waters are most pure, proceeding from the entrails of rocky
mountains.

The herbs and fruits are of many sorts and kinds, as alkermes,
curran[t]s, mulberries, vines, respises [raspberries], gooseberries,
plums, walnuts, chestnuts, small-nuts, pumpkins, gourds, strawberries,
beans, peas, and maize; a kind or two of flax, wherewith they make
nets, lines, and ropes, both small and great, very strong for their
quantities.

Oak is the chief wood, of which there is great difference, in regard of
the soil where it groweth, fir, pine, walnut, chestnut, birch, ash, elm,
cypress, cedar, mulberry, plum tree, hazel, sassafras, and many other
sorts.

Eagles, grips, divers sorts of hawks, herons, geese, brants, cormorants,
ducks, cranes, swans, sheldrakes, teal, mews, gulls, turkeys, dive-doppers,
and many other sorts whose names I know not.

Whales, grompus, porpoises, turbot, sturgeon, cod, hake, haddock,
coal[fish], cusk or small ling, shark, mackerel, herring, mullet, bass,
pinnacks, cunners, perch, eels, crabs, lobsters, mussels, wilks, oysters,
clams, periwinkles, and divers others, &c.

Moose, a beast bigger than a stag, deer red and fallow, beavers,
wolves, foxes both black and other, aroughcuns, wildcats, bears, otters,
martens, fitches, musquassus, and divers other sorts of vermin whose
names I know not.

All these and divers other good things do here for want of use
still increase and decrease with little diminution, whereby they grow
to that abundance, you shall scarce[ly] find any bay, shallow shore
or cove of sand, where you may not take many clams or lobsters, or
both at your pleasure, and in many places load your boat if you please;
nor isles where you find not fruits, birds, crabs, and mussels, or all of
them; for taking at a low water cod, cusk, halibut, skate, turbot,
mackerel, or such like are taken plentifully in divers sandy bays, store
of mullet, bass, and divers other sorts of such excellent fish as many
as their net can hold: no river where there is not plenty of sturgeon,

or salmon, or both, all which are to be had in abundance observing
but their seasons: but if a man will go at Christmas to gather cherries
in Kent, though there be plenty in summer, he may be·deceived; so
here these plenties have each their seasons, as I have expressed.

We for the most part had little but bread and vinegar, and though,
the most part of July when the fishing decayed [declined], they [the
members of Smith's party] wrought all day, lay abroad in the isles all
night, and lived on what they found, yet were not sick. But I would
wish none long [to] put himself to such plunges [hardships], except
necessity constrain it: yet worthy is that person to starve that here
cannot live if he have sense, strength and health, for there is no such
penury of these blessings in any place but that one hundred men may
in two or three hours make their provisions for a day, and he that hath
experience to manage these affairs, with forty or thirty honest industrious men, might well undertake (if they dwell in these parts) to
subject the savages, and feed daily two or three hundred men, with
as good corn, fish, and flesh as the earth hath of those kinds, and yet
make that labor but their pleasure: provided that they have engines
[equipment] that be proper for their purposes.

Who can desire more content that hath small means, or but only his
merit to advance his fortunes, than to tread and plant that ground he
hath purchased by the hazard of his life; if he have but the taste of
virtue and magnanimity, what to such a mind can be more pleasant
than planting and building a foundation for his posterity, got from the
rude earth by God's blessing and his own industry without prejudice
to any; if he have any grain of faith or zeal in religion, what can he
do less hurtful to any, or more agreeable to God, than to seek to
convert those poor savages to know Christ and humanity, whose labors
with discretion will tripl[y] requite thy charge and pain; what so truly
suits with honor and honesty, as the discovering things unknown,
erecting towns, peopling countries, informing the ignorant, reforming
things unjust, teaching virtue and gain to our native mother country
[and providing] a kingdom to attend her, find employment for those
that are idle, because they know not what to do: so far from wronging
any, as to cause posterity to remember thee; and remembering thee,
ever honor that remembrance with praise.

Consider what were the beginnings and endings of the monarchies
of the Chaldeans, the Syrians, the Grecians and Romans, but this one
rule; what was it they would not do for the good of their commonweal,

or their mother city? For example: Rome, what made her such a monarchess, but only the adventures of her youth, not in riots at home, but in dangers abroad; and the justice and judgment out of their experiences, when they grew aged: what was their ruin and hurt but this, the excess of idleness, the fondness of parents, the want of experience in magistrates, the admiration of their undeserved honors, the contempt of true merit, their unjust jealousies, their politi[cal] incredulities, their hypocritical seeming goodness and their deeds of secret lewdness; finally in fine, growing only formal temporists [time servers], all that their predecessors got in many years they lost in a few days: those by their pains and virtues became lords of the world, they by their ease and vices became slaves to their servants; this is the difference betwixt the use of arms in the field and on the monuments of stones, the golden age and the leaden age, prosperity and misery, justice and corruption, substance and shadows, words and deeds, experience and imagination, making commonweals and marring commonweals, the fruits of virtue and the conclusions of vice.

Then who would live at home idly, or think in himself any worth to live, only to eat, drink and sleep, and so die; or by consuming that carelessly, his friends got worthily; or by using that miserably that maintained virtue honestly; or for being descended nobly, and pine with the vain vaunt of great kindred in penury; or to maintain a silly show of bravery, toil out thy heart, soul and time basely, by shifts [subterfuges], tricks, cards and dice; or by relating news of other men's actions, shark [steal] here and there for a dinner or supper; deceive thy friends by fair promises and dissimulation, in borrowing where thou never meanest to pay; offend the laws, surfeit with excess, burthen thy country, abuse thyself, despair in want, and then cozen [cheat] thy kindred, yea even thy own brother, and wish thy parents death (I will not say damnation) to have their estates: though thou seest what honors and rewards the world yet hath for them that will seek them and worthily deserve them.

I would be sorry to offend, or that any should mistake my honest meaning; for I wish good to all, hurt to none: but rich men for the most part are grown to that dotage through their pride in their wealth, as though there were no accident could end it or their life.

And what hellish care do such take to make it their own misery and their country's spoil, especially when there is most need of their employment, drawing by all manner of inventions from the Prince and his honest subjects, even the vital spirits of their powers and estates: as if their [money] bags or brags were so powerful a defense, the malicious could not assault them, when they are the only bait to cause us not only to be assaulted, but betrayed and murdered in our own security ere we will perceive it.

May not the miserable ruin of Constantinople, their impregnable walls, riches and pleasures [at] last taken by the Turk, which were then but a bit in comparison of their mightiness now, remember [remind] us of the effects of private covetousness; at which time the good Emperor held himself rich enough, to have such rich subjects, so formal in all excess of vanity, all kind of delicacy and prodigality: his poverty when the Turk besieged the citizens (whose merchandising [engaged in trade] thoughts were only to get wealth) little conceiving the desperate resolution of a valiant expert enemy, left the Emperor so long to his conclusions [ends], having spent all he had to pay his young, raw, discontented soldiers, that suddenly he, they, and their city were all a prey to the devouring Turk, and what they would not spare for the maintenance of them who adventured their lives to defend them, did serve only their enemies to torment them, their friends and country, and all Christendom to this present day. Let this lamentable example remember you that are rich (seeing there are such great thieves in the world to rob you) not [to] grudge to lend some proportion to breed them that have little, yet willing to learn how to defend you, for it is too late when the deed is doing [when trouble comes].

The Romans' estate hath been worse than this, for the mere covetousness and extortion of a few of them so moved the rest, that not having any employment but contemplation, their great judgments grew to so great malice, as themselves were sufficient to destroy themselves by faction; let this move you to embrace employment for those whose educations, spirits and judgments want but your purses, not only to prevent such accustomed dangers, but also to gain more thereby than you have.

And you fathers that are either so foolishly fond, or so miserably covetous, or so willfully ignorant, or so negligently careless, as that you will rather maintain your children in idle wantonness till they grow your masters; or become so basely unkind that they wish nothing but your deaths; so that both sorts grow dissolute; and although you would wish them anywhere to escape the gallows and ease your cares; though they spend you here one, two or three hundred pound[s] a year; you would grudge to give half so much in adventure with them to obtain an estate, which in a small time, but with a little assistance of your providence, might be better than your own. But if an angel should tell you [that] any place yet unknown, can afford such fortunes, you would not believe it, no more than Columbus was believed [that] there was any such land as is now the well known, abounding America, mightless [much less] such large regions as are yet unknown, as well in America, as in Africa and Asia, and *terra incognita*.

I have not been so ill bred but I have tasted of plenty and pleasure, as well as want and misery; nor doth necessity yet, or occasion of discontent force me to these endeavors; nor am I ignorant [of] what small thanks I shall have for my pains, or that many would have the world imagine them to be of great judgment, that can but blemish these my designs, by their witty objections and detractions: yet (I hope) my reasons with my deeds will so prevail with some, that I shall not want employment in these affairs, to make the most blind see his own senselessness and incredulity, hoping that gain will make them affect that which religion, charity and the common good cannot. It were but a poor device in me to deceive myself, much more the King and State, my friends and country, with these inducements: which seeing His Majesty hath given permission, I wish all sorts of worthy, honest, industrious spirits would understand, and if they desire any further satisfaction, I will do my best to give it, not to persuade them to go only, but go with them; not leave them there, but live with them there.

I will not say but by ill providing and undue managing, such courses may be taken [that] may make us miserable enough: but if I may have the execution of what I have projected, if they want to eat, let them eat or never digest [understand] me. If I perform what I say, I desire but that reward out of the gains [which] may suit my pains, quality and condition; and if I abuse you with my tongue, take my head for satisfaction. If any dislike at the year's end, defraying their charge, by my consent they should freely return; I fear not want of company sufficient, were it but known what I know of these countries; and by the proof of that wealth I hope yearly to return, if God please to bless me from such accidents as are beyond my power in reason to prevent; for I am not so simple to think that ever any other motive than wealth will ever erect there a commonwealth, or draw company from their ease and humors at home, to stay in New England to effect my purposes.

And lest any should think the toil might be insupportable, though these things may be had by labor and diligence; I assure myself there are [those] who delight extremely in vain pleasure, that take much more pains in England to enjoy it, than I should do here [in New England] to gain wealth sufficient, and yet I think they should not have half such sweet content: for our pleasure here is still gains, in England charges and loss; here nature and liberty affords us that freely which in England we want, or it costeth us dearly. What pleasure can be more than being tired with any occasion ashore, in planting vines, fruits, or herbs, in contriving their own grounds to the pleasure of their own minds, their fields, gardens, orchards, buildings, ships, and other works, &c., to recreate themselves before their own doors in their own boats upon the sea, where man, woman and child, with a small hook and line, by angling may take divers sorts of excellent fish at their pleasures; and is it not pretty sport to pull up two pence, six pence, and twelve pence, as fast as you can haul and vere [raise up] a line; he is a very bad fisher[man] [that] cannot kill in one day with his hook and line one, two, or three hundred cods, which dressed and dried, if they be sold there for ten shillings a hundred, though in England they will give more than twenty, may not both servant, master and merchant be well content with this gain? If a man work but three days in seven, he may get more than he can spend unless he will be exceedingly excessive. Now that carpenter, mason, gardner, tailor, smith, sailor, forger, or what other, may they not make this a pretty recreation [employment], though they fish but an hour in a day, to take more than they can eat in a week; or if they will not eat it, because there is so much better choice, yet sell it or [ex]change it with the fishermen or merchants for anything you want; and what sport doth yield a more pleasing content, and less hurt and charge than angling with a hook, and crossing the sweet air from isle to isle, over the silent streams of a calm sea; wherein the most curious may find profit, pleasure and content.

Thus though all men be not fishers, yet all men whatsoever may in other matters do as well, for necessity doth in these cases so rule a commonwealth, and each in their several functions, as their labors in their qualities may be as profitable because there is a necessary mutual use of all.

For gentlemen, what exercise should more delight them than ranging daily these unknown parts, using fowling and fishing for hunting and hawking, and yet you shall see the wild hawks give you some pleasure in seeing them stoop [descending] six or seven times after one another an hour or two together, at the skulls [schools] of fish in the fair harbors, as those ashore at a fowl; and never trouble nor torment yourselves with watching, mewing, feeding, and attending them, nor kill horse and man with running and crying, See you not a hawk: for hunting also, the woods, lakes and rivers afford not only chase sufficient for any that delights in that kind of toil or pleasure, but such beasts to hunt, that besides the delicacy of their bodies for food, their skins are so rich, as they will recompense thy daily labor with a Captain's pay.

For laborers, if those that sow hemp, rape, turnips, parsnips, carrots, cabbage, and such like; give twenty, thirty, forty, fifty shillings yearly for an acre of land; and meat, drink, and wages to use it, and yet grow rich: when better, or at least as good ground may be had and cost nothing but labor; it seems strange to me any such should grow poor.

My purpose is not to persuade children from their parents, men from their wives, nor servants from their masters; only such as with free consent may be spared: but that each parish, or village, in city, or country, that will but apparel their fatherless children of thirteen or fourteen years of age, or young married people that have small wealth to live on, here by their labor may live exceeding[ly] well. Provided always, that first there be a sufficient power to command them, houses to receive them, means to defend them, and meet provisions for them, for [any]place may be overlaid [crowded]: and it is most necessary to have a fortress (ere this grow [in]to practice) and sufficient masters of all necessary mechanical qualities, to take ten or twelve of them for apprentices; the master by this may quickly grow rich, these may learn their trades themselves to do the like, to a general and an incredible benefit for King and country, master and servant.

It would be a history of a large volume, to recite the adventures of the Spaniards and Portuguese, their affronts and defeats, their dangers and miseries; which with such incomparable honor, and constant resolution, so far beyond belief, they have attempted and endured in their discoveries and plantations, as may well condemn us of too much imbecility, sloth, and negligence: yet the authors of these new inventions were held as ridiculous for a long time, as now are others that do but seek to imitate their unparalleled virtues. And though we see daily their mountains of wealth (sprung from the plants of their generous endeavors) yet is our sensuality and untowardness such, and so great, that we either ignorantly believe nothing, or so curiously contest, to prevent we know not what future events; that we either so neglect, or oppress and discourage the present, as we spoil all in the making, crop all in the blooming; and building upon fair sand rather than upon rough rocks, judge that we know not, govern that we have not, fear that which is not; and for fear some should do too well, force such against their wills to be idle, or as ill. And who is he [that] hath judgment, courage, and any industry or quality with understanding, will leave his country, his hopes at home, his certain estate, his friends, pleasures, liberty, and the preferment sweet England doth afford to all degrees, were it not to advance his fortunes by enjoying his deserts, whose prosperity once appearing, will encourage others: but it must be cherished as a child, till it be able to go and understand itself, and not corrected nor oppressed above it[s] strength, ere it know wherefore.

A child can neither perform the office nor deeds of a man of strength, nor endure that affliction he is able: nor can an apprentice at the first perform the part of a master. And if twenty years be required to make a child a man, seven years limited an apprentice for his trade: if scarce an age be sufficient to make a wise man a statesman, and commonly a man dies ere he hath learned to be discreet; if perfection be so hard to be obtained, as of necessity there must be practice as well as theor[y]: let no man then condemn this paradox[ical] opinion, to say that half seven years is scarce[ly] sufficient for a good capacity to learn in these affairs how to carry himself. And whoever shall try in these remote places the erecting of a colony, shall find at the end of seven years occasion enough to use all his discretion: and in the interim, all the content, rewards, gains, and hopes, will be necessarily required, to be given to the beginning, till it be able to creep, to stand, and go, and to encourage desert [merit] by all possible means; yet time enough to keep it from running, for there is no fear it will grow too fast, or ever to anything, except liberty, profit, honor, and prosperity there found, more bind the planters of those affairs in devotion to effect it; than bondage, violence, tyranny, ingratitude, and such double dealing, as binds free men to become slaves, and honest men turn knaves; which hath ever been the ruin of the most popular commonweals, and is very unlikely ever well to begin anew.

Who seeth not what is the greatest good of the Spaniard, but these new conclusions in searching those unknown parts of this unknown world; by which means he dives even into the very secrets of all his neighbors, and the most part of the world; and when the Portuguese and Spaniards had found the East and West Indies, how many did condemn themselves, that did not accept of that honest offer of noble Columbus, who upon our neglect brought them to it, persuading ourselves the world had no such places as they had found: and yet ever since we find, they still (from time to time) have found new lands, new nations, and trades, and still daily do find, both in Asia, Africa, *terra incognita,* and America, so that there is neither soldier nor mechanic, from the lord to the beggar, but those parts afford them all employment, and discharges their native soil of so many thousands of all sorts, that else by their sloth, pride, and imperfections, would long ere this have troubled their neighbors, or have eaten the pride of Spain itself.

Now he knows little that knows not England may well spare many more people than Spain, and is as well able to furnish them with all manner of necessaries; and seeing for all they have, they cease not still to search for that they have not, and know not; it is strange we should be so dull, as not [to] maintain that which we have, and pursue that we know.

Surely, I am sure many would take it ill, to be abridged of the titles and honors of their predecessors; when if but truly they would judge themselves, look how inferior they are to their noble virtues, so much they are unworthy of their honors and livings, which never were ordained for shows and shadows, to maintain idleness and vice; but to make them more able to abound in honor, by heroical deeds of action, judgment, piety, and virtue. What was it both in their purse and person they would not do, for the good of their commonwealth, which might move them presently to set out their spare children in these generous designs.

Religion above all things should move us, especially the clergy, if we are religious, to show our faith by our works, in converting those poor savages to the knowledge of God, seeing what pains the Spaniards take to bring them to their adultered faith. Honor might move the gentry, the valiant, and industrious; and the hope and assurance of wealth, all, if we were that we would seem, and be accounted: or be we so far inferior to other nations, or our spirits so far dejected from our ancient predecessors, or our minds so upon spoil, piracy, and such villainy, as to serve the Portuguese, Spaniard, Dutch, French, or Turk, (as to the cost of Europe too many do) rather than our God, our King, our country, and ourselves; excusing our idleness and our base complaints by want of employment, when here is such choice of all sorts, and for all degrees, in the planting and discovering these north parts of America.

My second voyage to New England.

In the year of our Lord 1615 I was employed by many [of] my friends of London, and Sir Ferdinando Gorges, a noble knight, and a great favorer of those actions, who persuaded the Reverend Dean of Exeter, Doctor [Matthew] Sutcliffe, and divers merchants of the west [country], to entertain this plantation.

Much labor I had taken to bring the Londoners and them to join together, because the Londoners have most money, and the western men are most proper for fishing; and it is near[ly] as much trouble, but much more danger, to sail from London to Plymouth, than from Plymouth to New England, so that half the voyage would thus be saved: yet by no means I could prevail, so desirous they were both to be lords of this fishing.

Now to make my words more apparent by my deeds, to begin a plantation for a more ample trial of those conclusions, I was to have stayed there but with sixteen men. . . .

I confess I could have wished them as many thousands, had all other provisions been in like proportion; nor would I have had so few, could I have had means for more: yet would God have pleased we had safely arrived, I doubted not but to have performed more than I promised, and that many thousands ere this would have been there ere now. The main assistance next [to] God I had to this small number, was my acquaintance amongst the savages, especially with Tahanedo, one of their greatest lords, who had lived long in England (and another called Tantum, I [had] carried with me from England, and set on shore at Cape Cod); by the means of this proud savage, I did not doubt but quickly to have got that credit amongst the rest of the savages and their alliance, to have had as many of them as I desired in any design I intended, and that trade also they had by such a kind of exchange of their country commodities, which both with ease and security might then have been used.

With him and divers others, I had concluded to inhabit and defend them against the *Tarrentines,* with a better power than the French did them; whose tyranny did enforce them to embrace my offer with no small devotion.

And though many may think me more bold than wise, in regard of their power, dexterity, treachery, and inconstancy, having so desperately assaulted and betrayed many others; I say but this (because with so many, I have many times done much more in Virginia than I intended here, when I wanted that experience Virginia taught me) that to me it seems no more danger than ordinary: and though I know myself [to be] the meanest of many thousands, whose apprehensive inspection can pierce beyond the bounds of my abilities, into the hidden things of nature, art, and reason: yet I entreat such, [to] give me leave to excuse myself of so much imbecility, as to say, that in these eighteen years [1606–1624] which I have been conversant with these affairs, I have not learned, there is a great difference betwixt the directions and judgment of experimental knowledge, and the superficial conjecture of variable relation: wherein rumor, humor, or misprision [scorn] have such power, that oft times one is enough to beguile twenty, but twenty not sufficient to keep one from being deceived. Therefore I know no reason but to believe my own eyes before any man's imagination, that is but wrested from the conceits of my own projects and endeavors, but I honor with all affection, the counsel and instructions of judicial directions, or any other honest advertisement, so far to observe, [if] they tie me not to the cruelty of unknown events.

These are the inducements that thus drew me to neglect all other employments, and spend my time and best abilities in these adventures, wherein though I have had many discouragements, by the ingratitude of some, the malicious slanders of others, the falseness of friends, the treachery of cowards, and slowness of adventurers [investors].

Now you are to remember, as I returned first from New England at Plymouth, I was promised four good ships ready prepared to my hand the next Christmas, and what conditions and content I would desire, to put this business in practice, and arriving at London, four more were offered me with the like courtesy. But to join the Londoners and them in one, was most impossible; so that in January [1615] with two hundred pound[s] in cash for adventure, and six gentlemen well furnished, I went from London to the four ships [which] were promised me at Plymouth, but I found no such matter: and the most of those that had made such great promises, by the bad return of the ship [that] went for gold, and their private emulations [rivalries], were extinct and qualified.

Notwithstanding at last, with a labyrinth of trouble, though the greatest of the burden lay on me, and a few of my particular friends, I was furnished with a ship of two hundred tons, and another of fifty. But ere I had sailed one hundred and twenty leagues, she brake all her masts, pumping each watch five or six thousand strokes; only her spritsail remained to spoon before the wind, till we had reaccommodated a jury-mast to return for Plymouth, or founder in the seas.

My vice admiral being lost [out of sight], not knowing of this, proceeded [on] her voyage.

Now with the remainder of those provisions, I got out again in a small bark of sixty tons with thirty men; for this of two hundred [tons], and provision for seventy: which were the sixteen before [mentioned] . . . and fourteen other sailors for the ship.

With those I set sail again the four and twentieth of June [1615]. Where what befell me (because my actions and writings are so public to the world) envy still seeking to scandalize my endeavors, and seeing no power but death can stop the chat of ill tongues, nor imagination of men's minds, lest my own relations of those hard events might by some constructors be made doubtful, I have thought it best to insert the examinations of those proceedings, taken by Sir Lewis Stucley, a worthy knight, and vice admiral of Devonshire, which was as followeth.*

---

* Smith was captured by pirates and after many adventures returned to England in December of 1615. See below, pp. 174 and 178.

PART TWO

Captain John Smith on the Theory and Practice of Colonization in the New World

4. A Virginia Indian Wordbook

From Book II of
*The Generall Historie of Virginia,
New England, and the Summer Isles*

*Because many do desire to know the manner
of their language, I have inserted these few words.*

Ka katorawincs yowo, What call you this?

Nemarough, a man.

Crenepo, a woman.

Marowanchesso, a boy.

Yehawkans, houses.

Matchcores, skins, or garments.

Mockasins, shoes.

Tussan, beds.

Pokatawer, fire.

Attawp, a bow.

Attonce, arrows.

Monacookes, swords.

Aumoughhowgh, a target.

Pawcussacks, guns.

Tomahacks, axes.

Tockahacks, pickaxes.

Pamesacks, knives.

Accowprets, shears.

Pawpecones, pipes.

Mattassin, copper.

Ussawassin, iron, brass, silver, or any white metal.

Musses, woods.

Attasskuss, leaves, weeds, or grass.

Chepsin, land.

Shacquohocan, a stone.

Wepenter, a cuckold.

Suckahanna, water.

Noughmass, fish.

Copotone, sturgeon.

Weghshaughes, flesh.

Sawwehone, blood.

Netoppew, friends.

Marrapough, enemies.

Maskapow, the worst of the enemies.

Mawchick chammay, the best of friends.

Cassacunnakack, peya quagh acquintan uttasantasough, In how many days will there come hither any more English ships?

Their numbers.
   Necut, 1. Ningh, 2. Nuss, 3. Yowgh, 4. Paranske, 5. Comotinch, 6. Toppawoss, 7. Nusswash, 8. Kekatawgh, 9. Kaskeke, 10.

They count no more but by tens as followeth.

Case, how many?

Ninghsapooeksku, 20. *Nussapooeksku,* 30. *Yowghapooeksku,* 40. *Parankestassapooeksku,* 50. *Comatinchtassapooeksku,* 60. *Nussswashtassapooeksku,* 70. *Kekataughtassapooeksku,* 90. *Necuttoughtysinough,* 100. *Necuttweunquaough,* 1000.

Rowcosowghs, days.

Keskowghes, suns.

Toppquough, nights.

Nepawweshowghs, moons.

Pawpaxsoughes, years.

Pummahumps, stars.

Osies, heavens.

Okees, gods.

Quiyoughcosoughs, petty gods, and their affinities.

Righcomoughes, deaths.

Kekughes, lives.

Mowchick woyawgh tawgh noeragh kaquere mecher, I am very hungry. What shall I eat?

Tawnor nehiegh Powhatan, Where dwells Powhatan?

Mache, neheigh yourowgh, Orapaks, Now he dwells a great way hence at *Orapaks.*

Vittapitchewayne anpechitchs nehawper Werowocómoco, You lie, he stayed ever at *Werowocómoco.*

Kator nehiegh mattagh neer uttapitchewayne, Truly he is there. I do not lie.

Spaughtynere keragh werowance mawmarynough kekatem wawgh peyaquaugh, Run you then to the King Mawmarynough and bid him come hither.

Utteke, e peya weyack wighwhip, Get you gone, and come again quickly.

Kekaten Pocahontas patiaquagh niugh tanks manotyens neer mowchick rawrenock audowgh, Bid Pocahontas bring hither two little baskets, and I will give her white beads to make her a chain.

5. A Check List for Virginia-Bound Colonists

From Book IV of
*The Generall Historie of Virginia,
New England, and the Summer Isles*

*A particular of such necessaries as either private
families, or single persons, shall have cause to provide
to go to Virginia, whereby greater numbers may in part
conceive the better how to provide for themselves.*

Apparel

	s.	d.
A Monmouth cap.	1s.	10d.
3 falling bands [collars].	1s.	3d.
3 shirts.	7s.	6d.
1 waistcoat.	2s.	2d.
1 suit of canvas.	7s.	6d.
1 suit of frieze [coarse wool].	10s.	
1 suit of cloth.	15s.	
3 pair of Irish stockings.	4s.	
4 pair of shoes.	8s.	8d.
1 pair of garters.		10d.
1 dozen of points [for lacing clothes].		3d.

1 pair of canvas sheets.		8s.	
7 ells of canvas to make a bed and bolster, to be filled in Virginia, serving for two men.		8s.	
5 ells of coarse canvas to make a bed at sea for two men.		5s.	
1 coarse rug at sea for two men.		6s.	

Victual for a whole year for a man,
and so after the rate for more.

8 bushels of meal.	2£.		
2 bushels of peas.		6s.	
2 bushels of oatmeal.		9s.	
1 gallon of aqua vitae.		2s.	6d.
1 gallon of oil.		3s.	6d.
2 gallons of vinegar.		2s.	
	3£.	3s.	

Arms for a man; but if half your men
be armed it is well, so all have
swords and pieces.

1 armor complete, light.		17s.	
1 long piece five feet and a half, near musket bore.	1£.	2s.	
1 sword.		5s.	
1 belt.		1s.	
1 bandolier.		1s.	6d.
20 pound[s] of powder.		18s.	
60 pound[s] of shot or lead, pistol and goose shot.		5s.	
	3£.	9s.	6d.

Tools for a family of six persons,
and so after the rate for more.

5 broad hoes at 2s. apiece.		10s.	
5 narrow hoes at 16d. apiece.		6s.	8d.
2 broad axes at 3s. 8d. apiece.		7s.	4d.
5 felling axes at 18d. apiece.		7s.	6d.
2 steel handsaws at 16d. apiece.		2s.	8d.
2 two-handsaws at 5s. apiece.		10s.	

		£	s.	d.
1	whipsaw, set and filed; with box, file and wrest [screw key].		10s.	
2	hammers [at] 12d. apiece.		2s.	
3	shovels at 18d. apiece.		4s.	6d.
2	spades at 18d. apiece.		3s.	
2	augers at 6d. apiece.		1s.	
6	chisels at 6d. apiece.		3s.	
2	percers stocked [at] 4d. apiece.			8d.
3	gimlets at 2d. apiece.			6d.
2	hatchets at 21d. apiece.		3s.	6d.
2	froes to cleave pale [make staves or shingles] [at] 18d. each.		3s.	
2	hand bills [at] 20d. apiece.		3s.	4d.
1	grindstone.		4s.	
	nails of all sorts to the value of	2£.		
2	pickaxes.		3s.	
		6£.	2s.	8d.

*Household implements for a family
and six persons, and so for more
or less after the rate.*

		£	s.	d.
1	iron pot.		7s.	
1	kettle.		6s.	
1	large frying pan.		2s.	6d.
1	gridiron.		1s.	6d.
2	skillets.		5s.	
1	spit.		2s.	
	platters, dishes, spoons of wood.		4s.	
		1£.	8s.	

For sugar, spice, and fruit, and at sea for six men. 12s.6d.

So the full charge after this rate for each person, will amount to about the sum of 12£.10s.10d.

The passage of each man is 6£.

The fraught of these provisions for a man, will be about half a ton, which is 1£.10s.

So the whole charge will amount to about 20£.

Now if the number be great; [not only] nets, hooks, and lines, but cheese, bacon, kine and goats must be added.

And this is the usual proportion the Virginia Company doe[s] bestow upon their tenants they send.

6. John Smith's Written Testimony to the Commission Appointed to Investigate the Affairs of the Virginia Company

From Book IV of
The Generall Historie of Virginia, New England, and the Summer Isles

Out of these observations it pleased His Majesty's commissioners for the reformation of Virginia, to desire my answer to these seven questions.

Quest. 1. *What conceive you is the cause the plantation hath prospered no better since you left it in so good a forwardness [prosperity]?*

Answ. Idleness and carelessness brought all I did in three years, in six months to nothing; and of five hundred I left, scarce[ly] three-score remained; and had Sir Thomas Gates not got from the Bermudas, I think they had all been dead before they could be supplied.

Quest. 2. *What conceive you should be the cause, though the country be good, there comes nothing but tobacco?*

Answ. The oft altering of governors it seems causes every man [to] make use of his time, and because corn was stinted at two shillings six pence the bushel, and tobacco at three shillings the pound; and they value a man's labor a year worth fifty or threescore pound[s], but in corn not worth ten pound[s], presuming tobacco will furnish them with all things: now make a man's labor in corn worth threescore pound[s], and in tobacco but ten pound[s] a man, then shall they have corn sufficient to entertain all comers, and keep their people in health to do anything; but till then, there will be little or nothing to any purpose.

Quest. 3. *What conceive you to have been the cause of the massacre [March 1622], and had the savages had the use of any pieces [guns] in your time, or when, or by whom were they taught?*

Answ. The cause of the massacre was the want of martial discipline; and because they would have all the English had by destroying those they found so carelessly secure, that they were not provided to defend themselves against any enemy; being so dispersed as they were. In my time, though Captain Newport furnished them with swords by truck [in trade], and many fugitives did the like, and some pieces they got accidentally: yet I got the most of them again; and it was death to him that should show a savage the use of a piece. Since, I understand, they became so good shot, they were employed [as] fowlers and huntsmen by the English.

Quest. 4. *What charge think you would have settled the government both for defense and planting when you left it?*

Answ. Twenty thousand pound[s] would have hired good laborers and mechanical men, and have furnished them with cattle and all necessaries; and 100 of them would have done more than a thousand of those that went: though the Lord De La Warr, . . . Sir Thomas Gates and Sir Thomas Dale were persuaded to the contrary; but when they had tried, they confessed their error.

Quest. 5. *What conceive you would be the remedy and the charge?*

Answ. The remedy is to send soldiers and all sorts of laborers and necessaries for them, that they may be there by next Michaelmas [1624], the which to do well will stand you in five thousand pound[s]: but if His Majesty would please to lend two of his ships to transport them, less would serve; besides the benefit of his grace to the action would encourage all men.

Quest. 6. *What think you are the defects of the government [of the Virginia Company] both here and there?*

Answ. The multiplicity of opinions here, and officers there, makes such delays by questions and formality, that as much time is spent in complement as in action; besides, some are so desirous to employ their ships, having six pounds for every passenger, and three pounds for every ton of goods, at which rate a thousand ships may now better be procured than one at the first, when the common stock defrayed all fraughts, wages, provisions and magazines, whereby the ships are so pestered, as occasions much sickness, diseases and mortality: for though all the passengers die they are sure of their fraught; and then all must be satisfied with orations, disputations, excuses and hopes.

As for the letters of advice from hence, and their answers thence, they are so well written, men would believe there were no great doubt of the performance, and that all things were well, to which error here they have been ever much subject; and there not to believe, or not to relieve the true and poor estate of that colony, whose fruits were commonly spent before they were ripe, and this loss is nothing to them here, whose great estates are not sensible of the loss of their adventures, and so they think, or will not take notice; but it is so with all men.

But howsoever they think or dispose of all things at their pleasure, I am sure not myself only, but a thousand others have not only spent the most of their estates, but the most part have lost their lives and all, only but to make way for the trial of more new conclusions: and he that now will adventure but twelve pounds ten shillings, shall have better respect and as much favor than he that sixteen year[s] ago [in 1609] adventured as much, except he have money as the other hath; but though he have adventured five hundred pound[s], and spent there never so much time, if he have no more and [be] not able to begin a family of himself, all is lost by order of court.

But in the beginning it was not so, all went then out of one purse, till those new devices have consumed both money and purse; for at first there were but six patentees, now more than a thousand; then but thirteen Councilors, now not less than a hundred: I speak not of all, for there are some both honorable and honest, but of those officers [who] did they manage their own estates no better than the affairs of Virginia, they would quickly fall to decay so well as it. But this is most evident, few officers in England it hath caused to turn bankrupts, nor for all their complaints would [they] leave their places; neither yet any of their officers there, nor few of the rest but they would be at home. But fewer adventurers here will adventure any more till they see the business better established, although there be some so willfully improvident they care for nothing but to get thither, and then if their friends be dead, or want themselves, they die or live but poorly for want of necessaries, and to think the old planters can relieve them were too much simplicity; for who here in England is so charitable to feed two or three strangers, have they never so much; much less in Virginia where they want for themselves. Now the general complaint saith, that pride, covetousness, extortion and oppression in a few that engross all, then sell all again to the commonality at what rate they please (yea even men, women and children for who will give most), occasions no small mischief amongst the planters.

As for the company, or those that do transport them, provided of necessaries, God forbid but they should receive their charges again with advantage, or that masters there should not have the same privilege over their servants as here: but to sell him or her for forty, fifty, or three-score pounds, whom the company hath sent over for eight or ten pounds at the most, without regard how they shall be maintained with apparel, meat, drink, and lodging, is odious, and their fruits suitable: therefore such merchants it were better they were made such merchandise them-selves, than suffered any longer to use that trade, and those are defects sufficient to bring a well settled commonwealth to misery, much more Virginia.

Quest. 7. *How think you it may be rectified?*

Answ. If His Majesty would please to entitle [resume] it [the Vir-ginia colony] to his crown, and yearly that both the governors here and there may give their accounts to you, or some that are not engaged in the business, that the common stock be not spent in maintaining one hundred men for the governor, one hundred for two deputies, fifty for the treasurer, five and twenty for the secretary, and more for the marshall and other officers who were never there nor adventured anything; but only preferred by favor to be lords over them that broke the ice and beat the path, and must teach them what to do. If anything happen well, it is their glory; if ill, the fault of the old directors, that in all dangers must endure the worst, yet not five hundred of them have so much as one of the others.

Also that there be some present course taken to maintain a garrison to suppress the savages, till they be able to subsist, and that His Majesty would please to remit his custom; or it is to be feared they will lose custom and all, for this cannot be done by promises, hopes, counsels and countenances, but with sufficient workmen and means to maintain them: not such delinquents as here cannot be ruled by all the laws in England. Yet when the foundation is laid, as I have said, and a commonwealth established, then such there may better be constrained to labor than here; but to rectify a commonwealth with debauched people is impossible, and no wise man would throw himself into such a society, that intends honestly, and knows what he undertakes. For there is no country to pillage as the Romans found, all you expect from thence must be by labor.

For the government I think there is as much ado about it as the kingdoms of Scotland and Ireland, men here conceiting Virginia as they are, erecting as many stately offices as officers with their attendants, as there are laborers in the country: where a constable were as good as twenty of their captains; and three hundred good soldiers and laborers better than all the rest, that go only to get the fruits of other men's labors by the title of an office. Thus they spend Michaelmas rent in midsummer moon, and would gather their harvest before they have planted their corn.

As for the maintenance of the officers, the first that went never demanded any, but adventured good sums: and it seems strange to me, the fruits of all their labors, besides the expense of a hundred and fifty thousand pounds, and such multitudes of people, those collateral officers could not maintain themselves so well as the old did; and having now such liberty to do to the savages what they will, [which] the others had not.

I more than wonder they have not five hundred savages to work for them towards their general maintenance; and as many more to return some content and satisfaction to the adventurers, that for all their care, charge and diligence, can hear nor see nothing but miserable complaints: therefore under your correction to rectify all, [it] is with all expedition to pass the authority to them who will relieve them, lest all be consumed ere the differences be determined.

And except His Majesty undertake it, or by Act of Parliament some small tax may be granted throughout his dominions, [such] as a penny upon every poll [taxable person], called a headpenny; two pence upon every chimney, or some such collection might be raised, and that would be sufficient to give a good stock, and many servants to sufficient men of any faculty, and transport them freely for paying only homage to the crown of England, and such duties to the public good as their estates increased, [as] reason should require. Were this put in practice, how many people of what quality you please, for all those disasters would yet gladly go to spend their lives there, and by this means more good might be done in one year, than all those petty particular under-takings will effect in twenty.

For the patent the King may, if he please, rather take it from them that have it, than from us who had it first; pretending to His Majesty what great matters they would do, and how little we did: and for any-thing I can conceive had we remained still as at first, it is not likely we could have done much worse; but those oft altering of governments are not without much charge, hazard and loss.

If I be too plain, I humbly crave your pardon; but you requested me, therefore I do but my duty. For the nobility, who knows not how freely both in their purses and assistances many of them have been to advance it, committing the managing of the business to inferior persons: amongst whom questionless [doubtless] also many have done their utmost best, sincerely and truly according to their conceit, opinion and understanding; yet gross errors have been committed, but no man lives without his fault. For my own part, I have so much ado to amend my own, I have no leisure to look into any man's particular [fault], but those [faults] in general I conceive to be true. And so I humbly rest.

Yours to command,
J[ohn] S[mith]

7. A Memorandum to John Winthrop and the Massachusetts Colonists

Selections from
*Advertisements For the unexperienced Planters of
New-England, or any where. OR The Path-way
to experience to errect a Plantation*

The Sea Mark.
Aloof, aloof; and come no near,
      the dangers do appear;
Which if my ruin had not been
      you had not seen:
I only lie upon this shelf
    to be a mark to all
    which on the same might fall,
That none may perish but myself.

If in or outward you be bound,
      do not forget to sound.
Neglect of that was cause of this
      to steer amiss.
The seas were calm, the wind was fair
    that made me so secure,
    that now I must endure
All weathers be they foul or fair.

> The winter's cold, the summer's heat
> > alternatively beat
> Upon my bruised sides, that rue
> > because too true
> That no relief can ever come.
> > But why should I despair
> > being promised so fair
> That there shall be a day of Doom.
> > > [apparently by John Smith]

CHAPTER I.

What people they are that begin this plantation:
the bane of Virginia: strange misprisions of wise men.

The wars in Europe, Asia, and Africa, taught me how to subdue the wild savages in Virginia and New England, in America; which now after many a stormy blast of ignorant contradictors, projectors, and undertakers, both they and I have been so tossed and tortured into so many extremities, as despair was the next we both expected, till it pleased God now at last to stir up some good minds, that I hope will produce glory to God, honor to His Majesty, and profit to his kingdoms: although all our plantations have been so foiled and abused, their best good willers have been for the most part discouraged, and their good intents disgraced, as the general history of them will at large truly relate [to] you.

Pardon me if I offend in loving that I have cherished truly, by the loss of my prime fortunes, means, and youth: if it over glad me to see industry herself adventure now to make use of my aged endeavors, not by such (I hope) as rumor doth report, a many of discontented Brownists, Anabaptists, Papists, Puritans, Separatists, and such factious humorists [fanatics]: for no such they will suffer among them, if known, as many of the chief of them [the Puritan leaders] have assured me; and the much conferences I have had with many of them, doth confidently persuade me to write thus much in their behalf.

I mean not the Brownists of Leyden and Amsterdam at New Plymouth, who although by accident, ignorance, and willfulness, have endured, with a wonderful patience, many losses and extremities; yet they subsist and prosper so well, not any of them will abandon the country, but to the utmost of their powers increase their numbers. But of those which are gone within this eighteen months [April 1629–October 1630] for Cape Ann, and the Bay of the Massachusetts. Those which are their chief undertakers are gentlemen of good estate, some of 500, some a thousand pound[s'] land a year, all which they say they will sell for the advancing [of] this harmless and pious work; men of good credit and well-beloved in their country [district], not such as fly for debt, or any scandal at home; and are good Catholic Protestants according to the reformed Church of England, if not, it is well they are gone. The rest of them [are] men of good means, or arts, occupations, and qualities, much more fit for such a business, and better furnished of all necessaries if they arrive well, than was ever any plantation [that] went out of England.

I will not say but some of them may be more precise [Puritan] than needs, nor that they all be so good as they should be; for Christ had but twelve apostles, and one was a traitor: and if there be no dissemblers among them, it is more than a wonder; therefore do not condemn all for some. But however they have as good authority from His Majesty as they could desire: if they do ill, the loss is but their own; if well, a great glory and exceeding good to this kingdom, to make good at last what all our former conclusions have disgraced.

Now they take not that course the Virginia company did for the planters there, their purses and lives were subject to some few here in London who were never there, that consumed all in arguments, projects, and their own conceits: every year trying new conclusions, altering everything yearly as they altered opinions, till they had consumed more than two hundred thousand pounds, and near[ly] eight thousand men's lives.

It is true, in the year of our Lord 1622, they were, the company in England say 7 or 8 thousand: the Council in Virginia say but 2200 or thereabouts, English indifferently well furnished with most necessaries, and many of them grew to that height of bravery, living in that plenty and excess, that went thither not worth anything, [that] made the company here think all the world was oatmeal there; and all this proceeded by surviving those that died: nor were they ignorant to use as curious tricks there as here, and out of the juice of tobacco, which at first they sold at such good rates, they regarded nothing but tobacco; a commodity then so vendible, it provided them [with] all things. And the loving savages their kind friends, they trained so well up to shoot [with] a piece, to hunt and kill them fowl, they became more expert than our own countrymen; whose labors were more profitable to their masters in planting tobacco and other business.

This superfluity caused my poor beginnings [to be] scorned, or to be spoken of but with much derision, that never sent ship from thence fraught, but only some small quantities of wainscot, clapboard, pitch, tar, rosin, soap ashes, glass, cedar, cypress, black walnut, knees for ships, ash for pikes, iron ore none better, some silver ore but so poor it was not regarded; better there may be, for I was no mineralist; some sturgeon, but it was too tart of the vinegar (which was of my own store, for little came from them which was good); and wine of the country's wild grapes, but it was too sour; yet better than they sent us any, [which was] in two or three years but one hogshead of claret. Only spending my time to revenge my imprisonment upon the harmless, innocent savages, who by my cruelty I forced to feed me with their contribution; and to send any [who] offended my idle humor to Jamestown to punish at mine own discretion; or keep their Kings and subjects in chains, and make them work. Things clean contrary to my commission; whilst I and my company took our needless pleasures in discovering the countries about us, building of forts, and such unnecessary fooleries, where an eggshell (as they writ) had been sufficient [protection] against such enemies; neglecting to answer the merchants' expectations with profit, feeding the company only with letters and tastes of such commodities as we writ the country would afford in time by industry, as silk, wines, oils of olives, rape [turnip or radish seed], and linseed, raisins, prunes, flax, hemp, and iron. As for tobacco, we never then dreamt of it.

Now because I sent not their ships full fraught home with those commodities; they kindly writ to me, if we failed the next return, they would leave us there as banished men, as if houses and all those commodities did grow naturally, only for us to take at our pleasure; with such tedious letters, directions, and instructions, and most contrary to that [which] was fitting, we did admire [wonder] how it was possible such wise men could so torment themselves and us with such strange absurdities and impossibilities: making religion their color, when all their aim was nothing but present profit, as most plainly appeared, by sending us so many refiners, goldsmiths, jewelers, lapidaries, stone-cutters, tobacco pipe makers, embroiderers, perfumers, silk men, with [not only] all their appurtenances but materials, and all those had great sums out of the common stock; and [were] so many spies and superintendents over us, as if they supposed we would turn rebels, all striving to suppress and advance they knew not what.

At last [they] got a commission [the charter of 1609] in their own names, promising the King custom within seven years, where[as] we were free for one and twenty; appointing the Lord De La Warr for Governor, with as many great and stately officers, and offices under him, as doth belong to a great kingdom, with good sums for their extraordinary expenses; also privileges for cities; charters for corporations, universities, free schools, and glebe land; putting all those in practice before there [were] either people, students, or scholars to build or use them, or provision or victual to feed them [that] were then there: and to amend this, most of the tradesmen in London that would adventure but twelve pounds ten shillings, had the furnishing [of] the company of all such things as belonged to his trade, such juggling there was betwixt them, and such intruding committees [committee men] their associates, that all the trash they could get in London was sent us to Virginia, they being [as] well payed [as] for that [which] was good.

Much they blamed us for not converting the savages, when those they sent us were little better, if not worse; nor did they all, convert any of those [natives] we sent them to England for that purpose. So doting of mines of gold, and the South Sea; that all the world could not have devised better courses to bring us to ruin than they did themselves, with many more such like strange conceits.

By this you [the Puritans] may avoid the like inconveniences, and take heed by those examples, you have not too many irons in the fire at once; neither such change of governors, nor such a multitude of officers; neither more masters, gentlemen, gentlewomen, and children, than you have men to work, which idle charge you will find very troublesome, and the effects dangerous: and one hundred good laborers better than a thousand such gallants as were sent me, that would do nothing but complain, curse, and despair, when they saw our miseries and all things so clean contrary to the report in England; yet must I provide as well for them as for myself.

CHAPTER II.

Needless custom, effect of flattery, cause of misery,
factions, careless government, the dissolving
[of] the company and patent.

This the mariners and sailors did ever all they could do to conceal; who had always good fare, and good pay for the most part, and part out of our own purses: never caring how long they stayed upon their voyage, daily feasting before our faces; when we lived upon a little corn and water, and not half enough of that, the most of which we had from amongst the savages. Now although there be deer in the woods, fish in the rivers, and fowls in abundance in their seasons: yet the woods are so wide, the rivers so broad, and the beasts so wild, and we so unskillful to catch them we little troubled them nor they us.

For all this, our letters that still signified unto them [in London] the plain truth, would not be believed, because they required such things as [were] most necessary: but their opinion was otherw[ise], for they desired but to pack over so many as they could, saying necessity would make them get victuals for themselves, as for good laborers they were more useful here in England.

But they found it otherw[ise]; the charge was all one to send a workman as a roarer [reveller]; whose clamors to appease, we had much ado to get fish and corn to maintain them from one supply till another came with more loiterers without victuals still to make us worse and worse, for the most of them would rather starve than work: yet had it not been for some few that were gentlemen, both by birth, industry, and discretion, we could not possibly have subsisted.

Many did urge I might have forced them to it, having authority that extended so far as death: but I say, having neither meat, drink, lodging, pay, nor hope of anything or preferment; and seeing the merchants only did what they listed with all they wrought for, I know not what punishment could be greater than that they endured; which miseries caused us always to be in factions: the most part striving by any means to abandon the country, and I with my party to prevent them and cause them [to] stay. But indeed the cause of our factions was bred here in England, and grew to that maturity among themselves that spoiled all, as all the kingdom and other nations can too well testify.

Yet in the year 1622 there were about seven or eight thousand English, as hath been said, so well trained, secure, and well furnished, as they reported and conceited. These simple savages, their bosom friends, I so much oppressed, had laid their plot how to cut all their throats in a morning: and upon the 22 of March [1622], so innocently attempted it, they slew three hundred [and] forty-seven, set their houses on fire, slew their cattle, and brought them to that distraction and confusion [that] within less than a year, there were not many more than two thousand remaining.

The which loss to repair the company did what they could, till they had consumed all their stock [capital] as is said: then they broke [became bankrupt], not making any account, nor giving satisfaction to the lords, planters, adventurers, nor any; whose noble intents had referred the managing of this intricate business to a few that lost not by it. So that His Majesty recalled their commission [charter] [June 1624]: and [that] by more just cause than they persuaded King James to call in ours [in 1609], [who] were the first beginners, without our knowledge or consent, disposing of us and all our endeavors at their pleasures.

CHAPTER III.

A great comfort to New England, it is no island. . . .

Notwithstanding since they [in Virginia] have been left in a manner, as it were, to themselves, they have increased [by October 1630] their numbers to four or five thousand, and near[ly] as many cattle, with plenty of goats: abundance of swine, poultry, and corn, that as they report, they have sufficient and to spare, to entertain three or four hundred people, which is much better than to have many people more than provision.

Now having glutted the world with their too much overabounding tobacco: reason, or necessity, or both, will cause them, I hope, [to] learn in time better to fortify themselves, and make better use of the trials of their gross commodities that I have propounded, and at the first sent over: and were it not a lamentable dishonor [that] so goodly a country after so much cost, loss, and trouble, should now in this estate not be regarded and supplied.

And to those of New England may it not be a great comfort to have so near a neighbor of their own nation, that may furnish them with their spare cattle, swine, poultry, and other roots and fruits, much better than from England. But I fear the seed of envy, and the rust of covetousness doth grow too fast, for some would have all men advance Virginia to the ruin of New England; and others the loss of Virginia to sustain New England, which God of His mercy forbid: for at first it was intended by that most memorable Judge Sir John Popham, then Lord Chief Justice of England, and the lords of His Majesty's privy council, with divers others, that two colonies should be planted, as now they be, for the better strengthening [of] each other against all occurrences; the which to perform, shall ever be my hearty prayers to Almighty God, to increase and continue that mutual love betwixt them forever.

By this you may perceive somewhat, what unexpected inconveniences are incident to a plantation, especially in such a multitude of voluntary contributers, superfluity of officers, and unexperienced commissioners. But it is not so, as yet, with those [of] New England; for they will neither believe nor use such officers, in that they are overseers of their own estates, and [as] well bred in labor and good husbandry as any in England: whereas few as I say [were] sent me to Virginia, but those [who] were naught here and worse there. . . .

CHAPTER IV.

*Our right to those countries, true reasons
for plantations, rare examples.*

Many good, religious, devout men have made it a great question, as a matter in conscience, by what warrant they might go to possess those countries, which are none of theirs, but the poor savages'.

Which poor curiosity will answer itself; for God did make the world to be inhabited [by] mankind, and to have His name known to all nations, and from generation to generation: as the people increased they dispersed themselves into such countries as they found most convenient. And here in Florida, Virginia, New England, and Canada, is more land than all the people in Christendom can manure [cultivate], and yet more to spare than all the natives of those countries can use and culturate. And shall we here [in England] keep such a coil [demand] for land, and at such great rents and rates, when there is so much of the world uninhabited, and as much more in other places, and as good or rather better than any we possess, were it manured and used accordingly.

If this be not a reason sufficient to such tender consciences; for a copper knife and a few toys, as beads and hatchets, they will sell you a whole country [district]; and for a small matter, their houses and the ground they dwell upon; but those of the *Massachusetts* have resigned theirs freely.

Now the reasons for plantations are many. . . .

The Portuguese and Spaniards that first began plantations in this unknown world of America till within this 140 years, whose everlasting actions before our eyes, will testify our idleness and ingratitude to all posterity, and neglect of our duty and religion we owe our God, our King, and country, and want of charity to those poor savages, whose countries we challenge, use, and possess: except we be but made to mar what our forefathers made; or but only tell what they did; or esteem ourselves too good to take the like pains where there is so much reason, liberty, and action offers itself. Having as much power and means as others, why should Englishmen despair, and not do so much as any? Was it virtue in those heroes to provide that [which] doth maintain us, and baseness in us to do the like for others to come? Surely no; then seeing we are not born for ourselves but each to help [an]other; and our abilities are much alike at the hour of our birth and minute of our death: seeing our good deeds or bad, by faith in Christ's merits, is all we have to carry our souls to heaven or hell: seeing honor is our lives' ambition, and our ambition after death, to have an honorable memory of our life: and seeing by no means we would be abated of the dignity and glory of our predecessors, let us imitate their virtues to be worthily their successors; or at least not hinder, if not further, them that would and do their utmost and best endeavor.

CHAPTER V.

My first voyage to New England, my return and profit.

To begin with the originals of the voyages to those coasts, I refer you to my general history; for New England by the most of them was esteemed a most barren, rocky desert.

Notwithstanding at the sole charges of four merchants of London and myself [in] 1614 with[in] eight weeks' sailing I arrived at *Monhegan,* an isle in America in 43 degrees, 39 minutes of northerly latitude.

Had the fishing for whale proved as we expected, I had stayed in the country: but we found the plots [charts] we had, so false; and the seasons for fishing and trade by the unskillfulness of our pilot so much mistaken; I was contented, having taken by hooks and lines, with fifteen or eighteen men at most, more than 60,000 cod in less than a month: whilst myself and eight others of them [that] might best be spared, by an hour glass of three months, ranging the coast in a small boat, got for trifles eleven hundred beaver skins besides otters and martens [skins]; all amounting to the value of fifteen hundred pound[s], and arrived in England with all my men in health, in six or seven months.

But northward the French returned this year [1614] to France five and twenty thousand beavers [skins] and good furs; whilst we were contending about patents and commissions, with such fearful incredulity that more dazzled our eyes than opened them.

In this voyage I took the description of the coast as well by map as writing, and called it New England: but malicious minds amongst sailors and others, drowned that name with the echo of *Nuskoucus, Canada,* and *Pemaquid;* till, at my humble suit, our most gracious King Charles, then Prince of Wales, was pleased to confirm it by that title, and did change the barbarous names of their principal harbors and habitations for such English, that posterity may say, King Charles was their godfather: and in my opinion it should seem an unmannerly presumption in any that doth alter them without his leave.

My second voyage was to begin a plantation, and to do what else I could, but by extreme tempests that tore near[ly] all my masts by the board, being more than two hundred leagues at sea, [I] was forced to return to Plymouth with a jury mast.

The third [voyage] was intercepted by English and French pirates, by my treacherous company that betrayed me to them; who ran away with my ship and all that I had: such enemies the sailors were to a plantation, and the greatest loss being mine, [they] did easily excuse themselves to the merchants in England, that still provided to follow the fishing.

Much difference there was betwixt the Londoners and the Westerlings to engross it, who now would adventure thousands, that when I went first would not adventure a groat. . . .

At my return from France [December 1615], I did my best to have united them; but that had been more than a work for Hercules, so violent is the folly of greedy covetousness. . . .

CHAPTER VII.

New England's yearly trials, the planting of New Plymouth, surprisals prevented, their wonderful industry and fishing.

For all those differences there went eight tall ships before I arrived [in December 1615] in England, from France, so that I spent that year in the West Country, to persuade the cities, towns, and gentry for a plantation; which the merchants very little liked, because they would have the coast free only for themselves, and the gentlemen were doubtful of their true accounts.

Oft and much it was so disputed, that at last they promised me the next year twenty sail well furnished, made me Admiral of the country for my life under their hands and the colony's seal for New England; and in renewing their letters patent, to be a patentee for my pains; yet nothing but a voluntary fishing was effected, for all this air.

In those years many ships made exceeding[ly] good voyages, some in six months, others in five: but one of two hundred ton[s] in six weeks, with eight and thirty men and boys had her fraught, which she sold at the first penny for one and twenty hundred pounds, besides her furs. Six or seven more went out of the west, and some sailors that had but a single share, had twenty pounds and [were] at home again in seven months; which was more than such a one should have got in twenty months, had he gone for wages anywhere: yet for all this, in all this time, though I had divulged to my great labor, cost, and loss, more than seven thousand books and maps, and moved the particular companies in London, as also noblemen, gentlemen, and merchants for a plantation, all availed no more than to hew rocks with oyster shells; so fresh were the living abuses of Virginia and the Summer Isles in their memories.

At last, upon those inducements, some well disposed Brownists, as they are termed, with some gentlemen and merchants of Leyden and Amsterdam, to save charges [the expense of employing Smith], would try their own conclusions, though with great loss and much misery till time had taught them to see their own error; for such humorists [fanatics] will never believe well, till they be beaten with their own rod.

They were supplied [reinforced] with a small ship with seven and thirty passengers, who found all them [that] were left after they were seated, well all but six that died, for all their poverties: in this ship they returned, the value of five hundred pounds, which was taken by a Frenchman upon the coast of England. . . .

Now you are to understand, the seven and thirty passengers miscarrying twice upon the coast of England, came so ill provided, they only relied upon that poor company they found [the Pilgrims], that had lived two years by their naked [simple] industry, and what the country naturally afforded. It is true, at first, there hath been taken a thousand bass at a draught, and more than twelve hogsheads of herrings in a night; of other fish when and what they would, when they had means; but wanting most necessaries for fishing and fowling, it is a wonder how they could subsist, fortify themselves, resist their enemies, and plant their plants.

In July [1622], a many of straggling forlorn Englishmen, whose wants they relieved, though [they] wanted themselves; the which to requite [them], destroyed their corn and fruits, and would have done the like to them, and have surprised what they had. The savages also intended the like, but wisely they slew the savage captains; and revenged those injuries upon the fugitive English, that would have done the like to them.

CHAPTER VIII.

Extremity next despair, God's great mercy, their estate;
they make good salt, an unknown rich mine.

At New Plymouth, having planted their fields and gardens, such an extraordinary drought ensued, all things withered, that they expected no harvest; and having long expected a supply, they heard no news, but [of] a wreck split upon their coast, they supposed their ship: thus in the very labyrinth of despair, they solemnly assembled themselves together nine hours in prayer. At their departure, the parching fair skies [were] all overcast with black clouds; and the next morning, such a pleasant moderate rain continued fourteen days, that it was hard to say, whether their withered fruits or drooping affections were most revived.

Not long after came two ships to supply them, with all their passengers well, except one, and he presently recovered: for themselves, for all their wants, there was not one sick person amongst them. The greater ship they returned fraught with commodities. . . .

In this plantation there [are] about a hundred and fourscore persons, some cattle, but many swine and poultry: their town contains two and thirty houses, whereof seven were burnt, with the value of five or six hundred pounds in other goods; impaled about half a mile, within which within a high mount, a fort, with a watchtower, well built of stone, loam, and wood, their ordnance well mounted: and so healthful, that of the first planters not one hath died this three years [1621–1624]: yet at the first landing at Cape Cod, being a hundred passengers, besides twenty they had left behind at Plymouth, for want of good take heed, thinking to find all things better than I advised them, [they] spent six or seven weeks in wandering up and down in frost and snow, wind and rain, among the woods, creeks and swamps, [so that] forty of them died; and threescore were left in most miserable estate at New Plymouth where their ship left them, and but nine leagues by sea from where they landed: whose misery and variable opinions for want of experience, occasioned much faction, till necessity agreed them.

These disasters, losses, and uncertain ties, made such disagreement among the adventurers in England, who began to repent, and [would] rather lose all than longer continue the charge, being out of purse six or seven thousand pounds; accounting my books and their relations as old almanacs.

But the planters, rather than leave the country, concluded absolutely to supply themselves, and to all their adventurers [to] pay them for nine years two hundred pounds yearly without any other account: where more than six hundred adventurers for Virginia, for more than two hundred thousand pounds, had not six pence.

Since they have made a salt works, wherewith they preserve all the fish they take; and have fraughted this year a ship of a hundred and fourscore tons: living so well they desire nothing but more company; and whatever they take, [they] return commodities to the value.

Thus you may plainly see, although many envying [that] I should bring so much from thence, where many others had been; and some, the same year, returned with nothing, reported the fish and beavers I brought home, I had taken from the Frenchmen of Canada, to discourage any from believing me, and excuse their own misprisions: some only to have concealed this good country (as is said) to their private use; others taxed me as much of indiscretion, to make my discoveries and designs so public for nothing, which might have been so well managed by some concealers, to have been all rich ere any had known of it.

Those, and many such likewise rewards, have been my recompenses: for which I am contented, so the country prosper, and God's name be there praised by my countrymen, I have my desire: and the benefit of this salt and fish, for breeding mariners and building ships, will make so many fit men to raise a commonwealth, if but managed, as my general history will show you, it might well by this have been as profitable as the best mine the King of Spain hath in his West Indies.

CHAPTER IX.

Notes worth observation:
miserableness no good husbandry.

Now if you but truly consider how many strange accidents have befallen those plantations and myself; how oft up, how oft down, sometimes near despair, and ere long flourishing; how many scandals and

Spaniolized [imbued with Spanish ideas] English have sought to disgrace them, bring them to ruin, or at least hinder them all they could; how many have shaven [fleeced] and cozened [cheated] both them and me, and their most honorable supporters and well-willers: [you] cannot but conceive God's infinite mercy both to them and me.

Having been a slave to the Turks, prisoner amongst the most barbarous savages, after my deliverance commonly discovering and ranging those large rivers and unknown nations with such a handful of ignorant companions that the wiser sort often gave me [up] for lost, always in mutinies [of others], wants, and miseries, blown up with gunpowder; a long time prisoner among the French pirates, from whom escaping in a little boat by myself, and adrift all such a stormy winter night, when their ships were split, more than a hundred thousand pound[s] lost [which] they had taken at sea, and most of them drowned upon the *Ile de Ré,* not far from whence I was driven onshore in my little boat &c. And many a score of the worst of winter months [have I] lived in the fields: yet to have lived near[ly] 37 years [1593–1630] in the midst of wars, pestilence and famine, by which many a hundred thousand have died about me, and scarce[ly] five living of them [who] went first with me to Virginia: and [yet to] see the fruits of my labors thus well begin to prosper: though I have but my labor for my pains, have I not much reason both privately and publicly to acknowledge it and give God thanks, whose omnipotent power only delivered me, to do the utmost of my best to make His name known in those remote parts of the world, and His loving mercy to such a miserable sinner.

Had my designs been to have persuaded men to a mine of gold, as I know many have done that knew no such matter; though few do conceive either the charge or pains in refining it, nor the power nor care to defend it: or some new invention to pass to the South Sea: or some strange plot to invade some strange monastery; or some chargeable fleet to take some rich carracks: or letters of mart [marque] to rob some poor merchant or honest fishermen: what multitudes of both people and money would contend to be first employed. But in those noble endeavors now, how few, unless it be to beg them as monopolies, and those seldom seek the common good, but the commons' goods. . . . But only those noble gentlemen and their associates, for whose better encouragements I have recollected these experienced memorandums, as an apology against all calumniating detractors, as well for myself as them.

Now since [those] called Brownists went (some few before them also having my books and maps, presumed they knew as much as they desired); many other directors they had as wise as themselves, but that was best, that liked their own conceits: for indeed they would not be known to have any knowledge of any but themselves, pretending only religion their governor, and frugality their council, when indeed it was only their pride, and singularity, and contempt of authority; because they could not be equals, they would have no superiors. In this fool's paradise, they so long used that good husbandry, they have payed soundly in trying their own follies: who undertaking in small handfuls to make many plantations, and to be several lords and kings of themselves, most vanished to nothing; to the great disparagement of the general business, therefore let them take heed that do follow their example.

CHAPTER X.

The mistaking of patents, strange effects, encouragements for servants.

Who would not think that all those certainties should not have made both me and this country have prospered well by this? But it fell out otherw[ise]. For by the instigation of some, whose policy had long watched their opportunity by the assurance of those profitable returns, procured new letters patent from King James [in 1609]; drawing in many noblemen and others to the number of twenty, for patentees; dividing my map and that tract of land from the North Sea to the South Sea, east and west, which is supposed by most cosmographers [to be] at least more than two thousand miles; and from 41 degrees to 48 of northerly latitude about 560 miles; the bounds Virginia to the south, and South Sea [Pacific Ocean] to the west, Canada to the north, and the main ocean to the east; all this they divided into twenty parts, for which they cast lots: but no lot for me but Smiths Isles, which are a many of barren rocks, the most overgrown with such shrubs and sharp whins [buckthorns] you can hardly pass them; without either grass or wood but three or four short shrubby old cedars.

Those patentees procured a proclamation, that no ship should go thither to fish but pay them for the public [as a tax], as it was pretended, five pound[s] upon every thirty tons of shipping; neither trade with the natives, cut down wood, throw their ballast overboard, nor plant without commission, leave, and content to the lord of that division or manor; some of which for some of them I believe will be tenantless this thousand year[s]. Thus whereas this country, as the contrivers of those projects, should have planted itself of itself; especially all the chief parts along the coast the first year, as they have oft told me: and chiefly by the fishing ships and some small help of their own, thinking men would be glad upon any terms to be admitted under their protections: but it proved so contrary, none would go at all. So, for fear to make a contempt against the proclamation, it hath ever since been little frequented to any purpose: nor would they do anything, but left it to itself.

Thus it lay again in a manner vast [waste], till those noble gentlemen [the Puritan leaders] thus voluntarily undertook it, whom I entreat to take this as a memorandum of my love, to make your plantations so near and great as you can; for many hands make light work, whereas yet your small parties can do nothing available; nor stand too much upon the letting, setting, or selling those wild countries, nor impose too much upon the commonalty either by your magazines [victualling ships or stores] which commonly eat out all poor men's labors; nor any other too hard imposition for present gain; but let every man [as] it be by order allotted him, plant freely without limitation so much as he can, be it by the halves or otherw[ise]. And at the end of five or six years, or when you make a division, for every acre he hath planted, let him have twenty, thirty, forty, or a hundred; or as you find he hath extraordinarily deserved, by itself to him and his heirs forever; all his charges being defrayed to his lord or master, and public good.

In so doing, a servant that will labor, within four or five years may live as well there as his master did here: for where there is so much land lie waste, it were a madness in a man at the first to buy, or hire, or pay anything more than an acknowledgement to whom it shall be due; and he is doubl[y] mad that will leave his friends, means, and freedom in England, to be worse there than here.

Therefore let all men have as much freedom in reason as may be, and true dealing; for it is the greatest comfort you can give them, where the very name of servitude will breed much ill blood, and become odious to God and man: but mildly temper correction with mercy, for

I know well you will have occasion enough to use both; and in thus doing, doubtless God will bless you, and quickly triple and multiply your numbers; the which to my utmost I will do my best endeavor.

CHAPTER XI.

The planting [of] Bastable or Salem and Charlton [Charlestown], a description of the Massachusetts.

In all those plantations, yea, of those that have done least, yet the most will say, we were the first; and so every next supply, still the next beginner: but seeing history is the memory of time, the life of the dead, and the happiness of the living; because I have more plainly discovered, and described, and discoursed of those countries than any as yet I know, I am the bolder to continue the story, and do all men right [as] near[ly] as I can in those new beginnings, which hereafter perhaps may be in better request [fashion] than a forest of nine days' pamphlets.

In the year 1629, about March, six good ships are gone with 350 men, women, and children; people professing themselves of good rank, zeal, means and quality: also 150 head of cattle, as horse[s], mares, and neat beasts; 41 goats, some conies, with all provision for household and apparel; six pieces of great ordnance for a fort, with muskets, pikes, corselets, drums and colors, with all provisions necessary for the good of man.

They are seated about 42 degrees and 38 minutes, at a place called by the natives *Naemkeck,* by our Royal King Charles, Bastable; but now by the planters, Salem: where they arrived for most part exceeding[ly] well, their cattle and all things else prospering exceedingly, far beyond their expectation.

At this place they found some reasonabl[y] good provision and houses built by some few of Dorchester, with whom they are joined in society with two hundred men.

A hundred and fifty more they have sent to the Massachusetts, which they call Charlton, or Charlestown.

I took the fairest reach in this bay for a river, whereupon I called it

[the] Charles River, after the name of our Royal King Charles; but they find that fair channel to divide itself into so many fair branches as make forty or fifty pleasant islands within that excellent bay, where the land is of divers and sundry sorts, in some places very black and fat, in others good clay, sand and gravel, the superficies neither too flat in plains, nor too high in hills. In the isles you may keep your hogs, horse[s], cattle, conies or poultry, and secure for little or nothing, and to command when you list; only having a care of provision for some extraordinar[il]y cold winter. In those isles, as in the main[land], you may make your nurseries for fruits and plants where you put no cattle; in the main[land] you may shape your orchards, vineyards, pastures, gardens, walks, parks, and cornfields out of the whole piece as you please into such plots, [one] adjoining to another, leaving every of them environed with two, three, four, or six, or so many rows of well grown trees as you will, ready grown to your hands, to defend them from ill weather, which in a champaign [open field] you could not in many ages; and this at first you may do with as much facility, as carelessly or ignorantly cut down all before you, and then after better consideration make ditches, pales, plant young trees with an excessive charge and labor, seeing you may have so many great and small growing trees for your mainposts, to fix hedges, palisades, houses, rails, or what you will. Which order in Virginia hath not been so well observed as it might: where all the woods for many a hundred mile[s] for the most part grow slight, like unto the high grove or tuft of trees upon the high hill by the house of that worthy knight Sir Humphrey Mildmay, so remarkable in Essex in the parish of Danbury, where I writ this discourse, but much taller and greater; neither grow they so thick together by the half, and much good ground between them without shrubs, and the best is ever known by the greatness of the trees and the vesture it beareth.

Now in New England the trees are commonly lower, but much thicker and firmer wood, and more proper for shipping, of which I will speak a little, [it] being the chief engine we are to use in this work; and the rather for that within a square of twenty leagues, you may have all, or most of the chief materials belonging to them, were they wrought to their perfection as in other places.

Of all fabrics [products of skilled workmen] a ship is the most excellent, requiring more art in building, rigging, sailing, trimming, defending, and moaring, with such a number of several terms and names in continual motion, not understood of any landsman, as none would think of, but some few that know them; for whose better instruction I writ my sea grammar [*An Accidence,* 1626]: a book most necessary for those plantations, because there is scarce[ly] anything belonging to a ship, but the sea terms, charge and duty of every officer is plainly expressed, and also any indifferent capacity may conceive how to direct an unskillful carpenter, or sailor to build boats and barks sufficient to sail those coasts and rivers, and put a good workman in mind of many things in this business he may easily mistake or forget.

But to be excellent in this faculty is the masterpiece of all most necessary workmen in the world. The first rule or model thereof being directed by God Himself to Noah for his ark; which He never did to any other building but His temple: which is tossed and turned up and down the world with the like dangers, miseries, and extremities as a ship, sometimes tasting the fury of the four elements, as well as she, by unlimited tyrants in their cruelty for tortures, that it is hard to conceive whether those in humanness exceed the beasts of the forest, the birds of the air, the fishes of the sea, either in numbers, greatness, swiftness, fierceness, or cruelty: whose actions and varieties, with such memorable observations as I have collected, you shall find with admiration in my history of the sea, if God be pleased I live to finish it.

CHAPTER XII.

Extraordinary means for building, many caveats,
increase of corn, how to spoil the woods for anything,
their healths.

For the building [of] houses, towns, and fortresses, where shall a man find the like conveniency, as stones of most sorts, as well [as] limestone, if I be not much deceived, as ironstone, smooth stone, blue slate for covering houses, and great rocks we supposed marble, so that one place is called the marble harbor.

There is grass plenty, though very long and thick stalked, which being neither mown nor eaten, is very rank; yet all their cattle like and prosper well therewith: but indeed it is weeds, herbs, and grass growing together, which although they be good and sweet in the summer, they will deceive your cattle in winter. Therefore be careful in the spring to mow the swamps, and the low islands . . . where you may have harsh shear grass enough to make hay of, till you can clear ground to make pasture; which will bear as good grass as can grow anywhere, as now it doth in Virginia: and unless you make this provision, if there come an extraordinary winter, you will lose many of them and hazard the rest; especially if you bring them in the latter end of summer, or before the grass be grown in the spring, coming weak from sea.

All things they plant prosper exceedingly: but one man of 13 gallons of Indian corn, reaped that year 364 bushels London measure, as they confidently report, at which I much wonder, having planted many bushels, but no such increase.

The best way we found in Virginia to spoil the woods, was first to cut a notch in the bark a hand broad round about the tree, which [peel] off and the tree will sprout no more, and all the small boughs in a year or two will decay: the greatest branches in the root they spoil with fire, but you with more ease may cut them from the body and they will quickly rot.

Betwixt those trees they plant their corn, whose great bodies do much defend it from extreme gusts, and heat of the sun; where that in the plains, where the trees by time they have consumed, is subject to both: and this is the most easy way to have pasture and cornfields, which is much more fertile than the other.

In Virginia they never manure their overworn fields, which [are] very few, the ground for [the] most part is so fertile: but in New England they do, sticking at every plant of corn, a herring or two; which cometh in that season in such abundance, they may take more than they know what to do with.

Some infirmed bodies, or tender educates [young children], complain of the piercing cold, especially in January and February; yet the French in Canada, the Russians, Swedes, Poles, Germans, and our neighbor Hollanders, are much colder and far more northward; [and] for all that, rich countries and live well. Now they have wood enough if they will but cut it, at their doors to make fires; and train oil with the splinters of the roots of fir trees for candles: where[as] in Holland they have little or none to build ships, houses, or anything but what they fetch from foreign countries, yet they dwell but in the latitude of Yorkshire; and New England is in the height of the north cape of

Spain, which is 10 degrees, 200 leagues, or 600 miles nearer the sun than we, where upon the mountains of Biscay I have felt [in 1604] as much cold, frost and snow as in England. And of this I am sure, a good part of the best countries and kingdoms of the world, both northward and southward of the line, lie in the same parallels of Virginia and New England. . . .

Thus you may see how prosperously thus far they have proceeded, in which course by God's grace they may continue; but great care would be had they pester [crowd] not their ships too much with cattle nor passengers, and to make good conditions for your people's diet, for therein is used much ledgerdemain: therefore in that you cannot be too careful to keep your men well, and in health at sea. In this case some masters are very provident, but the most part so they can get fraught enough, care not much whether the passengers live or die; for a common sailor regards not a landsman, especially a poor passenger; as I have seen too oft approved by lamentable experience, although we have victualled them all at our own charges.

CHAPTER XIII.

Their great supplies, present estate and accidents, advantage.

Who would not think but that all those trials had been sufficient to lay a foundation for a plantation; but we see many men many minds, and still new lords, new laws; for those 350 men with all their cattle that so well arrived and promised so much, not being of one body, but several men's servants, few could command and fewer obey, lived merrily of that they had, neither planting or building anything to any purpose, but one fair house for the governor, till all was spent and the winter approached; then they grew into many diseases, and as many inconveniences, depending only o[n] a supply from England, which expected houses, gardens, and cornfields ready planted by them for their entertainment.

It is true, that Master John Winthrop, their now governor, a worthy gentleman both in estate and esteem, went so well provided (for six or seven hundred people went with him) as could be devised; but at sea, such an extraordinary storm encountered his fleet, continuing ten days, that of two hundred cattle which were so tossed .and bruised, threescore and ten died, many of their people fell sick, and in this perplexed estate, after ten weeks, they arrived [June–July 1630] in New England at several times: where they found threescore of their people dead, the rest sick, nothing done; but all complaining, and all things so contrary to their expectation, that now every monstrous humor began to show itself.

And to second this, near[ly] as many more came after them, but so ill provided, with such multitudes of women and children, as redoubled their necessities.

This small trial of their patience caused among them no small confusion, and put the Governor and his Council to their utmost wits. Some could not endure the name of a bishop, others not the sight of a cross nor surplice, others by no means the Book of Common Prayer. This absolute crew, only of the elect, holding all (but such as themselves) reprobates and castaways, now make more haste to return to Babel as they termed England, than stay to enjoy the land they called Canaan: somewhat they must say to excuse themselves.

Those he found Brownists, he let go for New Plymouth; who are now betwixt four or five hundred, and live well without want.

Some two hundred of the rest he was content to return [to] England, whose clamors are as variable as their humors and auditors. Some say they could see no timber of two feet diameter, some the country is all woods; others they drunk all the springs and ponds dry, yet like to famish for want of fresh water; some of the danger of the rattlesnake; and that others sold their provisions at what rates they pleased to them that wanted, and so returned to England great gainers out of others' miseries: yet all that returned are not of those humors.

Notwithstanding all this, the noble Governor was no way disanimated, neither repents him of his enterprise for all those mistakes: but did order all things with that temperance and discretion, and so relieved those that wanted with his own provision, that there [are] six or seven hundred remained with him; and more than 1600 English in all the country, with three or four hundred head of cattle.

As for corn they are very ignorant, if upon the coast of America, they do not before the end of this October [1630] (for toys) furnish themselves with two or three thousand bushels of Indian corn, which is better than ours; and in a short time cause the savages to do them as good service as their own men, as I did in Virginia; and yet neither use cruelty nor tyranny amongst them: a consequence well worth putting in practice; and till it be effected, they will hardly do well.

I know ignorance will say it is impossible, but this impossible task, ever since the massacre in Virginia [22 March 1622], I have been a suitor to have undertaken but with 150 men, to have got corn, fortified the country, and discovered them more land than they all yet know or have demonstrated: but the merchants' common answer was, necessity in time would force the planters [to] do it themselves; and rather thus husbandly to lose ten sheep, than be at the charge of a half penny worth of tar.

Who is it that knows not what a small handful of Spaniards in the West Indies, subdued millions of the inhabitants, so depopulating those countries they conquered, that they are glad to buy Negroes in Africa at a great rate, in countries far remote from them; which although they be as idle and as devilish people as any in the world, yet they cause them quickly to be their best servants. Notwithstanding, there is for every four or five natural Spaniards, two or three hundred Indians and Negroes; and in Virginia and New England more English than savages that can assemble themselves to assault or hurt them, and it is much better to help to plant a country than unplant it and then replant it: but there Indians were in such multitudes, the Spaniards had no other remedy; and ours such a few, and so dispersed, it were nothing in a short time to bring them to labor and obedience.

It is strange to me, that Englishmen should not do as much as any; but upon every slight affront, instead to amend it, we make it worse. Notwithstanding the worst of all those rumors, the better sort there are constant in their resolutions, and so are the most of their best friends here; and making provision to supply them, many conceit they make a dearth here, which is nothing so; for they would spend more here than they transport thither.

One ship this summer [1630] with twenty cattle, and forty or fifty passengers, arrived all well; and the ship at home again in nine weeks: another for all this exclamation of want, is returned with 10,000 corfish, and fourscore kegs of sturgeon; which they did take and save when the season was near[ly] past, and in the very heat of summer; yet as good as can be.

Since another ship is gone from Bristol, and many more a[re] providing to follow them with all speed.

Thus you may plainly see for all these rumors, they are in no such distress as is supposed: as for their mischances, misprisions, or what accidents may befall them, I hope none is so malicious, as [to] attribute the fault to the country nor me: yet if some blame us not both, it were more than a wonder. For I am not ignorant that ignorance and too curious spectators, make it a great part of their profession to censure (however) any man's actions, who having lost the path to virtue, will make most excellent shifts to mount up any way; such incomparable connivance is in the devil's most punctual cheaters, they will hazard a joint, but where God hath His church they will have a chapel; a mischief so hard to be prevented, that I have thus plainly adventured to show my affection, through the weakness of my ability. You may easily know them by their absoluteness in opinions, holding experience but the mother of fools, which indeed is the very ground of reason; and he that condemns her in those actions, may find occasion enough to use all the wit and wisdom he hath to correct his own folly, that thinks to find amongst those savages such churches, palaces, monuments, and buildings as are in England.

CHAPTER XIV.

Ecclesiastical government in Virginia,
authority from the Archbishop,
their beginning at Bastable now called Salem.

Now because I have spoke[n] so much for the body, give me leave to say somewhat of the soul; and the rather because I have been demanded by so many, how we began to preach the gospel in Virginia, and by what authority; what churches we had, our order of service, and maintenance for our ministers; therefore I think it not amiss to satisfy their demands, it being the mother of all our plantations, entreating pride to spare laughter, to understand her simple beginning and proceedings.

When I went first to Virginia, I well remember we did hang an awning (which is an old sail) to three or four trees to shadow us from the sun, our walls were rails of wood, our seats unhewed trees till we cut planks, our pulpit a bar of wood nailed to two neighboring trees. In foul weather we shifted into an old rotten tent; for we had few better, and this came by way of adventure for new. This was our church, till we built a homely thing like a barn, set upon cratchets, covered with rafts, sedge, and earth; so [were] also the walls: the best of our houses [were] of the like curiosity; but the most part far much worse workmanship, that could neither well defend [from] wind nor rain.

Yet we had daily common prayer morning and evening, every Sunday two sermons, and every three months the holy communion, till our minister died: but our prayers daily, with a homily on Sundays, we continued two or three years after, till more preachers came: and surely God did most mercifully hear us, till the continual inundations of mistaking directions, factions, and numbers of unprovided libertines near[ly] consumed us all, as the Israelites in the wilderness.

Notwithstanding, out of the relics of our miseries, time and experience had brought that country to a great happiness; had they not so much doted on their tobacco, on whose fumish foundation there is small stability: there being so many good commodities besides. Yet by it they have builded many pretty villages, fair houses, and chapels, which are grown good benefices of 120 pounds a year, besides their own mundall industry. But Jamestown was 500 pounds a year, as they say, appointed by the Council here, allowed by the Council there, and confirmed by the Archbishop of Canterbury his Grace, Primate and Metropolitan of all England, *An.* 1605 to Master Richard Hakluyt, prebend[ary] of Westminster: who by his authority sent Master Robert Hunt, an honest, religious, and courageous divine; during whose life our factions were oft qualified, our wants and greatest extremities so comforted, that they seemed easy in comparison of what we endured after his memorable death.

Now in New England they have all our examples to teach them how to beware, and choose men, we [being] most ignorant in all things, or little better; therefore presage not the event of all such actions by our defailments: for they write, they doubt not ere long to be able to defend themselves against any indifferent enemy; in the interim, they have preachers erected among themselves, and God's true religion (they say) taught amongst them, the sabbath day observed, the common prayer (as I understand) and sermons performed, and diligent catechizing, with strict and careful exercise, and commendable good orders to bring those people with whom they have to deal withal into a Christian conversation, to live well, to fear God, serve the King, and love the country; which done, in time from both those plantations may grow a good addition to the Church of England: but Rome was not built in one day, whose beginnings [were] once as hopeful as theirs; and to make them as eminent shall be my humble and hearty prayers.

But as yet it is not well understood of any authority they have sought for the government and tranquillity of the church, which doth cause those suspicions of factions in religion; wherein although I be no divine, yet I hope without offence I may speak my opinion as well in this, as I have done in the rest.

He that will but truly consider the greatness of the Turk's empire and power here in Christendom, shall find the natural Turks are generally of one religion, and the Christians in so many divisions and opinions, that they are among themselves worse enemies than the Turks: whose disjointedness hath given him that opportunity to command so many hundred thousand of Christians as he doth; where had they been constant to one God, one Christ, and one church, Christians might have been more able to have commanded as many Turks, as now the Turks do poor miserable Christians. Let this example remember you to beware of faction in that nature: for my own part, I have seen many of you here in London go to church as orderly as any.

Therefore I doubt not but you will seek to the prime authority of the Church of England, for such an orderly authority as in most men's opinions is fit for you both to entreat for and to have, which I think will not be denied; and you have good reason, seeing you have such liberty to transport so many of His Majesty's subjects, with all sorts of cattle, arms, and provision as you please, and can provide means to accomplish: nor can you have any certain relief, nor long subsist, without more supplies from England. Besides, this might prevent many inconveniences [which] may ensue, and would clearly take away all those idle and malicious rumors, and occasion you many good and great friends and assistance you yet dream not of; for you know better than I can tell, that the maintainers of good orders and laws is the best preservation next [to] God of a kingdom: but when they are stuffed with hypocrisy and corruption, that state is not doubtful but lamentable in a well settled commonwealth, much more in such as yours, which is but a beginning, for as the laws corrupt, the state consumes.

CHAPTER XV.

*The true model of a plantation, tenure, increase
of trade, true examples, necessity of expert soldiers,
the names of all the first discoverers for plantations,
and their actions, what is requisite to be in the governor
of a plantation, the expedition of Queen Elizabeth's
sea captains.*

In regard of all that is past, it is better of those slow proceedings than lose all, and better to amend late than never. I know how hateful it is to envy, pride, flattery, and greatness to be advised, but I hope my true meaning wise men will excuse, for making my opinion plain: I have been so often and by so many honest men entreated for the rest, the more they mislike it, the better I like it myself.

Concerning this point of a citadel, it is not the least, though the last remembered: therefore seeing you have such good means and power of your own [as] I never had, with the best convenient speed maybe erect a fort, a castle or citadel, which in a manner is all one. Towards the building, provision, and maintenance thereof, every man for every acre he doth culturate to pay four pence yearly, and some small matter out of every hundred of fish taken or used within five or ten miles, or as you please about it; it being the center as a fortress forever belonging to the state, and when the charge shall be defrayed to the chief undertaker (in reason) let him be governor for his life: the overplus to go forward to the erecting [of] another in like manner in a most convenient place; and so one after another, as your abilities can accomplish, by benevolences, forfeitures, fines, and impositions, as reason and the necessity of the common good requireth; all men holding their lands on those manors as they do of churches, universities, and hospitals, but all depending upon one principal, and this would avoid all faction among the superiors, extremities from the commonalty, and none would repine at such payments, when they shall see it justly employed for their own defense and security. As for corruption in so small a government; you may quickly perceive, and punish it accordingly.

Now as His Majesty hath made you custom free for seven years, have a care that all your countrymen [who] shall come to trade with you, be not troubled with pilotage, buoyage, anchorage, wharfage, custom, or any such tricks as hath been lately used in most of new plantations, where they would be kings before their folly; to the discouragement of many, and a scorn to them of understanding: for Dutch, French, Biskinner, or any will as yet use freely the coast without control, and why not English as well as they.

Therefore use all comers with that respect, courtesy, and liberty [that] is fitting; which in a short time will much increase your trade, and shipping to fetch it from you: for as yet it were not good to adventure any more abroad with factors till you be better provided. Now there is nothing more enricheth a commonwealth than much trade: nor no means better to increase [it] than small custom. . . .

In this your infancy, imagine you have many eyes attending your actions, some for one end, and some only to find fault; neglect therefore no opportunity, to inform His Majesty truly [of] your orderly proceedings, which if it be to his liking, and contrary to the common rumor here in England, doubtless His Majesty will continue you custom free, till you have recovered yourselves, and are able to subsist.

For till such time, to take any custom from a plantation is not the way to make them prosper; nor is it likely those patentees shall accomplish anything, that will neither maintain them nor defend them, but with countenances, counsels, and advice, which any reasonable man there may better advise himself, than one thousand of them here who were never there: nor will any man, that hath any wit, throw himself into such a kind of subjection, especially at his own cost and charges; but it is too oft seen that sometimes one is enough to deceive one hundred, but two hundred not sufficient to keep one from being deceived.

I speak not this to discourage any with vain fears, but could wish every Englishman to carry always this motto in his heart; Why should the brave Spanish soldiers brag; the sun never sets in the Spanish dominions, but ever shineth on one part or other we have conquered for our King: who within these few hundred of years, was one of the least of most of his neighbors; but to animate us to do the like for ours, who is no way his inferior.

And truly there is no pleasure comparable to [that of] a generous spirit; as good employment in noble actions, especially amongst Turks, heathens, and infidels; to see daily new countries, people, fashions, governments, stratagems; [to] relieve the oppressed, comfort his friends, pass miseries, subdue enemies, adventure upon any feasible danger for God and his country. It is true, it is a happy thing to be born to strength, wealth, and honor; but that which is got by prowess and magnanimity is the truest luster: and those can the best distinguish content, that have escaped most honorable dangers; as if, out of every extremity, he found himself now born to a new life, to learn how to amend and maintain his age.

Those harsh conclusions have so oft plundered me in those perplexed actions, that if I could not freely express myself to them [who] doth second them, I should think myself guilty of a most damnable crime worse than ingratitude; however some overweening, capricious conceits may attribute it to vainglory, ambition, or what other idle epithet such pleased to bestow on me. But such trash I so much scorn, that I presume further to advise those, less advised than myself, that as your fish and trade increaseth, so let your forts and exercise of arms; drilling your men at your most convenient times, to rank, file, march, skirmish, and retire, in file, manaples, battalia, or ambushes, which service there is most proper; also how to assault and defend your forts, and be not sparing of a little extraordinary shot and powder to make them mark[s]men, especially your gentlemen, and those you find most capable, for shot must be your best weapon: yet all this will not do unless you have at least 100 or as many as you can, of expert, blooded, approved good soldiers, who dare boldly lead them; not to shoot a duck, a goose or a dead mark, but at men, from whom you must expect such as you send.

The want of this, and the presumptuous assurance of literal captains, was the loss of the French and Spaniards in Florida, each surprising [the] other; and lately near[ly] the ruin of Nevis, and Saint Christophers in the Indies: also the French at Port Royal, and those at Canada, now your next English neighbors: lastly Cape Breton not far from you, called New Scotland.

Questionless there were some good soldiers among them, yet somewhat was the cause they were undone by those that watched the advantage of opportunity: for as rich preys make true men thieves; so you must not expect, if you be once worth taking and unprovided, but by some to be attempted in the like manner: to the prevention whereof, I have not been more willing, at the request of my friends to print this discourse, than I am ready to live and die among you, upon conditions suiting my calling and profession to make good; and [to make] Virginia and New England, my heirs, executors, administrators and assignees.

Now because I cannot express half that which is necessary for your full satisfaction and instruction belonging to this business in this small pamphlet, I refer you to the general history of Virginia, the Summer Isles, and New England; wherein you may plainly see all the discoveries, plantations, accidents, the misprisions and causes of defailments of all those noble and worthy captains. . . .

This great work, though small in conceit, is not a work for everyone to manage such an affair, as [to] make a discovery, and plant a colony, it requires all the best parts of art, judgment, courage, honesty, constancy, diligence, and industry, to do but near well; some are more proper for one thing than another, and therein best to be employed, and nothing breeds more confusion than misplacing and misemploying men in their undertakings. Columbus, Cortez, Pizarro, De Soto, Magellan, and the rest, served more than an apprenticeship to learn how to begin their most memorable attempts in the West Indies, which to the wonder of all ages, successfully they effected; when many hundreds far above them in the world's opinion, being instructed but by relation, scorning to follow their blunt examples, but in great state, with new inventions, came to shame and confusion in actions of small moment, who doubtless in other matters, were both wise, discreet, generous and courageous. I say not this to detract anything from their nobleness, state, nor greatness; but to answer those questionless questions that keep us from imitating the others' brave spirits, that advanced themselves from poor soldiers to great captains, their posterity to great lords, and their king to be one of the greatest potentates on earth, and the fruits of their labors his greatest glory, power, and renown.

Till his [the Spaniard's] greatness and security made his so rich, remote, and dispersed plantations such great booties and honors, to the incomparable Sir Fr[ancis] Drake, [and] . . . Sir John Hawkins; . . . with many hundreds of brave English soldiers, captains, and gentlemen, that have taught the Hollanders to do the like. Those would never stand upon a demure who should give the first blow, when they [saw] peace was only but an empty name, and no sure league, but impuissance [powerless] to do hurt; found it better to buy peace by war, than take it up at interest of those [who] could better guide penknives than use swords. And there is no misery worse than [to] be conducted by a fool, or commanded by a coward; for who can endure to be assaulted by any, see his men and self imbrued in their own blood, for fear of a check, when it is so contrary to nature and necessity, and yet as obedient to government and their sovereign, as duty required.

Now your best plea is to stand upon your guard, and provide to defend as they did offend, especially at landing. If you be forced to retire, you have the advantage five for one in your retreat, wherein there is more discipline, than in a brave charge: and though it seem less in fortune, it is as much in valor to defend as to get; but it is more easy to defend than assault, especially in woods where an enemy is ignorant.

Lastly, remember as faction, pride, and security, produces nothing
but confusion, misery, and dissolution; so the con-
traries well practiced will in short time make you
happy, and the most admired people of all our
plantations for your time in the world.

John Smith writ this with his own hand.